Dimensions. Journal of Architectural Knowledge
02/2021

I0616398

Spatial Dimensions of Moving Experience

Issue Editors
Katharina Voigt and Virginie Roy

Advisory Board
Isabelle Doucet, Uta Graff, Susanne Hauser,
Klaske Havik, Jonathan Michael Hill, Wilfried Kühn,
Ferdinand Ludwig, Meike Schalk, Katharina Voigt

Editorial Context
BauHow5
Bartlett University College London, Great Britain
Chalmers University Gothenburg, Sweden
Delft University of Technology, Netherlands
Swiss Federal Institute of Technology Zurich, Switzerland
Technical University of Munich, Germany

Associated Institutions
Music and Arts University of the City of Vienna, Austria
Royal Technical University of Stockholm, Sweden
Technical University of Vienna, Austria
University of the Arts Berlin, Germany

[transcript]

Dimensions. Journal of Architectural Knowledge
is initiated and founded by Uta Graff, Ferdinand Ludwig and Katharina Voigt.
Initial funding for the journal is provided by the Technical University of Munich.

Coordination and organization by Katharina Voigt.
Contact: mail@dimensions-journal.eu

This journal is published bianually (in spring and autumn). The printed editions are available for annual subscription directly from the publisher. The retail price incl. shipment within Germany is 75,00 € and for international purchases 85,00 €. The electronic version is available free of charge (Open Access). All information regarding notes for contributors, subscriptions, Open Access, back volume and orders is available online at https://www.transcript-publishing.com/dak

Bibliographic information published by the Deutsche Nationalbibliothek
The Deutsche Nationalbibliothek lists this publication in the Deutsche Nationalbibliografie; detailed bibliographic data are available in the Internet at http://dnb.de

First published by 2021 transcript Verlag, Bielefeld
© **Katharina Voigt and Virginie Roy (eds.)**

Cover layout: Uta Graff, Technical University of Munich
Copy-editing: Madison Erdall and Katharina Voigt, Technical University of Munich
Proofreading: Lisa Goodrum, London
Typeset: Katharina Voigt, Technical University of Munich

ISSN 2747-5085
eISSN 2747-5093
Print-ISBN 978-3-8376-5831-6
PDF-ISBN 978-3-8394-5831-0

Contents

TRACES

Introduction

»What interests me most is how I can use creativity to maintain openness and curiosity. I have never discarded my yearning for change.«

Rebecca Horn 1997: 19.

Horn, Rebecca/Haenlein, Carl (1997):
The Glance of Infinity, Zurich: Scalo.

Dimensions of Architectural Knowledge, 2021-02 ∂
https://doi.org/10.14361/dak-2021-0201

Editorial: Spatial Dimensions of Moving Experience

Katharina Voigt and Virginie Roy

Theme

»Spatial Dimensions of Moving Experience«, Issue 02/2021, investigates the relevance of the senses, the body, and movement in the discipline of architecture. The movements triggered by the experiences as well as the sensations of being moved are explored. While the inaugural issue of *Dimensions. Journal of Architectural Knowledge* initiated the discussion on the spectrum of methodologies and ways of working within architecture research, this second issue is concerned with the investigation of perception- and experience-based research questions and methods of applied and practice-based ways of working. Focusing on the movements of corporeal and spatial exploration and the experience of being moved by sensations, the issue analyzes and balances such concepts against each other. The issue goes into detail on observations and reflections in research, while paying particular attention to the ways in which architecture affects the experiencer, on how corporeality and sensuality are stimulated by architectural experience, and how body-knowledge is at work in this process.

This issue invites its readers to be inspired toward perspectives of thinking, acting, and conveying the implication of corporeality, the senses, and the subjective insights of experiencing architecture. Architecture, here, is understood in the broadest sense of the term: addressing both the discipline and the built environment, and any kind of conceived space, including all scales from landscape architecture and urbanism, to architectural spaces in the city, to buildings and interiors, furniture and objects. The presented research and reflections include the creative process of architectural design as well as the making and experience of the built environment; furthermore, notions of sociological, psychological, and anthropological or ethnological parameters involved in the perception, conception, or conveyance of architecture are addressed.

Corresponding authors: Katharina Voigt (Technical University of Munich, Germany); katharina.voigt@tum.de; http://orcid.org/0000-0002-2547-8292; Virginie Roy (Music and Art University, Vienna, Austria); v.roy@muk.ac.at; http://orcid.org/0000-0003-2879-1839.

We were eager to explore the questions: How are corporeal sensations of spatial and architectural experience perceived, and how can they be observed and described? How does the resonance of the perceptive awareness raise situational attention in particular, and how can it be the subject of reflective or practice-oriented research?

Structure

This issue resembles a layered landscape, inviting the readers to explore it as a journey, unraveling its different dimensionalities, exploring both its entirety and its individual components. It suggests opening up to the emergence of manifold perspectives and observations, and encourages their discovery and exploration. It aims to set out the terrain, to examine the rims and edges, as well as to look at the anchoring points and crystallizations of specific positions. This issue addresses moving experience in the context of the perception and conception of architectural space.

Theorists and practitioners from different disciplines reflect upon »Spatial Dimensions of Moving Experience« and present their findings, obtained in theoretical research, practice-based investigations or teaching, in order to contribute to the architectural discourse and add to the body of architectural knowledge. The presented contributions differ in methodology and format, ranging from field studies to doctoral theses, as well as practice-related and theoretical forms of research. They take reference to relevant theoretical positions in the field, highlight teaching methods and student projects, or refer to observations of actual lived experience and the sensations evoked by it.

All full paper contributions responded to this issue's »Call for Contributions« and were selected in a double-blind peer review procedure. The assembly of different positions and objectives in research entails their embedding in different contextual forms of research and their reflection against the background of their relevance to teaching, practice, and research in architecture. As proceedings from lived experience and their reflection provide notions of research and design methods rooted in sensual and corporeal experience, they bring forth the discourse already initiated in the inaugural issue of *Dimensions*, seeking perception- and experience-based methodologies.

Due to the challenges of our time, the peculiarities of modified spatial and moving experience due to the Covid-pandemic have become apparent in certain contributions as well. As this issue emerges from the background of a time of unique experiences, new and extended questions about the nature of life and its emphases are raised and enhanced methods of reflection are encouraged. The relationship to the body and to space has undergone a significant change as it has been restrained in multiple ways; what was previously taken for granted, now comes more clearly into consciousness. This increased awareness of space and body is the basis of this issue, aiming to bring sensual and bodily forms of perception to the forefront of architectural discourse.

This issue unfolds the **Layered Landscape** of knowledge in which this discourse is embedded, depicting anchoring points in the vastness of this landscape – like specific *places* or *situations* – to elaborate and investigate further. Particular attention, here, is given to the contributions, which concern the creative process in architecture. Many of the papers emphasize the importance of perceptual training, addressing ways of perceiving architecture in relation to the (moving) body, thereby highlighting their relevance for architectural design and teaching.

The first chapter explores the **Terrain** of investigation, providing the basis for the following contributions, which delve deeper into more detailed aspects. Under the overarching term of **Traces**, the second chapter elaborates on traces left in space and incorporated to the body upon spatial and moving experience. It retraces sensual, emotional, and associative events of experience. An **Assemblage** of gathered observations and sensations from lived experience constitutes the third section, which explores methods and practices of addressing moving experience and corporeal perception, bringing bodily ways of knowing to the fore. The last section of this issue expands the field of investigation further, exploring a possible **Extension** of the topic and versatile ways to adaptat it to different research contexts.

All contributions are intended to enrich the interdisciplinary discourse and to provide **Addition to the Architectural Body of Knowledge** in versatile dimensions. Indeed, with its assemblage of suggestions, this edition aims to inspire readers to rethink sensual experience and creative processes in architecture, as well as the notion of architectural design and, in doing so, to pave the way for new forms of conception in architecture.

Layered Landscape

»*Choreographing is embodying an abstraction.* Or, to put it another way: *a choreography is a calligraphy of embodiment.*«

Anne Teresa de Keersmaeker 2020: 60.

Keersmaeker, Anne Teresa de (2020): *Incarner une Abstraction.* – English translation: *Embodying an Abstraction,* transl. by Isobel Mackie and Joris van Leemput, Arles: Actes Sudes, édition bilingue.

Layered Landscape

Katharina Voigt and Virginie Roy

In resembling a multi-layered landscape, with manifold interlacements, sedimentations, and crystallizations of specificities, this issue unfolds the vastness of moving experience and its spatial dimensions. Setting this field of investigation in analogy to a landscape, the issue invites the reader to explore it in a journey of discovery. In this sense, this issue encourages the reader to actively engage: exploring an uncertain terrain requires openness to probe it and to let insights and impulses emerge from it. Accordingly, this issue does not necessarily demand a chronological reading.

Discovery takes time, and it is part of an on-going process of detection – taking the book in hand again and again in order to rediscover the content in light of the respective situation. Based on ever-changing experience, the reading of the different positions changes every time, as information is perceived differently according to the circumstances of its context. Taking time to discover also indicates allowing time to let the contents affect you in manifold ways, retracing perceptions in different situations anew.

Terrain

Along with contributions from different disciplinary fields, the first section of this issue explores the terrain of discourse, recounting the state of research and establishing different contexts of specific experience. In reference to the history and theory of architecture, the moving, sensual, or perceptual effects that architectural spaces have on the human body are addressed. Furthermore, movement and the sensation of being moved are examined under varying parameters; either in regard to somatic practice or the physicality of movement – with focus on the sensuality of movement, and the sensation of being moved, linked to emotional, mental, and associative movements of the mind – or in regard to the aesthetics of space and movement, with the attempt to interlink the disciplinary fields of architecture and dance as artistic and conceptual practices dedicated to space and movement.

Traces

Different positions are elaborated within the terrain of investigation that address the reciprocity and interaction of body, movement, and space. Within the framework of specific architectural contexts, they address the dialogue between the body and its environment. Furthermore, they investigate the traces that sensual and corporeal perceptions leave in the body, emphasize how they are incorporated and anchored in the body. Moving in space, the experiencers are also moved by their experience; the indications and sensations gathered are influential to the way in which we move and how we perceive. The moving experience regards varying modes of perception: Being moved evokes sensual, motional, and emotional resonance with the space, which are explored with the body. In this sense, the body can be regarded as an embodied resonating space in dialogue with the space of experience. Also, it forms the medium and tool to perceive what is there, to anchor in lived experience, and to take up a position in space.

Assemblage

Here, proceedings and observations from a teaching cycle on lived experience are documented and reflected in order to present the plurality of narrations derived from individual subjective experience. This contribution focuses on observations of the participating master's students, assembling experiential descriptions and photographically documented gestural, bodily expressions to bring forth their experience of architecture. As *trouvailles* – chance encounters and windfalls of finding that emerge from the situation without further attempts to foster them – these observations witness the individual processes of discovery in the exploration of architecture, with attuned awareness to bodily sensation, corporeal gesture, and movement. This section closes with a reflection on the constitution, conveyance, and relevance of such moments of particular attention in lived experience and their versatility in architectural design.

Extension

Beyond the experiential and sensual aspects of moving experience, this field is further expanded to address the question of how an enactive approach to memory and experience allows for change and transition in its prospective ways of adaption and anticipation in architectural design. The contributions assembled in this section take modes and procedures of perception into account, addressing proceedings achieved through the investigation of perceptive, bodily, or sensual processes, and observations on how the perception of space and movement is constituted. Furthermore, they investigate the appropriation, socio-cultural implications, and the politics of space that are derived from movement and moving experience. The matter of subjectivity and methodologies to address subjective, situational, and descriptive perspectives in architectural research are addressed throughout the contributions and propose different ways of working and investigative strategies to examine them.

Addition to the Architectural Body of Knowledge

This issue's contributions relate to different subjective and descriptive approaches to lived experience. Through tangible observations and investigation in research, they address moving experiences – which either emerge from the actual experience, or are connected to the memory or imagination of experiential events – and examine them with particular attention paid to their dimensionality and spatiality, as well as their relation to the body and the senses. To broaden the discourse, particular cases and research objectives take shape – just like places, cities, and other distinctive anchoring points – within the geographical landscape. Different concrete examples, which are located in and crystallize out of this terrain of knowledge, are used to illustrate the manifold forms in which it is expressed.

As the contributions suggest, sensual perception inevitably relies on corporeal experience. Body-based practices explore bodily ways of knowing as a pre-condition and an inherent part of experiencing space – and, vice-versa investigating the spatial dimension of body-based practice. Pre-reflective observations find their expression in corporeal gesture before they consciously come to attention. When encountering certain aspects of given situations or events, impressions are either left out during a sudden coming to awareness or are specifically addressed.

The aspect of being moved by experience is addressed in the multi-lateral sense of the term: experience evokes and triggers movement, while moving in space contributes constitutively to the experiencing of the space as such. Sensations of being moved are investigated in their associative, emotional, and sensual dimensions. Ultimately, the stream of perceptual experience is conveyed as a movement of thoughts, consolidating into memory and inheriting an inventory potential to envision ideas in the future.

Many of the challenges we face today – in the general global debates as well as in architectural discourse – are superordinate and so large that they tend to only be perceived as overwhelming and impossible to solve because of their sheer vastness and complexity. Questions about how we want to be in the world and how we want to live together have never been as urgent as they are today. An answer, here, could be to investigate the subjectivity embedded in architecture. It is an achievement of research approaches that acknowledge individual and subjective needs, experiences, and narratives to increase the plurality and diversity of perspectives considered in academic discourse.

»Spatial Dimensions of Moving Experience« stimulates further dimensions of research, knowledge constitution, and practice in architecture and its related disciplines, and strives to promote transdisciplinary exchange in order to widen the perspectives under consideration.

Terrain

»There are two things about ›Figure a Sea‹:
the body is the figure and inside is the sea.«

Deborah Hay 2015.

Hay, Deborah (2015): »Interview Deborah
Hay«, conducted by Josh Ronsen, in:
Monk Mink Pink Punk 27. http://ronsen.
org/monkminkpinkpunk/27/hay.html,
accessed September 20, 2021.

Cullberg Ballet/Deborah Hay:
»Figure a Sea«. Stokholm, 2015.

Dimensions of Architectural Knowledge, 2021-02 ʚ
https://doi.org/10.14361/dak-2021-0204

Architecture and/as Choreography:
Concepts of Movement and the Politics of Space

Lisa Beisswanger

Abstract: Dance projects exploring and interpreting architecture through choreography have become increasingly popular over the past two decades. This article takes a similar but theoretical approach, using the concept of choreography as a lens to look at the underlying scripts that shape the ways in which subjects move in, and are being moved by, architecture. Typically associated with the field of dance, choreography refers to spatial ordering principles, evoking highly political questions of authorship and authority, interpretation, improvisation, appropriation, accessibility, inclusion, and exclusion. Applying historical and comparative analysis, this article focuses on seminal examples from the fields of 20th-century Western dance and architecture. By mapping out evolving concepts and constellations of architecture and/as choreography, it aims to help create awareness of the spatial politics of architecture and their historical situatedness.

Keywords: Architecture Theory; Choreography; Dance; Motion; Movement; Politics; Space; Spatial Politics.

Introduction[1]

Let us begin with a sequence of images from Maribeth Romslo's short film *Kitchen Dance* (2020). We watch a woman entering a kitchen with a shopping net full of groceries. She opens a window at the far end of the room, briefly enjoying the breeze coming in through flowing white curtains. Soon, it becomes clear that the woman we are watching is not a regular »housewife« but a professional dancer. In fact, she is more than one. Her identity

---

1 The examples discussed in this text formed the basis for a seminar titled »Architecture as Choreography«, which I lead in the summer semester of 2020 in the Department of Architecture at the Technical University of Darmstadt. Some of the arguments presented here evolved out of the seminar discussions. Also, some of the literature referenced has been researched by participating students. I would like to thank all participants in the seminar for our stimulating discussions and for their contributions.

Corresponding author: Lisa Beisswanger (Technical University Darmstadt, Germany);
beisswanger@atw.tu-darmstadt.de; https://orcid.org/0000-0003-0331-7241

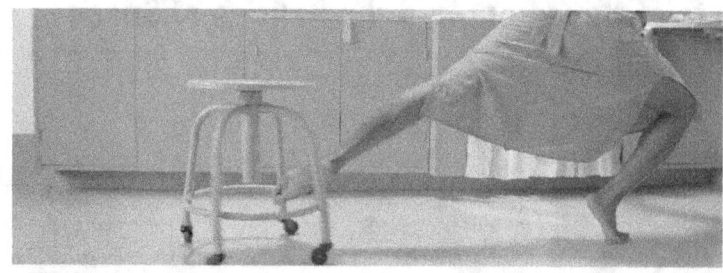

1.
Three stills from: Maribeth Romslo, Kitchen Dance, 2020, 7:30 min.
Online: https://web.archive.org/web/20201027232218/https://www.
kitchendanceproject.com/, accessed October 1, 2021 © Maribeth Romslo.

changes with every shot. In total, there are six dancers, each with different ethnic features. The ever-transforming protagonist puts away the groceries and begins to routinely move around the space, opening and closing cabinets and drawers. Sitting down on a stool she peels some potatoes, then sets them on a stove to cook. A stopwatch begins to tick. Now the woman's movements become more expansive and increasingly experimental. For example, she climbs onto the countertop and balances on the edge of the sink, she twirls on the floor like a break-dancer, and playfully pours flour out of a chute and swirls it around with her bare feet. The ringing of the stopwatch eventually ends this brief burst of creativity (fig. 1).

Architecture enthusiasts will immediately identify the film set as a *Frankfurt Kitchen*. They will know it was designed in 1927 by Austrian architect Margarete Schütte-Lihotzky (1897–2000) for the large-scale housing project *Neues Frankfurt*. Observers lacking this knowledge may notice the confined space and rationality of the kitchen's design and assume a historical context due to the somewhat outdated technological equipment. At the same time, the dancing women with their individual traits and styles, surely do not conform to the idea of a housewife in 1920s Germany. Neither do their movements follow the patterns prescribed by the architecture. By transgressing the standards inscribed into this kitchen, Romslo's film questions how architecture prefigures movement and constructs its user's subject, by means of choreography.

Dance projects like this have become increasingly popular over the past two decades. They explore and interpret both contemporary and historical architecture. In this article, I propose a similar but theoretical approach, using the concept of choreography as a lens to look at the underlying scripts that shape the ways in which subjects move in, and are being moved by, architecture. Traditionally associated with the field of dance, the term choreography comes from the Greek *choros* (=dance, dancing place) and *graphein* (=to write, writing) (cf. Brandstetter 2016). From here, two different, yet closely related spheres of inquiry unfold. On the one hand, there is the staging and performance of a choreography, the dimension of event and experience. On the other hand, there is the writing and prescribing of moving bodies in space, the dimension of notation, and the script (cf. Spier 2005; Brandstetter/ Hofmann/Maar 2010). In both cases, choreography refers to spatial ordering principles, evoking highly political questions of authorship and authority, interpretation, improvisation, appropriation, accessibility, inclusion, and exclusion.

Working with the medium of space, the disciplines of dance and architecture are both invested in the experiential and diagrammatic dimensions of choreography.[2] Yet, while in the field of dance the question of movement through space has always been central, in architecture it has only become prominent over the course of the 20th century (Jöchner 2004). This was closely related to technical and scientific innovations, for example, in transportation or telecommunications, and a concomitant change in the experience of mobility from the second industrial revolution around 1900 (Noell 2004) up until today's digital age of global »flows« (Delalex 2006). In this process, the way that movement in space is conceived in architecture changed along with notation techniques, for example, axonometry and 3-D-modeling (Krausse 1999).

It is against this backdrop that architectural theory has turned to questions of experiencing architecture in motion, some scholars addressing it in a more general sense (Zürn 2014; Blundell-Jones/Meagher 2015), and others, explicitly through the lens of choreography (Meisenheimer 1999), while a parallel discourse is dealing with architecture itself becoming kinetic and performative (cf. Vogt/Schaeffer/Schumacher 2012; Malkawi/Kolarevic 2005). Closer to the field of dance and combining the questions of performing and writing, Isa Wortelkamp argues that choreography makes it possible to achieve a sensory awareness of the »movement script« of architecture and to explore its »choreographic potential« (Wortelkamp 2006, author's translation). Kirsten Maar explores the reciprocal relationship of choreography and architecture, discussing the »situational potential« of both disciplines (Maar 2019: 31, author's translation). She rightly points out that their impact as both »models of thought that determine space« goes beyond the aesthetic sphere (Maar 2019: 28, author's translation). This performative and potentially disruptive dimension of choreography has been addressed by dance scholars with varying degrees of reference to architecture (Hewitt 2005; Lepecki 2013; Klein 2014, 2015). Here, questions about the political dimension of choreography arise. The scripting of movement and the organization of bodies in space evokes power structures and points to architecture's (bio-)political dimensions. Gerko Egert addresses this question from a global perspective in his current project on »Choreopower« (Egert 2020).

---

2 For a more in-depth look at architecture and choreography in etymological terms, see Maar 2019: 29–30.

In this article I will focus on such political dimensions of architecture and/ as choreography rather than its phenomenological or experiential aspects. I will do so from a historical and comparative perspective. The two parts of the article provide an overview of canonical positions – more precisely, canonical in Western discourse – from the fields of architecture and dance in the 20th century, which at the same time connect to each discipline in different ways. The first part will focus on the era of modernist rationalism and the second part will deal with the era of deconstructivism and the early digital age. On the basis of this overview I will sketch out how conceptions of space and the moving body have been subject to historical change and in what way they answered questions of authority and interpretation. By doing so, I intend to demonstrate how the concept of choreography can be a viable tool for a critical approach to architecture and spatial politics.

Norms, Efficiency, and Dynamics in the Era of the Second Industrial Revolution

Margarete Schütte-Lihotzky's *Frankfurt Kitchen* was the first serially produced fitted kitchen, a mass product built into thousands of homes. The standard variant is a small space of 6.5 square meters, connected to the living room by a kitchen pass-through. The kitchen is constructed from pre-fabricated components like work boards, floor and wall cabinets, an electric stove, a sink with running water, and accessories such as a dish drainer over the sink, a folding ironing board, an adjustable rolling metal stool, and handy chutes pre-labeled for the standard German cooking ingredients.

Developing her design, Schütte-Lihotzky aimed to »apply the principles of labor-saving economical management« (Schütte-Lihotzky 1927: 120). She looked at train and ship kitchens for inspiration and conducted movement studies – a method famously refined by Frank and Lillian Gilbreth in the early 1900s (cf. Corwin 2003) – resulting in diagrams resembling choreographic scripts (cf. Zürn 2014: 43). In favor of Taylorist efficiency, Schütte-Lihotzky championed short and linear movements in order to minimize the required effort. Implicitly, her studies were based on the idea of a prototypical well-functioning modern woman.[3]

---

3 What this woman may have looked like we see in a promotional film from 1927 where a young Caucasian woman with a short bob-haircut demonstrates the kitchen's functions. Die Frankfurter Küche, 1927, Online: https://web.archive.org/web/20211001173423/https://www.filmportal.de/node/123351/video/1445356, accessed October 1, 2021.

The architect stressed the emancipatory and health-relevant aspects of her design. She argued that speeding up a housewife's work in the kitchen would save her time and energy for more important tasks (Schütte-Lihotzky 1927: 120). However, apart from the fact that only women are considered possible kitchen users here, this stop-clock efficiency comes at the cost of limitation and de-individualization. A woman's workplace in the kitchen, separated from family life, resembles a factory setup or a giant machine, incorporating its user. In other words, by directing her every movement, the architect-choreographer's authority over the user is enormous, while space for interpretation shrinks to a minimum. What is true for the individual applies collectively as well. Imagining the women of *Neues Frankfurt* in their identical kitchens cooking standard German meals may remind one of the synchronized mass choreographies that became popular in the field of dance at the time. In the process, not only the kitchen design is standardized but also the bodies and lives of its users. Based on a normative image of women as care-workers in their families and in society, in this choreography, private space succumbs to the dictum of the machine age.

In parallel, some 500 kilometers northeast at the Bauhaus School in Dessau, *Neues Bauen* and dance were joined even more explicitly. At the very heart of the newly built school was a stage for interdisciplinary experimentation. It was here that »Bauhaus Master« and leader of the stage workshop, **Oskar Schlemmer** (1888–1943), created the so-called *Bauhaus Dances* (cf. Kaldrack 2011).[4] These short choreographies for up to three dancers could take different forms. Some involved props that were handled by the performers (e.g. *Baukastenspiel*, 1929) or devices strapped to their bodies (e.g. *Stäbetanz*, 1927–28), others, such as *Raumtanz* (1926), involved no props at all.[5] The stage setting for these dances was minimalist and performers wore de-individualizing masks and padded bodysuits. As in *Raumtanz*, where three dancers follow marked lines in the shape of a square, the dancer's steps and gestures were strictly timed, often mechanical. In this respect they are reminiscent of the movement patterns within the *Frankfurt Kitchen*.

---

4 Schlemmer developed the Bauhaus Dances with students and professional dancers (Siebenbrodt/Schöbe 2012: 179). Schlemmer taught at the school as a »Bauhaus Master« from 1921 to 1929. In 1923 he took over the Bauhaus Stage. Only after moving to Dessau was a professional stage available.

5 English translations of German titles: *Baukastenspiel* = Building-Block-Game, *Stäbetanz* = Stick-Dance, *Raumtanz* = Space-Dance.

These seemingly simple dances are embedded in a complex theoretical framework, propelled by Schlemmer's studies – as a visual artist rather than an architect – of abstract configurations of color, figure, and space. Dance and the stage played an important role here. A central problem for Schlemmer was the incompatibility of space, which he understood as a mathematical-abstract and geometric construct, and organic nature, as part of which he saw the human body (Schlemmer 1961[1926]: 25). Schlemmer visualized this in a drawing showing an abstracted stage crisscrossed by geometric lines, with a human figure at the center (fig. 2). According to Schlemmer, »man as dancer« (»*Tänzermensch*«) obeying »the law of the body as well as the law of space« is the ideal medium to bridge this divide (ibid.). Therefore, it was his interest in abstract space that made him turn to »body-mechanical« and »mathematical dance« (Schlemmer 1968[1926]: 129, author's translation, orig.: körpermechanischen/mathematischen Tanz). By using costumes and devices, Schlemmer aimed to help the transformation toward abstraction. In the process, he stated that »natural man, in deference to abstract space, is recast to fit its mold.« (Schlemmer 1961[1926]: 23). In this sense, Schlemmer's quest for abstraction has a limiting effect on the dancing subject. It conceptualizes non-individual dancers with limited freedom of movement to make them fit into his box-like concept of space.

Schlemmer's Bauhaus Dances were not about dancerly expression but rather analytical testing arrangements. It has been noted, that this brought him close to movement analysis and body-mechanical studies (Kaldrack 2011: 129 pp.). Schlemmer himself stressed his interest in »mechanization« and »technology« which he saw as two guiding principles of his time (Schlemmer 1961[1926]: 17). He was convinced that »theater, which should be the image of our time [...] must not ignore these signs« (ibid.: 18). However, as opposed to economically motivated movement studies, Schlemmer was not interested in technological efficiency, nor was it his aim to create a man-machine. It was rather his metaphysical search for universal truth that led him to de-individualization and standardization, giving his choreographies their mechanical character.

In what way is this relevant to architecture and/as choreography? First of all, Schlemmer's teaching formed part of a curriculum for architects, introducing dance and experience-based approaches into architecture education (Ersoy 2011). This teaching was not about actual design tasks but again, Schlemmer was pursuing larger goals: to reveal to his students the universal

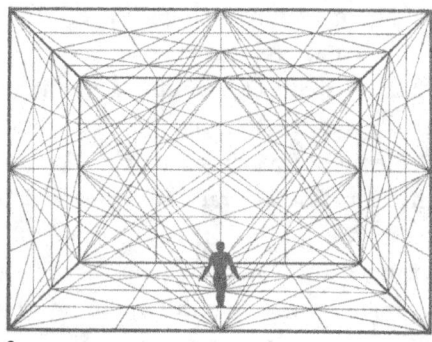

2.

Oskar Schlemmer, drawing of the abstract stage. From: Schlemmer, Oskar (1965[1925]): Mensch und Kunstfigur, in: Oskar Schlemmer et al.: Die Bühne im Bauhaus, Mainz: Kupferberg, 13.

3.

Dancer inside Rudolf von Laban's icosahedron, 1910s. Photographer unknown. From: Laban, Rudolf von (1926): Choreographie, Jena: Diederichs, n. p. Reproduction: Jürgen Schreiter, Darmstadt.

principles of man and space.[6] The idea of man as a universal prototype reveals an anthropocentric and essentialist world quite typical for this era. If we now think of the image of the architect conveyed in the process, they are pictured as keepers of universal knowledge, equipped with quasi omnipotent authority to create a universal theater or *Gesamtkunstwerk*, a popular idea at the Bauhaus. It seems important to consider this concept of artistic authority when thinking about the rationalist and rule-based design with which the Bauhaus of the 1920s is associated. Not unlike the *Frankfurt Kitchen*, this is an architecture that intentionally regulates and prescribes the choreographies of its users, all in the name of an essentialist vision of a »greater good«.

Negotiating the relationship between bodily movement and space was also central to the work of the influential dance scholar and »father« of *Ausdruckstanz*, **Rudolf von Laban** (1879–1951). Having studied architecture at the École des Beaux-Arts in Paris, Laban took a truly architectural approach to dance, understanding »movement« as a form of »living architecture« (Laban 2011[1966]: 5). Laban shared with Schlemmer the belief in a »law-governed inner unity of man and nature« and that the »dancer directly expresses the essence of the world« (Dörr/Lantz 2003: 9). However, Laban did not follow mechanical abstraction but chose a more expression-oriented approach. Himself a dancer, his thinking started from the individual moving body and he frequently stressed that the source of movement is a subject's »inner volition« (Laban 2011[1966]: 10). From here, he looked for spatial concepts flexible enough to deal with dynamic and complex movement. Focusing mostly on the individual dancer in his theoretical work, in his practice as a choreographer he took a strong interest in group dynamics and even mass choreographies. Good examples for this are his so-called *movement choirs* that he developed with amateurs (cf. Maletić 1987: 14f).

Similar to Schlemmer, Laban's basic idea of space followed the Euclidian box-model. But instead of »confronting« the dancing subject directly with the geometry of space, he defined the space within reach of the body's limbs as the *kinesphere*, surrounding the dancer like an invisible bubble.[7] To represent this sphere visually, Laban frequently used the platonic shape of the

---

6 The image of man was also the subject of Schlemmer's class *Der Mensch (The Human)* in which he included drawing exercises, biological, and anatomical studies as well as philosophy, aesthetics, ethics, and metaphysics.

7 Complementing the *kinesphere*, he defined the *dynamosphere* as a register for dynamics.

icosahedron. For example, for a series of photographs illustrating his 1926 manual on choreography, he had a dancer perform inside a human-scale icosahedron model (fig. 3, previous page). Laban's idea of the *kinesphere* freed the individual moving body from the »confines« of abstract space without giving up a geometric model of space. In comparison to Schlemmer's dances, this allowed Laban to conceptualize movement much more freely while holding on to the modernist essentialist image of man representing the harmony of the universe (cf. Dörr/Lantz 2003: 9).[8]

Laban became famous for his pioneering system of dance notation, today known as *Labanotation* (cf. Guest 2005). Inspired by the then new media of film and motion photography, this system was based on the idea of making movement visible through sequences of »snapshots« (Laban 2011[1966]: 3). At the same time *Labanotation* is deeply rooted in architectural diagrammatics. Laban argued that a »ground-plan, and at least two elevations« were necessary to convey »a plastic image of the three-dimensional whole« (ibid.: 5). The icosahedron model helped him arrive at reliable measuring points on the *kinesphere*. By means of a specifically developed system of signs, individual movements from one point to another could be noted. Additionally, he developed a register for the quality of movement, like speed or intensity. This he referred to as the *dynamosphere*.

Developing tools to systematically measure and describe movement in space is a highly political act. Movement ceases to be something that »just happens«, becoming prescriptible and plannable. With his pioneering work, Laban laid the foundation for increasingly sophisticated choreographic planning strategies that would later gain importance in both dance and architecture. Laban's case also exemplifies how the application of such choreographic knowledge can be highly ambivalent. For example, he cooperated with the National Socialist regime, creating a mass choreography for the opening of the 1936 Olympic Games (cf. Kew 1999). After falling out of favor with the regime and fleeing Germany in the 1940s, he lent his expertise to industrial movement studies in Great Britain (Davies 2006[2001]; Rothe 2012). As opposed to the Gilbreths or Schütte-Lihotzky, who saw short and mechanical movements as most effective, he experimented with dynamic movement

---

8 Laban frequently turned to the geometry of crystals, an image corresponding to his icosa-hedron model, to exemplify the universal order of nature.

patterns, making use of the body's inner drive for motion.[9] This focus on dynamism and processuality, and the intention to stimulate and channel intrinsic motivation in the name of increasing economic productivity, anticipates the tendency toward immaterial labor in the age of neoliberalism.

Where previous examples were mostly concerned with the relationship of bodily movement to space, movement *through* space and architecture is key to **Le Corbusier's** (1887–1965) *promenade architecturale*. The architect coined this term in 1934 when writing about his *Villa Savoye* (late 1920s). He claimed that to correspond to the dynamism of man, architecture should be experienced »*à la marche*« (Corbusier/Boesiger 2015[1934]: 24). He argued for a »living« architecture, challenging the central perspective directed toward a single immobile viewer that had prevailed – according to Le Corbusier – since the Baroque period (ibid.).

Le Corbusier describes the *Villa Savoye* as a walk-in scenography. From the recipient's arrival by car to following the double-flight ramp or spiral staircase up to the roof terrace, to a view of the surrounding nature opening up through a strategically placed opening in the wall. Movement is necessary to fully grasp and experience the building. Le Corbusier also stressed the activating elements of suspense and surprise along the way to prevent passive consumption (ibid.). By replacing the term »circulation« – a term he had previously used – with »*promenade*«, he favors aspects of spatial flow and dynamics over more technical questions of access (cf. Samuel 2010).

Compared to Schütte-Lihotzky's kitchen-choreography, the *promenade* evokes openness and freedom. Instead of efficient work flows it focuses on creating an inspiring and pleasant experience. Considering that the villa was designed as a place of relaxation and leisure for busy upper-class Parisians, this was certainly deliberate. At the same time, the moving experience is not left to chance. On the contrary, its linear progression is carefully scripted (cf. Blum 1988: 21). This leads us to consider the role of the architect in this choreography. To my knowledge, Le Corbusier did not conduct movement studies to arrive at this choreography but relied on his artistic intuition and sense of space as an architect. This makes the underlying concept more difficult to detect and contributes to Le Corbusier's image of himself as an artistic genius. Thereby, his role as a choreographer becomes less visible,

---

9 With reference to Schütte-Lihotzky's movement studies, it seems interesting, that he developed this approach to help women workers in post-war Great Britain lift heavier loads.

despite the degree of authority over this meticulously choreographed experience remaining similarly high, as it was in the design of the *Frankfurt Kitchen*.

Le Corbusier was not only the creator of villas, but he engaged in urban planning and mass housing such as his *Unité d'habitation* in Marseille (1940s). It seems interesting to compare the qualities of movement and the underlying conceptions of the users that come with this shift in scale. For the *Unité*, at least at first sight, the more technical concept of circulation seems more apt than the *promenade*. However, the design does follow a similar idea of curated progression, providing inhabitants with stimulating situations of space and light (cf. Janson 2007). Granting »ordinary citizens« the same experiences as wealthy villa owners points to the utopian idea of prosperity across classes, with design playing a major role in achieving this goal. At the same time, in the light of rational typification and standardization, the quasi-individuality of the *promenade* is brought to the fore. This oscillation between individuality and prototypical standardization is also reflected in Le Corbusier's *Modulor*, the human-scale model he developed as a reference for his own work. In keeping with the long-standing tradition of human modeling in architecture (cf. Zöllner 2014), its measurements are based on a standardized male (white) body.[10] This points to a modernist essentialism underlying Le Corbusier's buildings in general and the concept of the *promenade* in particular. The concept reveals itself to be indebted to the master narrative of linear progression and testifies to a belief in the possibility of projecting and controlling movement in space. At the same time, by introducing the individual user experience as a relevant concern, the *promenade* deviates from the rigorous »machine choreographies« of the early 20th century. As we will see in the following paragraphs, it is this aspect in particular that will be developed further in the second half of the century.

Deconstructing Authority and Approaching the Digital Age in the Postmodern Era

In the United States of the post-World War II period, dance pioneer **Anna Halprin** (1920–2021) and landscape architect **Lawrence Halprin** (1916–2009) tackled classical and modernist approaches in their respective fields. They did so individually and in collaborative projects. For example, building on

---

10 Federica Buzzi speaks of »an updated version of […] masculinist and ableist universalism« (Buzzi 2017). In this there is an overlap with the concepts of Ernst Neufert (Meister 2016).

the Bauhaus spirit they taught interdisciplinary workshops for dancers and architects, which were based on the idea of »movement as the primary impetus in form-making« (Wasserman 2012: 34) and focused on fostering active participation in planning processes (ibid.: 44f).[11]

An apt architectonic representation of the Halprins' methods is the so-called *Dance Deck* (1950), an irregularly shaped wooden platform built on a forested slope near the couple's home in San Francisco (fig. 4). The deck was designed by Lawrence Halprin and intended for Anna Halprin's dance classes and workshops. Its shape deviated radically from traditional rectilinear stages with a clear front and back, as exemplified by Oskar Schlemmer's design for an abstract stage. This, according to Anna Halprin, led to a »complete reorientation on the dancer. The customary points of reference are gone [...] the space explodes and becomes mobile« (A. Halprin, in: L. Halprin 1956: 24). Anna Halprin's dancing and choreography evolved in relation to this transgressive concept of space. Instead of linear and regulated movement, she favored intuition and improvisation based on an understanding of anatomy, but also visceral and spiritual knowledge. In her teaching she worked with professional dancers,[12] as well as amateurs, aiming to democratize dance by letting »everyone have mastery of movement« while »making it possible to go beyond the conformity of behavior« (Bal-Blanc 2020).

For Lawrence Halprin, his profession of landscape architecture was just as much about »making space« as it was about dance. Writing about *The Choreography of Gardens* he criticizes baroque central perspective – just as Le Corbusier had done – and promotes designing »with the moving person in mind« (L. Halprin 1949: 32). In his eyes, design should be organic and playful, enriching everyday life with »a continuous sense of dance« (ibid.: 34). In this, he goes beyond Le Corbusier's scripted activation of the recipient/ user, aiming to create environments that prompt improvised responses and active participation. His water fountain designs, for example, are constructions of large concrete blocks and platforms of varying shapes and sizes on which visitors can sit and play (i.e. *Ira Keller Fountain*, 1970, Portland, Oregon). Participation was also key to his concept of *RSVP cycles* (cf. Hirsch 2014: 185f), a multi-step method for community involvement in planning processes.

---

11   Lawrence Halprin had studied at Harvard where Bauhaus architects Walter Gropius and Marcel Breuer were teaching.

12   Among them, Yvonne Rainer and Trisha Brown who later went on to be part of *Judson Dance Theater* in New York.

4.
Dance Deck with one person standing with hands on hips, possibly Anna Halprin, 1970s. Photographer unknown. Anna Halprin Papers, The Elyse Eng Dance Collection, Museum of Performance + Design.

This method was for »breaking down traditional distinctions between architect/dweller and choreographer/audience« (Merriman 2010: 436) and made him a forerunner of today's participatory planning approaches in architecture.

»In a world intensely involved in the development of motion through space«, Lawrence Halprin writes in 1966, little has been done to express it graphically« (L. Halprin 1966: 26). This is why he came up with the notation system of *Motation* (= motion + notation), »a tool for choreography [...] in the broadest sense – meaning design for movement« (ibid.: 31). This system is somewhat complementary to *Labanotation* – which Lawrence Halprin was well aware of. He points out that *Motation* does not record gestures in space but motion through space and the relationships of people, objects, and their environment (ibid.: 27). He used this system for noting Anna Halprin's choreographies, as well as for his architectural designs, from parks to shopping malls, and even highway systems (Merriman 2010: 434). In focusing on relational aspects and communication, *Motation* shows a sensibility for the growing complexity of societies and environments.

The Halprins set the Euclidean box-like space into motion. Rejecting traditional stage environments, in dance and – in a more metaphorical sense – in architecture, they were interested in the performance of everyday life. In Schlemmer's words, »natural man« takes over, rendering the idea of man as a prototype or programmable machine obsolete. Instead, individual experience and creation are brought to the fore. Compared to Le Corbusier's concept of the *promenade architecturale*, which reveals itself as a concept closer to consumption than self-initiated action, active participation and appropriation is encouraged. The Halprins' participatory approach drastically shifts authority from the hands of the choreographer to the choreographed. Historically, this democratization of choreography is embedded into greater sociopolitical processes, navigating the balance of individuality and collectivity in the post-war pluralist democracy of the United States.

Architect **Bernard Tschumi** (*1944) is equally interested in shifting authority from choreographers to the choreographed. Initially unfolding his practice as a theoretician and »paper architect«, he explores the fringes and limits of architecture in all of his projects. In the spirit of post-structuralist thought he takes particular interest in deconstructing the conventions and ordering systems of the discipline. »Movement«, »action«, and »event« are among the keywords most frequently used in his writing. A statement he continues to make is that »there is no architecture without action, without program, and without event. Architecture must deal with movement and action in space. If one does not understand architecture in this complex way, [...] there will be no architecture anymore« (Tschumi/Ruby 1993: 70, author's translation).

With his *Manhattan Transcripts* (1976–81), a series of graphic compositions in several parts (fig. 5), Tschumi created a method for spatial and movement notation that corresponded to his deconstructivist approach (cf. Tschumi 1994). The *Transcripts* combine line drawings and photographs which are abstractions of architectural spaces (represented through plans), movements (represented through movement diagrams) and events (represented through photographs) (ibid.: 7). Each part of the series deals with a different aspect of urban space and follows a loose narrative (ibid.: 8–9). Borrowing the terminology of cinema, Tschumi speaks of »a form of architectural jump-cut« (ibid.: 12). Unlike *Labanotation* or Motation, the *Transcripts* are not for scripting or recording movement sequences. Instead, Tschumi aimed to »transcribe things normally removed from conventional architectural representation, namely the complex relationship between spaces and their use« (ibid.: 7). In this way he »contaminated« or disrupted architecture's conventional plan drawings with the movements and events of everyday life. According to Tschumi, it is the negotiations of indifference, reciprocity, and conflict (ibid.: XXI) which produce space and architecture. The *Transcripts* as an experimental form of mapping make this reciprocal and conflicting relationship of built and lived space visible, without dissolving its complexity.

With the large-scale project of the *Parc de la Villette*, a 35 hectare park in the northeast of Paris, Tschumi put his theoretical approach into practice. The concept for the park is based on the basic constructivist shapes of points, lines, and surfaces. On a 10 × 10 × 10 meter grid of points, bright red steel structures – Tschumi calls them *Folies* – are scattered throughout the park. These small buildings are intended for cultural and recreational activities, but their design, which is somewhat reminiscent of playful and dysfunctional machines (Gugeler 2005: 50), does not make this function immediately apparent. The lines are paths cutting through the park: two intersecting main axes and a »cinematic promenade« – a sequence of smaller gardens – that meanders through the entire park. The *surfaces* in between are to be used freely (Tschumi 1988: 7–8). By moving the main routes off the axis and allowing paths to run into the void, architectural conventions are destabilized in order to deconstruct their »inbuilt ideology« (ibid.: VII) in the name of an »architecture that means nothing« (ibid.: VIII).

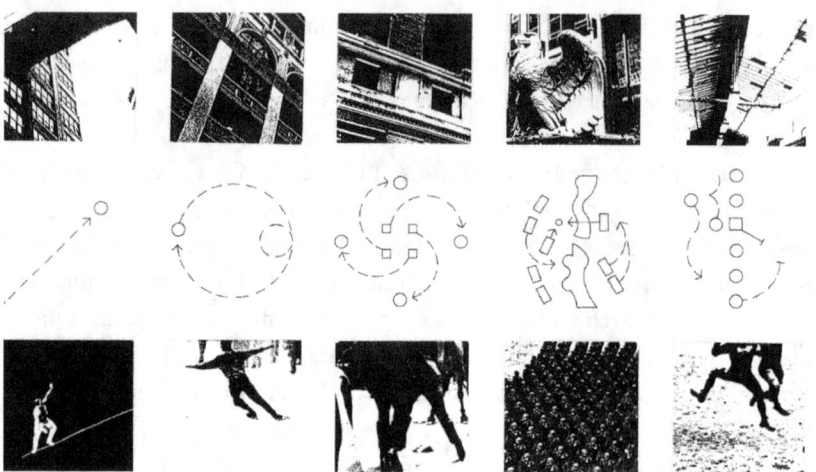

5.
Bernard Tschumi, The Manhattan Transcripts, *Episode 4: The Block, 1981.*
© Bernard Tschumi.

6.
William Forsythe with Dana Caspersen and Joel Ryan,
White Bouncy Castle, 1997, plastic, ventilators,
sound. Photo: Julian Gabriel Richter.

Tschumi thinks of architecture in close relation to its users, but instead of functionality he emphasizes an openness toward unforeseen dynamics and processes. If one now asks for the human subject at the centre of this conception, the image remains strangely obscure. Tschumi speaks about events and bodies, but not about individual participants or their identities. His is a cinematic perspective, a view from the outside, making the park appear as a kind of open film set or laboratory in which everything and nothing can happen. Compared to Le Corbusier, the architect here is less a designer than a facilitator of experience, while compared to Lawrence Halprin's communicative landscape architecture, his projects appear decentralized and neutral. It also seems significant that Tschumi, despite his focus on movement and events, does not refer to himself as a choreographer. One may even say that he is a choreographer who refuses to choreograph, very much in tune with Roland Barthes' prominent theory of the »death of the author«. With this radical renunciation of authority, Tschumi transfers all responsibility to the users or the choreographed, even at the risk of confusing or overwhelming them.

Deconstruction and participation are also major concerns for the choreographer **William Forsythe** (*1949). Forsythe became known for revolutionizing (neo-)classical ballet as the director of the Frankfurt Ballet in the 1980s, and later the *Forsythe Company*. It would be going too far to examine the breadth of his work here. Instead, a few focal points that correspond with the preceding examples in different ways will be highlighted. These concern questions of space and movement in space, the question of participatory choreography, and movement notation in the digital age.

Forsythe's ballets usually take place on minimalist stages, which may remind one of Oskar Schlemmer's stage concepts. Unlike Schlemmer, however, Forsythe's is a decentral concept of space that negates the central stage perspective, for example, when dancers turn away from the audience or disappear from their field of vision (e.g. *Heterotopia*, 2006, where there are two stages which are not visible at once), or when the audience is integrated in the stage action (e.g. *You Made Me a Monster*, 2005). Such choreographic twists transform the audience into active performers, blurring the conventional role attributions of theater (cf. Spier 2011). Similar to Tschumi, Forsythe also defines space not abstractly, but as a place of negotiation between aesthetic and social processes. Highly aware of choreography's inbuilt power dynamics, he aims to make these dynamics visible by turning its principles against themselves. As Mark Franko notes, Forsythe sees »choreography as an enabling practice [...] From this vision emerges a political potential that also becomes visible in performance« (Franko 2006).

In relation to architecture, Forsythe's so-called *Choreographic Objects* are of particular interest. These objects – often large installations – follow an interventionist strategy that literally sets bodies in motion. These works are created for amateur dancers, illustrating basic principles of choreography which to Forsythe are never monocausal, but always relational. By incorporating objects into his choreographic thinking, Forsythe also breaks with the notion – which for example was key to Laban's *kinesphere* – that movement must necessarily come from a single center or body. Instead, he tries to figure out what happens when there are multiple centers of movement (Gilpin 2011: 120). Forsythe's *White Bouncy Castle* (1997)[13] which is a giant, inflated castle-shaped playground/stage made of a white plastic fabric (fig. 6), may demonstrate this approach best (cf. Maar 2019: 285). When participants enter this elastic space, they are not only moved by the architecture that surrounds them but also they also influence each other's movements. There is no predetermined choreography, no dancers, and no audience, but everything dissolves in an anarchic and playful choreography. Similar to Tschumi's projects, a refusal of choreographic authority can be observed here. At the same time, both experiment with decentralizing not only space but also the idea of the subject, including architecture and objects as non-human actors in their choreographies. This marks a turn away from modernist anthropocentrism and toward perspectives of new materialism. Offering a playground without specifying the rules of the game is a highly political and also ambivalent gesture. Similar to Tschumi's *Parc de la Villette*, Forsythe's *White Bouncy Castle* turns every movement into an event. Instead of passively consuming, the audience is forced into the role of the performer. The radical openness to everybody and anything that may happen signals inclusion, and at the same time, points to an increasing »eventization« of all areas of life.

Forsythe is, finally, a pioneer of digital dance notation. Looking for an adequate medium to communicate his ideas on dance and dissatisfied with *Labanotation* that requires a high degree of expert knowledge, he turned instead to computer-assisted visualization techniques. One result of this research is the *Motion Bank* project (founded in 2010 with David Kern), that uses motion capture technology to record dance. This form of notation makes

13 The project's initial Title was Tight Roaring Circle and it was a collaboration with Dana Caspersen and Joel Ryan (cf. Spier 2011: 140f.).

it possible to work beyond a fixed repertoire of gestures, as did Lawrence Halprin's *Motation*, but also, to display a four-dimensional all-round view on a two-dimensional screen.[14] In principle, this is a cinematic approach indebted to historical movement studies (Fingerle/Woeste 1999: 31). At the same time, working with digital data opens op the possibility of processing and displaying the same material in many different ways. From a historical perspective this approach responds to the growing complexity of choreography (as exemplified in the *White Bouncy Castle*), and experiences of simultaneity and multi-causality in the age of global flows. Similar digital design tools have been developed and used in the field of architecture. A particularly interesting example in terms of choreography is the so-called *Space Syntax* project. In the tradition of economical movement studies, the project provides the software and methods to study complex movement patterns for efficient infrastructural planning.[15]

Conclusion: Concepts of Movement and the Politics of Space

This article's tour de force through the shared histories of architecture and dance focuses on three aspects: conceptions of movement in space and the underlying construction of the subject (1), questions of authorship and authority (2), and the corresponding design tools or forms of notation (3). To conclude, these aspects will be summarized and put into historical context, to then come back to the initial question concerning architecture and/as choreography and the politics of space.

(1) The examples demonstrated how, over the course of the 20th century, conceptions of space and movement became increasingly fluid and complex. Drawing a line from Oskar Schlemmer's geometrical stage concept via Anna and Lawrence Halprin's multi-faceted *Dance Deck* to William Forsythe's mobile *Choreographic Objects*, reveals a shift from the Euclidean box model toward a radically decentral conception of space. The imagined or projected quality of movement changed in close correspondence. The mechanical movement patterns embedded in Margarete Schütte-Lihotzky's *Frankfurt Kitchen* or Oskar Schlemmer's *Bauhaus Dances*, in keeping with geometric

---

14 In parallel, the so-called Piecemaker software makes it possible to annotate the recorded scenes in writing.

15 The project's website is: https://web.archive.org/web/20211001173704/https://spacesyntax.com/, accessed October 1, 2021.

space, were countered by the more dynamic movement concepts of Rudolf von Laban or Le Corbusier. From here, approaches, as in Anna Halprin's decentral choreographies or Bernard Tschumi's open park design, open up toward free improvisation. When it comes to the conception of the subject/ dancer/user, earlier examples such as Schütte-Lihotzky or Schlemmer tended to rely on a one-size-fits-all prototype, while later examples, such as the Halprins, took a strong interest in individuality. Following this path, the concepts of Bernard Tschumi or William Forsythe go even further, pointing toward an increasingly autonomous and self-designed subject. This freedom can be demanding in that it comes at the cost of high personal responsibility and a prerequisite to perform creatively in even the most mundane situations. In performance studies this phenomenon has been theorized as a state of »permanent performance«. When architecture becomes event-like, it reflects but also supports this process.

(2) Concepts of authority and authorship changed along with the sketched-out decentralization of space, movement, and subject. The examples discussed point to a continuous decrease in regulation or control on the part of the architect/choreographer. For example, compared to Margarete Schütte-Lihotzky's authoritarian kitchen design, the moving experience Le Corbusier's *promenade* offers is much more open, albeit still meticulously curated. Lawrence Halprin went on to create increasingly open-ended choreographies, and finally, Bernard Tschumi or William Forsythe intentionally avoided making any prescriptions. This process was accompanied by a decrease in the significance of singular authorship, an artistic self-image that was still prominent among actors such as Oskar Schlemmer or Le Corbusier. In the era of the »death of the author«, the concept of the choreographer as an unchallenged authority lost its appeal. The example of the Halprins best shows how participatory approaches and questions of shared authorship gained popularity in turn. Historically, this mirrors a paradigm shift in the ways that subjectivity and collectivity are negotiated in Western democracies. Spaces for improvisation and interpretation on the part of the users/choreographed radically increased, until, as in the projects of Tschumi and Forsythe, roles are reversed and participants become the authors of their own experience. Appearing at first as non- or even anti-authoritarian, such approaches rely on self-regulation. Therefore, they are inscribed with very complex and less visible forms of authority. In today's age of neoliberalism, where »shared spaces«, »inclusion«, or »access« have become popular buzzwords for investors and project developers, a sensibility toward these hidden

forms of authority and the related question of responsibility for our built environment is of particular importance.

(3) The tools or forms of notation in dance and architecture mirror the sketched-out development, becoming increasingly complex and multi-perspectival. Where the system of *Labanotation* focuses entirely on individual movements in space, *Motation* is able to note motion through space along with the design and quality of this space. Bernard Tschumi's deconstructive diagrammatics abandoned any linearity or narrative in favor of open-ended association. Finally, digital notation tools as developed by William Forsythe or the above-mentioned *Space Syntax* program are designed to capture increasingly individual and complex movement patterns in a decentralized space. A striking phenomenon in relation to the development of choreographic strategies and notation tools are the recurring overlaps with economically motivated movement studies. Be it the machine-like movement patterns applied by Schütte-Lihotzky, the dynamic movement concept of Rudolf von Laban, or the design of relational movement by Lawrence Halprin and Space Syntax, all of these approaches demonstrate a close connection between choreographic knowledge and economic value. The changing conceptualization of movement reflects the economic paradigm shift from physical to immaterial labor. In a more general sense, it refers to the ambivalence of (artistic) movement research between empowerment and exploitation. Along with changing concepts of the moving subject, this points to the biopolitical dimension of architecture and/as choreography.

The examples here have shown how choreographies in dance and architecture have been subject to historical change. From today's perspective, Schlemmer's mechanical dances or Le Corbusier's meticulously planned *promenade* may appear somewhat narrow and authoritarian, and we may sympathize more with the open-ended choreographies of Bernard Tschumi or William Forsythe. However, it is not the intention of this article to tell a story of progress. It seems well worth noting that within their historical contexts, all of the protagonists pursued emancipatory goals. Margarete Schütte-Lihotzky's aim was to save women time and energy, Oskar Schlemmer followed a quest for metaphysical truth, Le Corbusier worked on comfortable living for the masses, and the Halprins were looking for better ways of working together. At the same time, it became clear that any concept of movement in space is inevitably linked to questions of authority and therefore inherently political. By explicitly addressing those political questions of the ordering of space, the prescription of movement and the shifting degrees of authority and participation involved, the concept of choreography helps us to reveal and understand the power dynamics built into architecture. Finally, the *Kitchen Dance* project points toward choreography's important potential as a practice. Whether dealing with modernist master narratives or today's fluid concepts of authority, it reminds us of the necessity to constantly re-read and re-evaluate our built environment.

References

Bal-Blanc, Pierre (2020): »Anna Halprin's Dance Deck«, in: *Flash Art*, 29 May, https://web.archive.org/web/20210525165446/https://flash---art.com/2020/05/anna-halprins-dance-deck/, accessed May 25, 2021.

Blum, Elisabeth (1988): *Le Corbusiers Wege: Wie das Zauberwerk in Gang gesetzt wird (Le Corbusier's Paths: How the Magic Work is Set in Motion)*, Braunschweig: Vieweg.

Blundell-Jones, Peter/Meagher, Mark, eds. (2015): *Architecture and Movement: The Dynamic Experience of Buildings and Landscapes*, London/ New York: Routledge.

Brandstetter, Gabriele (2016): »Choreographie«, in: Erika Fischer-Lichte/Doris Kolesch/Matthias Warstat (eds.), *Metzler Lexikon Theatertheorie*, Stuttgart: J. B. Metzler, 54–57.

Brandstetter, Gabriele/Hofmann, Franck/Maar, Kirsten, eds. (2010): *Notationen und choreographisches Denken (Notations and Choreographic Thinking)*, Freiburg/Berlin/Wien: Rombach Verlag.

Buzzi, Federica (2017): »›Human, All Too Human‹: A Critique on the Modulor«, in: *FA Failed Architecture*, https://web.archive.org/web/20210908213607/https://failedarchitecture.com/human-all-too-human-a-critique-on-the-modulor/, accessed September 8, 2021.

Corwin, Sharon (2003): »Picturing Efficiency: Precisionism, Scientific Management, and the Effacement of Labor«, in: *Representations 84/1*, 139–165.

Davies, Eden (2006[2001]): *Beyond Dance: Laban's Legacy of Movement Analysis*, New York: Routledge.

Delalex, Gilles (2006): *Go with the Flow: Architecture, Infrastructure and the Everyday Experience of Mobility*, Helsinki: University of Art and Design.

Dörr, Evelyn/Lantz, Lori (2003): »Rudolf von Laban: The ›Founding Father‹ of Expressionist Dance«, in: *Dance Chronicle 26/1*, 1–29.

Egert, Gerko (2020): »Migration, Kontrolle und Choreomacht«, in: *Archplus 53*, 210–219.

Ersoy, Zehra (2011): »›Building Dancing‹: Dance within the Context of Architectural Design Pedagogy«, in: *JADE 30/1*, 123–132.

Fingerle, Kay/Woeste, Eghard (1999): »Phrasieren im Raum« (Phrasing in Space), in: *Archplus 148*, 31–33.

Franko, Mark (2006): »Dance and the Political States of Exception«, in: *Dance Research Journal 38/1–2*, 3–28.

Gilpin, Heidi (2011): »Aberrations of Gravity«, in: Steven Spier (ed.), *William Forsythe and the Practice of Choreography*, New York: Routledge, 112–127.

Guest, Ann Hutchinson (2005): *Labanotation: The System of Analyzing and Recording Movement*, 4th edition, Florence: Taylor & Francis.

Gugeler, Michaela (2005): »Der Parc de la Villette – Würfelwurf der Architektur: Das Zusammenwirken von Bernard Tschumi und Jacques Derrida beim Parc de la Villette in Paris« (Parc de la Villette – Architecture's Throw of the Dice: The Collaboration of Bernard Tschumi and Jacques Derrida at the Parc de la Villette in Paris), in: *Kritische Berichte 33/2*, 44–57.

Halprin, Lawrence (1949): »The Choreography of Gardens«, in: *Impulse Dance Magazine*, 30–43.

Halprin, Lawrence (1966): »Motation«, in: *Impulse Dance Magazine* [First published in: *Progressive Architecture*, 1965], 26–33.

Hewitt, Andrew (2005): *Social Choreography: Ideology as Performance in Dance and Everyday Movement*, Durham, NC: Duke University Press.

Hirsch, Alison Bick (2014): *City Choreographer: Lawrence Halprin in Urban Renewal America*, Minneapolis: University of Minnesota Press.

Janson, Alban (2007): »›Émouvant de jour et magique la nuit.‹ The architectural reality of the Unité d'habitation« (›Moving by Day and Magical by Night.‹ The Architectural Reality of the Unité d'habitation), in: Axel Menges (ed.), *Le Corbusier. Unité d'habitation*, Marseille : Opus 65, Stuttgart : Edition Axel Menges, 18–39.

Jöchner, Cornelia (2004): »Wie kommt ›Bewegung‹ in die Architekturtheorie? Zur Raum-Debatte am Beginn der Moderne« (How Does ›Movement‹ Enter Architectural Theory? On the Space Debate at the Beginning of Modernism), in: *Wolkenkuckucksheim 9/1*, https://web.archive.org/web/20160926041908/http://www.cloud-cuckoo.net/openarchive/wolke/deu/Themen/041/Joechner/joechner.htm, accessed October 1, 2021.

Kaldrack, Irina (2011): »Die Bauhaustänze Oskar Schlemmers« (Oskar Schlemmer's Bauhaus Dances), in: *Maske und Kothurn* 57/1–2, 123–140.

Kew, Carole (1999): »From Weimar Movement Choir to Nazi Community Dance: The Rise and Fall of Rudolf Laban's ›Festkultur‹«, in: *Dance Research Journal 17/2*, 73–96.

Klein, Gabriele (2014): »Dancing Politics. Worldmaking in Dance and Choreography«, in: Gabriele Klein/Sandra Noeth (eds.), *Emerging Bodies*, Bielefeld: transcript, 17–28.

Klein, Gabriele (2015): »Ordnung und Krawall. Choreografien in urbanen Räumen« (Order and Riot. Choreographies in Urban Spaces), in: Marianne Bäcker/Mechthild Schütte (eds.), *Tanz Raum Urbanität (Dance, Space, Urbanity)*, Leipzig: Henschel, 121–135.

Krausse, Joachim (1999): »Raum aus Zeit: Architektur aus der Bewegung«, in: *Archplus 148*, 22–29.

Laban, Rudolf von (2011[1966]): *Choreutics*, edited by Lisa Ullman, Hampshire: Dance Books Ltd.

Le Corbusier/Boesiger, Willy (2015[1934]): *Le Corbusier - Oeuvre complete, Vol. 2, 1929 – 1934*, 18th edition, Basel: Birkhäuser.

Lepecki, André (2013): »Choreopolice and Choreopolitics: Or, the Task of the Dancer«, in: *The Drama Review 57/4*, 13–27.

Maar, Kirsten (2019): *Entwürfe und Gefüge: William Forsythes choreographische Arbeiten in ihren architektonischen Konstellationen* (Designs and Structures: William Forsythe's Choreographic Works in their Architectural Constellations), Bielefeld: transcript.

Maletić, Vera (1987): *Body, Space, Expression: The Development of Rudolf Laban's Movement and Dance Concepts*, Berlin/New York: Mouton de Gruyter.

Malkawi, Ali/Kolarevic, Branko (2005): *Performative Architecture: Beyond Instrumentality*, New York: Spon Press.

Meisenheimer, Wolfgang (1999): *Choreografie des architektonischen Raumes: Das Verschwinden des Raumes in der Zeit*, (Choreography of Architectural Space: The Disappearance of Space in Time) Düsseldorf: Fachhochschule.

Meister, Anna-Maria (2016): »Formatting the Modern Dream«, in: *Harvard Design Magazine »Shelf Life«, 43/Fall*, 122 –124.

Merriman, Peter (2010): »Architecture/Dance: Choreographing and Inhabiting Spaces with Anna and Lawrence Halprin«, in: *Cultural Geographies 17/4*, 427–449.

Noell, Matthias (2004): »Bewegung in Zeit und Raum: Zum erweiterten Architekturbegriff im frühen 20. Jahrhundert« (Movement in Time and Space: On the Expanded Concept of Architecture in the Early 20th Century), in: Franck Hofmann/Jens E. Sennewald/Stavros Lazaris (eds.), *Raum – Dynamik: Beiträge zu einer Praxis des Raums*, Bielefeld: transcript, 301–314.

Rothe, Katja (2012): »Economy of Human Movement. Performances of Performance Research«, in: *Economic Knowledge* 17/6, 32–39.

Samuel, Flora/Le Corbusier (2010): *Le Corbusier and the Architectural Promenade*, Basel: Birkhäuser.

Schlemmer, Oskar (1961[1926]): »Man and Art Figure«, in: Walter Gropius/Arthur S. Wensinger (eds.), *The Theater of the Bauhaus*, Middleton: Wesleyan University Press, 15–46.

Schlemmer, Oskar (1968[1926]): »Tänzerische Mathematik« (Dance Mathmatics), in: Hans Maria Wingler (ed.), *Das Bauhaus: 1919 – 1933: Weimar, Dessau, Berlin und die Nachfolge in Chicago seit 1937*, Bramsche: Rasch, 128–130.

Schütte-Lihotzky, Margarete (1927): »Rationalisierung im Haushalt« (Rationalization in the Household), in: *Das Neue Frankfurt*, 5/April–June, 120–123. doi: 10.11588/DIGLIT.17290.41

Siebenbrodt, Michael/Schöbe, Lutz (2012): *Bauhaus: 1919–1933*, New York: Parkstone International.

Spier, Steven (2005): »Dancing and Drawing: Choreography and Architecture«, in: *The Journal of Architecture* 10/4, 349–364.

Spier, Steven (2011): »Choreographic Thinking and Amateur Bodies«, in: Steven Spier (ed.), *William Forsythe and the Practice of Choreography*, New York: Routledge, 139–150.

Tschumi, Bernard (1994): *The Manhattan Transcripts*, Robert Young (ed.), London: Academy Editions.

Tschumi, Bernard (1999): *Architecture and Disjunction*, 5th edition, Cambridge, MA: The MIT Press.

Tschumi, Bernard/Ruby, Andreas (1993): »Die Aktivierung des Raums: Bernard Tschumi im Gespräch mit ARCH+« (The Activation of Space: Bernard Tschumi in Conversation with ARCH+), in: *Archplus* 119/120, 70–121.

Tschumi, Bernard/Derrida, Jacques/Vidler, Anthony (2014): *Tschumi: Parc de la Villette*, London: Artifice.

Vogt, Michael-Marcus/Schaeffer, Oliver/Schumacher, Michael, (eds.) (2012): *MOVE. Architektur in Bewegung – Dynamische Komponenten und Bauteile (MOVE. Architecture in Motion – Dynamic Components and Building Elements)*, Basel: De Gruyter.

Wasserman, Judith (2012): »A World in Motion: The Creative Synergy of Lawrence and Anna Halprin«, in: *Landscape Journal* 31/1–2, 33–52.

Wortelkamp, Isa (2006): »Choreographien der Architektur: Bewegung schreiben, Wege lesen« (Choreographies of Architecture: Writing Movement, Reading Paths), in: Kerstin Hausbei (ed.), *Erfahrungsräume: Configurations de l'expérience*, Munich: Fink, 174–181.

Zöllner, Frank (2014): »Anthropomorphism: From Vitruvius to Neufert, from Human Measurement to the Module of Fascism«, in: Kirsten Wagner/Jasper Cep (eds.), *Images of the Body in Architecture: Anthropology and Built Space*, Tübingen: Wasmuth, 47–75.

Zürn, Tina (2016): *Bau Körper Bewegung. Prozessuale Raumaneignung in der Moderne (Building Body Movement. Processual Appropriation of Space in Modernity)*, Berlin/Munich: Deutscher Kunstverlag.

Dimensions of Architectural Knowledge, 2021-02 ⊕
https://doi.org/10.14361/dak-2021-0205

Principles of Somatic Movement Education for Architectural Design

Wiktor Skrzypczak

Abstract: An architect trying to predict the spatial effect of their design on its inhabitants often faces a dilemma. Their professional experience and personal feeling allows them to intuit its effect. Such intuition, however, might lack legitimacy in the dominant design practice. For over a century, the question of the felt space in architecture has been a topic of theoretical discussion, which led to the insight that the answer might lay not so much in studying the architectural structures, but rather in studying the bodies that inhabit them. And still the dominant architectural practice follows the outdated dualistic (mis-)understanding of the felt space. Another historical development took place in dance. Here, since the 1960s, the traditionally formalistic and objectifying understanding of dance has been strongly influenced by techniques of bodily sensitization, stemming from the field of somatics. In themselves rather diverse, these techniques have been institutionally delineated through the principles of somatic movement education. One of their characteristics is that somatic techniques are constantly re-emerging – not from a priori knowledge but from the study of one's own body and its interactions with the environment. This article envisages how such principles might be applied to architectural design practice and give rise to new embodied design practices – which might foster architects' sensory expertise and thus legitimize the felt knowledge in professional contexts.

Keywords: Empathy Theory; Phenomenology; Somatics; Practice; Sensory Expertise.

As a practicing architect, while designing, I often ask myself: *What would it feel like to be in that space?* Apparently a simple question, which entails however further questions – »Is it more about the feeling of *being*, or rather the feeling of the *space* itself?« In the tradition of the Enlightenment, questions of being were reduced to questions of thinking, the questions of the mind – the Cartesian »I think therefore I am«. In the same tradition, the architecture was not addressed as space at all, but rather as materials, forms, ornaments, and symbols (Friedrich/Gleiter 2007: 8) – as the merely »apparent elements of architecture« (Pallasmaa 2009: 145). If we try to answer the question

Corresponding author: Wiktor Skrzypczak (HafenCity University Hamburg, Germany);
research@stadtliebe.eu; http://orcid.org/0000-0002-9445-1712

of the feeling of being in the space from the rational perspective of the Enlightenment, we would have to deal with an allegedly autonomous, disembodied mind on one hand and lifeless architectural forms on the other – and with the yawning gap between them. For how could a meaning communicated between the mind and the matter? How could the architectural matter communicate with the mind without being reduced to signs and representations of something else than it is in itself? What is there to be found between the mind and the matter, which could help to overcome their strict distinction?

This article briefly sketches the historical developments in architectural theory, which proposed some methods of answering the question: *How would it feel to be in that space?* and which identified the body as the place where the answers might hide. It will become apparent that we still face a knowledge gap in architectural theory because we lack pragmatic methods of studying the body and applying bodily knowledge in design practice. Despite a robust philosophical framework, we are missing the practical methodology. What then, could be the principles of a bodily inquiry within architectural practice? One answer could be found among the principles of somatic movement education – which this article focuses on.

Psychophysics, Empathy Theory, and Phenomenology

How has the body, the missing link between mind and matter, been studied in the past? Briefly, since the mid-19th century, psychophysics studied the sensory organs and the nervous system, inextricably linking the stimuli with percepts. Soon after, Empathy Aesthetics absorbed these insights and attempted to explain our ability to perceive the expression of architecture with the ability to feel our own bodies. Moreover, it reduced the gap between the mind and the matter by placing the body *within* architectural space, instead of *in front* of the architectural object. Then, Husserl's phenomenology, although initially studying the consciousness and not explicitly the body, recognized the pre-logical ways of knowing and thus allowed for more adequate addressing of the bodily knowledge and of the role of the bodily movement in the constitution of perceptions. Merleau-Ponty's phenomenology then studied the body as a feeling body, as a center of our being-toward-the-world. His idea that there is no being without the world has given the word its own agency, and again reduced the gap by demonstrating that the human is one agent among many. This very brief sketch shows that the lineage of embodiment research in architectural theory has a rhythm of zooming out, drawing from empirical research and zooming in, immersing in experiential study, and each time closing the Cartesian gap a little bit: Psychophysics linked the stimulus with the percept, the Empathy Theory linked the architectural expression with bodily impression, and phenomenology linked logical knowing with bodily knowing and being with the world. How somatics, which is an approach in movement education, closes the gap between the mind and body is addressed in the following section.

Somatics

What would it feel like to be in that space? Now we know that we have to question the body itself in order to arrive at a detailed and tangible answer. The problem is that as much as the dominant Cartesian perspective distanced us from the felt qualities of the environment, it also distanced us from the felt reality of our bodies. This implies that if this predominant perspective shapes our design practice, our attitude to our own body might be shaped in this way too, at least in the professional, non-private context. In this moment the architect's body becomes relevant to their profession and the intimacy of the body therewith becomes an explicit component of the professional design process.

One of the fields in which professionals engage their whole bodily selves is dance. And also here, similarly to phenomenology in philosophy, postmodernism has changed the attitude toward the body. The rejection of form and embracing of improvisation, the rejection of the visual effect and embracing of the atmospheric affect, the rejection of the objective reception criteria and embracing of the intersubjective perception of meaning – these new values produced new dances and new aesthetics, which were closer to the audience and closer to the place of performance (cf. Novack 1990). In the 1970s this new interest in the felt body strongly contributed to the popularization of somatic movement techniques in dance education. Somatics itself is a field of bodily movement practices, mostly developed throughout the 20th century. It grounds itself in the notion of soma as a felt body that is aware of itself – a continuum of minding body and embodied mind as inseparable aspects of a human being (Skrzypczak 2018). The term *somatics* was coined in the 1970s by Thomas Hanna, a philosopher, movement practitioner, and movement theorist:

> »A soma is any individual embodiment of a [life] process, which endures and adapts through time, and it remains soma as long as it lives. The moment that it dies, it ceases to be a soma and becomes a body« (Hanna 1976: 31).

Hanna uses the Greek term *soma* to foreground the dynamic, evolutionary, self-determining processes – the sense of being alive. Soma, perceived from the first-person-perspective, is a phenomenon diametrically different from the objectified body perceived from the third-person-perspective (Hanna, in: Hanlon Johnson 2012: 371). The similarity to Merleau-Ponty's sensed body, *Leib*, is self-evident. However, the main difference between phenomenology and somatics as disciplines can be grasped as the difference between an embodied mind and an enminded body. Both phenomenology and somatics can be understood as perceptual approaches which organize and systematize our interactions with the environment in the everyday life, however the dominant mode of inquiry in phenomenology is thinking, in somatics it is moving. Phenomenology uses thought experiments (such as phenomenological analysis), which might lead to new sensations and insights, whereas somatics, being a movement education approach, uses movement experiments which might also lead to new sensations and insights.

Historically, somatics evolved from numerous sources and diverged into three main »branches: somatic bodywork, somatic psychology, and somatic movement« (Eddy 2016: 8). As a field, it is highly decentralized and still growing while delivering new somatic methods and new applications, but also undertaking attempts at institutional self-definition and delineation. The following outline of somatic movement principles is based on the requirements for membership of the International Somatic Movement Education and Therapy Association (ISMETA) – which is an umbrella association publicly representing both somatic education organizations and individual somatic educators and practitioners.

Similarly to sport education in the general movement education curricula, somatic movement education is grounded in natural sciences and includes the principles of »movement observation and analysis; efficient alignment; spatial awareness; perceptual and motor development; neuromuscular, skeletal, tissue, and fluid awareness« (ISMETA 2017: 2–3, cf. also ISMETA 2003 in Eddy 2009). However, the core of somatic inquiry is the interrelations between the objective and subjective processes of the soma. In practical terms, somatic movement is guided through the observation of the interrelations between one's own »*subjective processes*« (ibid.: 1) of the psyche (primarily but not exclusively the processes of attention) and »*objective processes*« (ibid.: 1) of the physique.

Somatic movement is foremost a »pedagogical approach« (ibid.: 2). It can be understood as bodily literacy – it teaches the techniques of »reading« the body-mind and expressing it. By definition, it is learning through movement and touch (Eddy 2016). The particular contents and insights of such reading and expression vary strongly and depend on the particular case, the technique used, and how it was specifically applied. Yet, in general, somatic movement aims at finding »ease, support and pleasure« (Eddy 2009: 6) in the experience of movement. It is a methodology of sensory sensitization which prioritizes the kinesthetic, tactile, and proprioceptive cues.

Somatic movement practitioners learn to recognize the »habitual patterns of perceptual, postural and movement interaction with [their] environment« (ISMETA 2017: 1). They learn that such habits cannot be attributed exclusively to the alleged »body« or »mind«, but instead are expressions of a specific somatic state. Practitioners also learn how to attain the new, non-habitual possibilities of interaction.[1] Another principle of somatic movement is releasing the practitioner's »movement inhibition and resistance« (ISMETA 2017: 2). Often, such patterns are experienced as muscular and mental tension. The release of such patterns is intended, because they often mask the internal proprioceptive sensations and narrow the perceived possibilities of action. These principles aim at both novel choices of interaction with the environment, but also at the »structural, functional, and expressive integration« (ISMETA 2017: 1) of the practitioner.

Somatic movement education is by definition non-authoritarian. Because many of its insights are phenomenological and pre-objective, the education consists of both learning from the teacher and constant rediscovery of the material by the student – learning from one's own knowing body. It demands that »teachers and students are co-active in the process of learning, discovering, and self-inquiry« (ISMETA 2017: 2) – students learn through guided exploration and learn how to guide their own explorations.

Because somatic movement education normally takes place in spaces shared by physically present participants, a large part of the communication

---

1 The non-habitual and novel choices are not explicitly included in ISMETA principles but have been emphasized by approaches such as critical somatics. Cf. Thomas Kampe (2015) »Eros and Inquiry: The Feldenkrais Method® as a Complex Resource«, in: *Theatre, Dance and Performance Training*, 6/2, 200–218, doi: 10.1080/19443927.2015.1027451.

about what is happening within the practice is a non-verbal, direct, and inter-corporeal communication. However, somatic movement education usually offers specific verbal communication formats and teaches »communication and guidance through touch and verbal cues« (ISMETA 2017: 1) which help to explicitly communicate the implicit observations. The higher purpose of somatic movement is often described as »homeostasis, co-regulation, and neuroplasticity« and »an embodied sense of vitality« (ISMETA 2017: 1).

This was a brief delineation of phenomenological traditions in architecture and movement education. They are systematic approaches pointing at the knowledge gaps which impede our understanding of the nature of interactions between the »subject« and the »world«, and between the »body« and »mind«. Architectural phenomenology and somatics are interested in understanding a specific kind of interactions, mainly, those which are pre-objective. Both approaches have been established as opposition, and then as extensions of objectifying knowledge traditions – Empathy Theory opposing the formal aesthetics, the phenomenology opposing the empiricist psychology, and somatics opposing the highly formalized and objectifying dance forms. Without pursuing a specific novel aesthetic both architectural phenomenology and somatics turn toward the aesthetics of everyday life and its direct, intuitive, and intimate character. Phenomenology and somatics try to transcend the habitual perceptions, the phenomenology turning toward the direct, present precepts, with somatics often turning to the evolutionary old, sensorimotor mechanisms.

A Somatic Design Practice?

The principles described above have a general character and admittedly lack the instructive precision which somatic *movement* techniques themselves have. But this general character allows for a deductive imagining, not of a somatic movement practice but a somatic *design* practice. The following are guidelines for a design practice that places the principles of the movement practice (emphasized in the text below) in the context of design practice. They are not based in any existing application of somatic movement for architectural design, although such attempts have been made (e.g. by Galen Cranz, Auxiliadora Gálvez, and Jader Tolja) they are much more of an aprioristic introduction to the theory of somatic design practice. Being a theory, the proposed principles remain general, but they also suggest some particular starting points:

- Take the ergonomics seriously. In terms of posture, do you prefer to be static or agile at your workplace? How do you physically prepare yourself for work? Do you have specific physical routines or rituals?

- Observe your *psycho-physical states* as you work on a design. Are there bodily states which support your design process? Do you prefer repose or arousal? Mind wandering or concentration? Find ways of facilitating these states.

- What media do you use in your design practice and how do they stimulate your sensory organs? Include mediums other than visual media in your design practice. How does the choice of medium affect your posture and movement? How does it limit what is thinkable and imaginable?

- As a private person – on a walk or on an excursion, observe your spatial behavior. Learn about your habitual interactions with the environment. How do you respond to narrow spaces? To wide spaces? To the crossing of boundaries? To voids above you and below you? To light and sound sources? To the presence of others? What other patterns of behavior do you notice?

- *Keep moving.* As you are *learning about your perceptual, postural, and movement interactions* with the environment keep moving, keep noticing the change, keep differentiating between the successive patterns and states.

- *Think with your hands.* Touch your environment, your design materials, and your media and tools attentively.

- Touch yourself attentively. Learn to feel what is underneath the skin surface, the internal space of your body. Observe how it resonates with the environment you are in.

- *Document your observations* and share them with your peers. Be as specific as possible. Listen to your peers as they share their observations with you. *Develop a vocabulary* for the spatial and bodily phenomena that you experience. Find the intersubjective common ground of your perception processes but acknowledge the idiosyncrasies.

- In your explorations, notice the moments of *spatial and bodily* ease. Learn inducing this state through adequate movement facilitation and spatial design.

- In your explorations, notice the moments of *spatial and bodily* challenge. Learn to induce this state through adequate movement facilitation and spatial design. Make it stimulating and disruptive but be kind.

- Question your habitual interactions with the environment. *Release your restriction patterns.* Question your habitual design choices. Release what restricts your creative process.

- *Interact with the environment non-habitually.* Increase your range of spatial choices. Go for novel experiences and imaginations of space.

- Learn to empathize with the spatial behavior of the future inhabitants of your designs.

- Observe how the practice changes you. Cultivate the moments in which you experience a *postural, functional, and expressive re-organization and integration.*

- Study both natural and human sciences. Often, you will learn that your little private discoveries have already been made by others. Contextualize your felt knowledge. Be critical about what you know and how you know it.

To recap, this article argues that neither architectural practice nor dance practice is independent from the dominant philosophical worldview of the era. And while dance makers learned to make use of non-Cartesian movement techniques – to physically apply phenomenology and embodiment philosophy, architects often used phenomenology as a reflective, intellectual practice without explicitly studying their bodies and their role in the design process. It lead to the hypothesis that, as dancers learned to make less formal and more sensitively choreographed dances, architects might learn to cultivate their bodily selves in the design practice and thus answer the question: *What would it feel like to be in that space?* with a greater sensory expertise. Such cultivation of the body-mind could lead to the emergence of new somatic methods within the profession of architecture, because, as most somatic techniques are constantly re-emerging from actual movement practice, it is conceivable that a new somatic technique might emerge from design practice, if the designer approaches the practice not as a purely intellectual but as an embodied activity.

The remaining question then, is what difference might such embodied design practice make? Besides gaining expertise in questions about the sense of space, what effects on the architectural practice are thinkable? Sondra Frailegh, a dancer and philosopher, contrasted the objectifying knowledge with the subjectifying knowledge and characterized the first one as affecting the world through control, and the latter as affecting it through transformation (Fraleigh 1996). Thus, in order to comprehend the effects of somatic design practices we would have to find methods of observing and documenting such transformations, which can be expected to be more gradual and nuanced than those of objectifying knowledge. Accompanying research is necessary in order to identify the qualitative and quantitative differences between architecture imagined by a sensitive architect versus largely analytically generated architecture.

From a global vantage point, through the general critique of modernity, one effect, that almost has a political relevance, could be a shift in architects' value systems, or maybe a greater appreciation of the humanists among the engineers. Undoubtedly, fields such as somatics are value-driven communities, thus their place in supposedly value-free universities has to be questioned. However, somatic education might find its place in architectural education, because, as a pragmatic approach, it does not presuppose a philosophical indoctrination. To put it boldly, that is because its core values are not transcendental, but immanent. They emanate from attentive bodily practices. As architects, we are neither philosophers nor movers, but by learning to cultivate our bodily selves and training our senses, we might understand better how our designs affect their inhabitants and thus increase the quality of the built environment.

References

Eddy, Martha (2009): »A Brief History of Somatic Practices and Dance: Historical Development of the Field of Somatic Education and its Relationship to Dance«, in: *Journal of Dance and Somatic Practices 1/1*, doi: 10.1386/jdsp.1.1.5/1

Eddy, Martha (2016): *Mindful Movement: The Evolution of the Somatic Arts and Conscious Action*, Chicago: University of Chicago Press.

Fraleigh, Sondra Horton (1996), »The Spiral Dance: Toward a Phenomenology of Somatics«, in: *Dance Faculty Publications 8*. http://digitalcommons.brockport.edu/dns_facpub/8, accessed July 15, 2021.

Friedrich, Thomas/ Gleiter, Jörg (2007): *Einfühlung und phänomenologische Reduktion: Grundlagentexte zu Architektur, Design und Kunst (Empathy and Phenomenological Reduction: Foundational Texts on Architecture, Design, and Art)*. Berlin: Lit Verlag.

Hanna, Thomas (1976): »The Field Of Somatics«, in: *Somatics: Magazine-Journal of the Bodily Arts and Sciences 1/1*.

ISMETA (2017): *Registered Somatic Movement Educator and Therapist Training Requirements*, https://ismeta.org/wp-content/uploads/2017/06/ISMETA_Registered-Professional-Member-Requirements.pdf, accessed July 15, 2021.

Jacquet, Benoît (2012): »The State of Architectural Phenomenology«, in: *Environmental & Architectural Phenomenology 23/2*.

Johnson, Don Hanlon/ Rytz, Thea/ Mauch, Christine, eds. (2012): *Klassiker der Körperwahrnehmung. Erfahrungen und Methoden des Embodiment (Classics of Body Awareness. Experiences and Methods of Embodiment)*, Bern: Huber Verlag.

Novack, Synthia (1990): *Sharing the Dance: Contact Improvisation and American Culture*, Madison: University of Wisconsin Press.

Pallasmaa, Juhani (2009): *The Thinking Hand: Existential and Embodied Wisdom in Architecture*, Chichester: John Wiley & Sons Ltd.

Robinson, Sarah/Pallasmaa, Juhani, eds. (2017): *Mind in Architecture: Neuroscience, Embodiment, and the Future of Design*, Cambridge, MA: The MIT Press.

Skrzypczak, Wiktor (2018): »Introduction to a Somatic Inquiry of Architectural Space«, in: Matthias Balestrem/Ignacio Borrego/Donatella Fioretti/Ralf Pasel/ Jürgen Weidinger, *CA²RE – Conference for Artistic and Architectural (Doctoral) Research*, https://www.pep.tu-berlin.de/wp-content/uploads/2020/11/ABSTRACTS-CA2RE-BERLIN.pdf, accessed October 5, 2021.

Dimensions of Architectural Knowledge, 2021-02 ᴆ
https://doi.org/10.14361/dak-2021-0206

Lived Experience as a Basis for Design:
A Design Studio Kindergarten Project

Katja Vaghi, Tijana Vojnović Ćalić, and Anja Ohliger

Abstract: This research is motivated by our belief that artistic practices have a great potential for exchange and so can promote innovations in the creative processes. In particular, we are interested in how the corporeal lived experience can be integrated into the design process and used as a conceptual basis for an architectural design. Within this article, we propose an inter-disciplinary approach to architectural design that includes somatic exercises taken from dance, and associated with a phenomenological recollection of the experiences in space. At the same time, in teaching, we recognize the challenge of bringing the design process closer to the second-semester architecture students of the Coburg University of Applied Sciences and Arts. The research was carried out as part of a studio project which focused on the design of a kindergarten. We found that the corporeal approach to design helped the students to immerse themselves in the role of the different users, and so relate to the design in an intimate way. Consequently, the designs were surprisingly imaginative and showed a considerable variation in typology.

Keywords: Space and Movement; Architectural Design; Design Studio Project; Design Process; Memory; Corporeal Experience; Empathy; Interdisciplinarity.

Introduction

Each artistic practice develops specific approaches and procedures to achieve the desired results. These different artistic worlds sometimes meet, but often run parallel without considering the potential for mutual exchange. Considering further developments in the architectural discipline, we realize the benefits of adopting creative methods from diverse artistic disciplines to promote an interdisciplinary approach to design. Common to architecture and dance is the body in motion and the variables of space and time. Techniques used in contemporary dance can awaken the senses and

Corresponding author: Katja Vaghi (Coburg University of Applied Sciences and Arts);
katja.vaghi@hs-coburg.de. Co-authors: Tijana Vojnović Ćalić (Coburg University of Applied Sciences and Arts); tijana.vojnovic-calic@hs-coburg.de; Anja Ohliger (Coburg University of Applied Sciences and Arts); anja.ohliger@hs-coburg.de

the spatial imagination, as well as help to picture possible scenarios for the usage of space. A sensory experience of space can serve as the initial inspiration for an architectural design and become an integral part of the design process. This kind of approach has the potential to take architectural design in a different direction.

In the context of architectural education and teaching a studio project, the problem of introducing the first-year students to the design process and the search for the initial concept that guides the design stands in the foreground. Here, we recognize the significant potential in a design process that starts with the analysis of an environment they are familiar with, or the insight into their personal experience. This starting point can provide the students with the initial confidence to choose an individual design direction.

The primary aim of this article is to investigate the role of the corporeal experience within the design process and its influence on the design itself. The article describes a concrete design process that was tested with a design studio for second-semester architecture students at the Coburg University of Applied Sciences and Arts in the summer semester of 2021. The task assigned to the students was to design a kindergarten module and an assembly appropriate for children from the age of three to six years old. This project was led with the expertise of the authors – the dance researcher and movement specialist, Katja Vaghi as well as of the architects Anja Ohliger and Tijana Vojnović Ćalić.

This research, carried out as part of a studio project, deals with the question of how the corporeal lived experience could be integrated into the design process and used as a conceptual basis for an architectural design. The lived experience, in this case, refers to the memory of prior sensorimotor experiences, as well as the present experiential explorations of space intended to provide a deeper understanding of the users' needs and various sensory and emotional situations. The initial phase of the design process was to recall spatial, sensorial, and emotional childhood experiences. As the task set was to design a kindergarten, we decided that besides present embodied experiences to access and include those from the past as well. To this, the production of new experiences in the imagined roles of child or teacher was also central to the approach. Upon reflection of this teaching approach and the work with the students in the design studio, this research proposes the following hypothesis: incorporating lived experience in the design process leads to an imaginative, well-informed, and well-grounded design. Bearing in mind that each person experiences an individual, and therefore distinctive, spatial and sensory event, the starting point of this design process leads to the development of a range of unconventional and innovative kindergarten typologies.

Theoretical Grounds

When entering a building, the play of light and shadow, spatial configuration and sequencing, the depth of visual plans and plasticity of the various elements, and the density and quality of the materials, only to mention a few factors, are experienced through the whole of the body. Besides the visual sense, we also experience space through acoustic, olfactory, haptic, proprioceptive, and kinesthetic senses. At the beginning of their book, the scholars Joy Monice Malnar and Frank Vodvarka ask about the senses in design: »What if we designed for all our senses?« (2004: IX). The focus of our pedagogical experimentation and interdisciplinary exchange is clearly expressed by Juhani Pallasmaa in his article »Architecture as Experience«, as he draws a parallel between the nature of the experience of architecture and that of art:

> »Works of architecture and art are encounters and lived rather than understood intellectually. Architecture is commonly understood, taught, practiced, and evaluated primarily as a visual art form. However, we encounter buildings and environments through our entire sense of being« (Pallasmaa 2018: 9).

He points to something akin to what in Maurice Merleau-Ponty's terminology would be called »bodily intentionality« (as mentioned in Hale 2017: 14) or the pre-conscious awareness that allows us to cope and function in space despite the overload of sensory information granted by our sensorial experiences. This is a state of awareness in which intellectual reasoning is yet to begin. What would the influence on planning be if this were the departing state from which to generate the main design concept?

The design studio and the introductory workshop aimed to put the experience of the users in focus and consider how they can be addressed in the design process. The methodology of the interdisciplinary workshop foregrounded a practical, embodied approach through guided experiences for the students to picture the possibilities for movements depending on the users' typology. The exercises allowed for the engagement of the whole body shifting the focus away from the usual catalog of activities (or the needs) that take place in space and putting the sensory experiences (or the sensorial pleasure) at the center at least in the initial phase. Taking – current or past – lived embodied experiences as the departing point, stimulated the students in generating ideas beyond the general and unjustified use of geometrical forms. We asked the participants to access their memories, so past embodied lived experiences, to stimulate an empathic response to the children's point of view and experiences.

With experience, or lived experience as in Merleau-Ponty's approach, the constant exchange between the individual and the surroundings, between the perception and the actions taking place in a particular space is intended. The embodied self is considered for its possibility for actions, while, conversely, the space is seen as »a field of opportunities for action« (Hale 2017: 18). The embodied self (or agent to highlight its ability for action along with that of the passive perceiver) is thus in continuous exchange with the surroundings. The context allows for determinate movements and actions to take place. It is then for the agents to determine if these are appropriate in the context. In their design of the space, the students had to consider at least a dual approach from the users – on the one hand, the children, on the other the adults, staff members, and parents – allowing for two different sets of possibilities for embodiments to coexist (Hale 2017: 28). The module's objective was to move from phenomenology in architecture as being a form of discourse to a design method (so going against Hale's argument in 2017: 5).

As mentioned earlier, memory played an important role in connecting the students to their own experiences as children – mostly pleasurable experiences of movement and of what Bachelard calls »images of felicitous space« (Bachelard 1994[1958]: XXXV). Bachelard sees space as laden with memories and imagination. These are »spaces of intimacy« (ibid.: 12), which promote well-being and are generally associated with the childhood house. Bachelard defines them as »well-tempered matter of the material para-dise«, stating: »This is the environment in which the protective beings live« (ibid.: 7). For Bachelard, memories are associated with space rather than with time: »Memories are motionless, and the more securely they are fixed in space, the sounder they are« (ibid.: 9).

Depending on the complexity of the childhood house, there are usually memories and imagination attached to it – »if it has a cellar and a garret, nooks and corridors, our memories have refuges that are all the more clearly delineated« (ibid.: 8). In his description though, memories are not pure memories but could also be identified as daydreams in which the space is purified, devoid of all that could cause discomfort. It is, so to speak, an idealized memory that it is recalled: »memory recaptured through daydreams, it is hard to say through what syncretism the attic is at once small and large, warm and cool, always comforting« (ibid.: 10). They are closely associated with dreams:

> »The house we were born in is more than an embodiment of home, it is also an embodiment of dreams. Each one of its nooks and corners was a resting-place for daydreaming« (ibid.: 15).

Bachelard claims that bodily memories of this idealized space are stored in our embodied being, as Bachelard claims: »But over and beyond our memories, the house we were born in is physically inscribed in us« (ibid.: 14). Preceding language and these embodied memories and associations are inter-subjective and »communicate poetically from soul to soul« (ibid.: 17). We asked the students to recall and locate these spaces of intimacy in the house or outside the house. We started by inviting them to remember their favorite games, how they were moving while playing them and how they felt afterwards, by re-embodying them and then tracing them in sketches. We then asked them to recall spaces from their memory that they were particularly fond of. Once in contact with this archive of personal experiences they were given the task to design spatial elements, landscapes, and spaces in which the children could re-experience these states (Hale 2017: 21).

Why Dance and Somatics in Architecture?

In an article entitled »Art As Action or Art As Object? The Embodiment of Knowledge in Practice As Research«, the dance researcher Anna Pakes argues for an expansion of what is generally thought of as knowledge beyond the »traditional deductive or inductive logic grounding scientific thinking« to also encompass »practical reasoning« and consider »other thinking processes and forms of knowledge as equally rigorous though they do not conform to conventional logical models« (Pakes 2004). Resting her argument on the phenomenology philosopher David Carr's reflections on Aristotle's distinction »between techne (the skill of craftsmanship) and phronesis (the practical wisdom of acting well within the social and moral domains«

(ibid.), she points to research in dance practice as relying on the latter, so that artists are exercising a certain type of »sensitivity to materials and the evolving situation« of social interactions. We would argue that this could also be extended to architects, as they are required to foresee the impact that certain materials would have on the users and furthermore anticipate exchanges among individuals, which a particular design would or would not facilitate. Dance can also be seen as intentional action, highlighting the fact that choreographers and dance researchers operating with practice are experts in mobilizing this type of practical knowledge, which is highly inter-subjective. Architects can thus be seen as setting the scene for these (good) actions to take place.

The years of training that go into becoming a dancer and a choreographer grant them with a particularly refined way of perceiving movement, space, and non-verbal human interactions. It is »knowledge of«, associated with craftsmanship, rather than a »knowledge about«, associated with academia (Pakes 2009). This knowledge often remains non-verbalized. Dance is not simply dance but different dance genres foreground different types of specialization which in turn might be applied for different outcomes. Current concepts and exercises in Western theatrical dance forms and somatic processes used by dancers to fine-tune their bodies can be repur-posed to propose sensory-motor experiences to the students and improve their embodied understanding of architectural and social spaces around them (we limited ourselves to Western theatrical dances but other tra-ditions could also be considered). We draw from several different traditions in Western theatrical dance to heighten these capacities, bringing to the fore – to consciousness – what is generally intuitively understood, and thus in turn ready to be implemented into design.

Somatic and Phenomenological Exploration of Motion and Space

To allow the students to familiarize themselves with the perspective of children, the interdisciplinary workshop was composed of three sections – motion, proportion, and fantasy. The classes had to be held via *Zoom* with short theoretical inputs that gave the students background information on particular aspects and practical exercises related to it that they could execute individually and in small groups outside. The exercises were taken from improvisation, somatic practices, and community dance activities. For example, the section on motion was divided into action and non-action (or rest), and the students were given a short introduction to the »movement analysis model« (1988) by dance researcher Janet Adshead Lansdale, highlighting the categories of spatial elements in a movement. They also were introduced to Rudolf von Laban's concept of kinesphere and movement dynamics in which he distinguishes eight basic movement efforts (Laban 2011[1966]). Macro and micro movements were considered in relation to the different ages that need to be accommodated in a kindergarten (from three to six years old). As we were still in partial lockdown, the students were given short films to observe the difference in the children's movement proficiency depending on their age. Considering the other parts of the workshop: the section on proportion was geared toward highlighting the problems and discomfort that one type of embodiment can experience while inhabiting a space that is not designed to consider their needs. The section on fantasy, on the other hand, considered the activities children engage in spontaneously and which foster their neurological development. This topic was also partly covered in the section on motion, as there is a significant connection between movement and brain development. The students were also asked to move beyond the category of right or wrong in their experience of the exercises so as to foreground playfulness.

The thematic units of the three consecutive workshops were combined with exercises geared toward remembering one's own experiences as a child. Behind this is Merleau-Ponty's notion that embodied experiences are not to be easily forgotten, even though they might require some time to be re-accessed. In the discussion and reflection, it became clear that the exchange with other students was particularly helpful, because the more the students shared their own experiences, the more memories seemed to emerge (pointing to remembering as a collective act). Each exercise was documented, either through pictures or drawings that were then shared on the communal digital pin board and so were easily accessible to everyone. The students were asked to describe the situation (of the exercise or memory) and their actions in a specific space, including the feelings and emotions that these actions and/or spaces brought with them.

Including subjective experiences through the description of feelings and emotions is a common activity in dance and somatic practices. We used the discussion sessions to reflect on the experience as a guide for embodied research, as this was where participants could associate a particular feeling with a particular movement or situation. During the workshop we took particular care in allowing space for this. The students were at first

1.
Kindergarten module, Lovedeep Chauhan and Jenny Klemmer.

2.
Interior space of a kindergarten module, Mara Förster and Lena Markert.

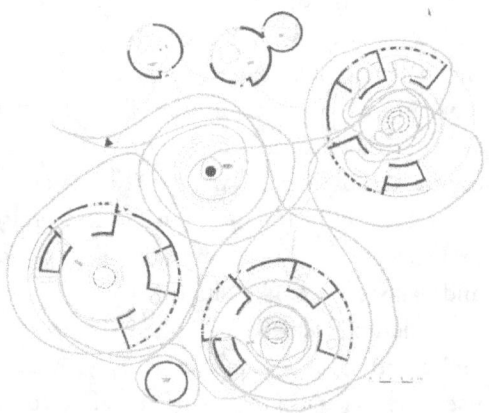

3.
Diagram of children's movement pattern, Rebecca Olimpio and Theresa Weis.

disorientated as generally the personal experience is glossed over and dismissed as not important as relative to the individual. Instead, the phenomenological approach gives credit to the individual's experience as representative of a plurality (of some sort as variations of this experience are valid for a small group). The workshop thus became a mixture of playful individual exercises and collective remembering.

Designing Spaces

Inspired by the interdisciplinary workshop, students in pairs designed two conceptually related simple spatial elements – one to be used for activity (physical activity) and one for non-activity (rest, retreat, and concentrated work). They did so by reconstructing the spatial situations that evoked sensory and emotional experiences in their childhood or those that were explored during the initial workshop and translated them into an appropriate design. In the next step, every group developed a matching pair of conceptual landscapes – one landscape for activity and one for non-activity, which could optionally be joined into one. During the design of both spatial elements and landscapes, attention was paid to the justification for and clarity of concepts and narratives, abstraction, and open associations that evoked multiple stories and images (especially those which are archetypical, such as stones, trees, and hills), multi-functionality (potentials to be interpreted and used freely in various ways), and haptic sensations. The formed pair of landscapes – playscapes, was a starting point for the interior organization of the kindergarten module as well as a conceptual basis that informed the following design decisions and determined the design principles to be pursued throughout the successive steps of this project (in terms of consistent formal expression, composition principles, and spatial organization).

Following the established concept and narrative of the landscape, it was necessary to design a spatial structure – an independent kindergarten module of 50–60 square meters for 20 children, which included the zones for activity and non-activity described above, as well as supporting functions like a cloakroom, a sanitary block and a kitchen (fig. 1, fig. 2). Particular attention was paid to the functional logic of reasonable conjunctions and the creation of appropriate relationships between the different zones. Furthermore, students were asked to design an appropriate envelope that follows the proposed concept, develops sensitive relationships between the interior and exterior spaces, and enables quality daylight and ventilation.

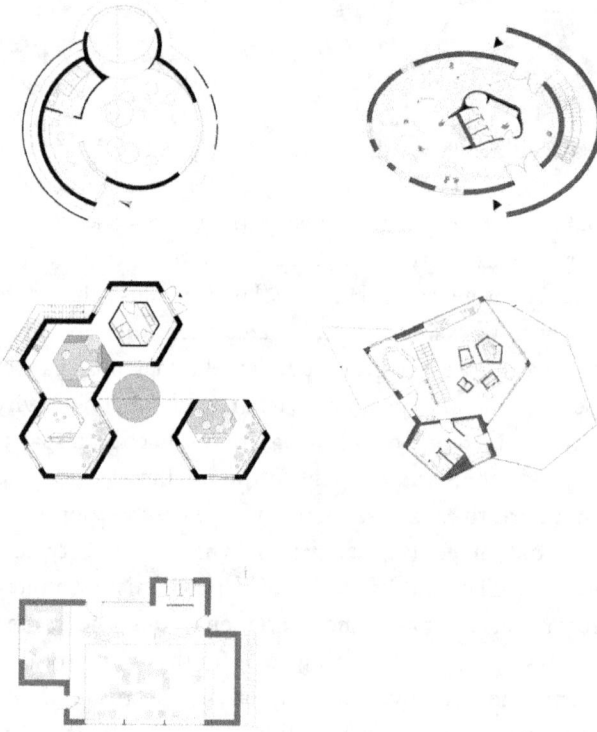

4.

Typology of the kindergarten modules, Julia Stoll and
Helen Walz, Lara Geh and Juliane Graf, Leonie Hassmann
and Marie Hofmann, Jessica Bauer and Sophie Fößel,
Sena Akboga and Özge Yilmaz.

This spatial structure provided the basic module for the further process of architectural assembly.

In the next step, it was necessary to form a cluster using the designed modules (and one auxiliary containing additional spaces for teachers and parents) that would finally form the kindergarten as a pavilion or enclosed structure. The kindergarten was located on the top of the individually chosen multi-story car park and otherwise designed free from the surrounding context. Here, the focus was on the overall positioning (in regard to the spatial possibilities – size and shape, of the chosen flat roof) and orientation of the structure on the car park deck (in regard to the seasonal and daily movement of the sun), as well as the organizational principles of the assembly. Further attention was paid to the functional and quality circulation areas, as well as pleasant and activated interspaces that were indicated by the various surface materialization and textures showing differentiation in their use.

To synthesize the project and their knowledge, the students were asked to illuminate their concepts through a series of diagrams. For example, to understand the movement pattern within the kindergarten cluster, it was necessary to imagine and represent possible circulation paths from the perspective of the child, the teacher, and the parent (fig. 3). The notation of imaginary movement paths was practiced through sketches and inspired by a Bauhaus exercise developed by Johannes Itten – »Figure skating on paper – avoiding points« (Holländer/Wiedemeyer 2019: 32–33) presented and practiced during the initial workshop.

All steps were accomplished using simple working mockups and drawing freehand sketches, as well as by other means of architectural representation such as plans, sections, elevations, and image-ground plans. The quality of the outer space was shown on a collage and of the interior spaces on an atmospheric photograph of the mockup. At the end of the course, we exchanged experiences with the students. During this project, which lasted a total of 4 weeks and 13 meetings, the succession of steps could be monitored on the shared digital pin board (*Miro*), and the interaction with students took place with the help of a virtual meeting platform (*Zoom*).

Results

One of the main results of this research is the invention of a teaching method and specific design process which successfully integrated an own lived experience as the basis for design. The second-semester students reported higher motivation to work resulting from the approach that included participation, i.e. play, improvisation, intuition, and group work. They developed greater confidence in their work by relying on their own experiences, including memory and sensory experimentation, as well as on feedback from their partners. The students acknowledged the significant impact of the interdisciplinary workshop on the design. They stated that it strongly influenced the design process and determined the design focus which was based on the user's experience.

During the initial workshop, students developed intense empathy toward the users and their needs. Immersing themselves in the role of a child, then a teacher and a parent, they realized the diversity of users' needs and routines. They further recognized the spatial consequences that arise from these insights. This understanding is best reflected in the variety of spatial scales and movement diagrams.

The process and the studio project resulted in a variety of kindergarten modules and cluster typologies. The module designs limited by the precondition of a flat accessible roof took cubic, prismatic or rounded shapes as reminiscent of archetypal and abstracted images and concepts like stones, crystals, honeycombs, and trees. Nevertheless, concerning the formal expression, organic, rounded forms prevailed. The open question remains if it had something to do with the shape of the body, which was the central instrument for investigation during this design process.

The formal language of the design is well-grounded. The imagined forms mirror the inner sensorial-emotional landscape of each student. The produced designs were evaluated as consistent from the initial spatial element and landscape to the kindergarten module and assembly, following the concept idea deeply anchored in an individual's corporeal understanding of the world.

Discussion and Conclusion

Conventionally, the architectural design is informed by means of observation, example analysis, and imagination. Exploring alternative points of departure to design, we proposed a corporeal approach. Through the phenomenological lens offered by Merleau-Ponty and Bachelard, somatic exercises taken from dance were introduced. The participatory nature of the corporeal input had a straightforward influence on the final studio designs. The initial workshop, positioned at the beginning of the course, placed the students in a playful and intuitive state through specifically devised exercises that allowed for a corporeal exploration of spatial scenarios. This shift in state resulted in a shift in their focus that foregrounded the experiential qualities of space and gave the design process a clear direction from then on.

The approach to each architectural design task implies a comprehensive understanding of the user, along with assumptions and imaginings of their requirements. Concerning our research, from the perspective of an adult, we can no longer easily understand the sensorimotor (and the cognitive) needs of children. At this initial stage, the workshop using corporeal means helped the participants to immerse themselves into this role. The performative processes triggered memories and conceptualizations, and served to collect new sets of sensations. Based on previous pedagogical experience and conversations with students, our conclusion regarding the described process is that it led, on a personal level, to a closer relationship to the project, higher motivation, noticeable conceptual independence, and on the level of design to imaginative, unconventional, and well-justified designs that are characterized by great diversity.

Concerning further research, we are interested in how and to what extent the experience and knowledge informed by the design process based on corporeal experience would stay with students and if it would change their approach to design permanently (memory plasticity). We would like to investigate how various corporeal approaches can lead to the advancement of kindergarten and other building typologies. Finally, we are interested in the development of alternative didactic methods and design processes that can be put into practice.

This study highlights how embodied knowledge can be transferred from one context to the next. This is innovative, on the one hand, in terms of understanding the design process as an activity closely linked to our everyday bodily perceptions and not somehow detached from the physical experience as constantly mediated by abstract models. As Pallasmaa points out: »an architectural project is not only a result of a problem-solving process« (Pallasmaa 2009: 108), since »buildings are not abstract, meaningless constructions, or aesthetic compositions, they are extensions and shelters of our bodies, memories, identities and minds« (ibid.: 117). On the other hand, from a dance studies perspective, it is extremely interesting to make the knowledge inscribed in dance available to other disciplines. As a »silent« knowledge, transmitted orally, and documented through traces, dance is enacted by the transience of the lived moving body. Dance resists the written form of the general academic discourse and necessitates alternative formats for its potential to unfold with further teasing needed for each field. The body and embodiment are still a blind spot in many disciplines, and dance can help bring this unexplored dimension to the fore.

References

Adshead-Lansdale, Janet (1988): *Dance Analysis : Theory and Practice*, London: Dance Books.

Bachelard, Gaston (1958) *La Poétique de l'Espace*. – English translation: *The Poetic of Space: The Classic Look at How We Experience Intimate Places*, transl. by Maria Jolas, 1994, Boston: Beacon Press.

Hale, Jonathan (2017): *Merleau-Ponty for Architects*, Oxon/New York: Routledge.

Holländer, Friederike/Wiedemeyer, Nina (2019): *Original Bauhaus Übungsbuch (Original Bauhaus Practice Book)*, Munich/London/New York: Prestel.

Laban, Rudolf von (2011[1966]): *Choreutics*, edited by Lisa Ullman, Hampshire: Dance Books Ltd.

Malnar, Joy Monice/Vodvarka, Frank (2004): *Sensory Design*, Minneapolis: University of Minnesota Press.

Pakes, Anna (2004): »Art as Action or Art as Object? The Embodiment of Knowledge in Practice as Research«, in: *Working Papers in Art & Design*, https://www.herts.ac.uk/__data/assets/pdf_file/0015/12363/WPIAAD_vol3_pakes.pdf, accessed September 22, 2021.

Pakes, Anna (2009): »Knowing through Dancemaking: Choreography, Practical Knowledge and Practice as Research«, in: Jo Butterworth/Liesebeth Wildschut (eds.) *Contemporary Choreography: A Critical Reader*. London: Routledge, doi: 10.4324/9780203124918

Pallasmaa, Juhani (2005): *The Eyes of The Skin: Architecture of the Senses*, Chichester: John Wiley & Sons Ltd.

Pallasmaa, Juhani (2009): *The Thinking Hand: Existential and Embodied Wisdom in Architecture*, Chichester: John Wiley & Sons Ltd.

Pallasmaa, Juhani (2018): »Architecture as Experience«, in: *Architectural Research in Finland 2/1, 9–17*.

Rogers, Brian (2017): *Perception: A Very Short Introduction*, Oxford: Oxford University Press.

Shilling, C. (1993): *The Body and Social Theory*, London: SAGE.

Tuan, Yi-Fu (1975): »Place: An Experiential Perspective«, in: *Geographical Review 65/2*, 151–165.

Wittmann, Franziska (2019): *Körper in Räumen (Bodies in Spaces)*, Luzern: Quart Verlag.

Traces

»What do you want from the body? What can it give you?«

Jonathan Burrows 2010: 100.

Burrows, Jonathan (2010). *A Choreographer's Handbook*, New York: Routledge.

Dimensions of Architectural Knowledge, 2021-02 ⓐ
https://doi.org/10.14361/dak-2021-0208

The Thread of the Virtual Movement
from Wölfflin to Lynn

Fabio Colonnese

Abstract: All buildings move under the effect of physical forces of the earth. It is unperceivable, but they move. Some of them are also designed to move to perform their functions. However, most of them look absolutely still. Nevertheless, architects, critics, and historians of architecture often borrowed terms from scientific disciplines to describe a building or parts of it as if it is actually moving. Since antiquity, artistic literature has been full of »dynamized« descriptions of artwork virtually set in motion to enhance the narrative quality of the communication, but in architecture this happens only from the end of the 18th century onward. Since the end of the 19th century, a sequence of scholars and architects Heinrich Wölfflin, Colin Rowe, Peter Eisenman, and Greg Lynn have been developing a series of analytical and design tools that were used to introduce (or to query) time and motion in architecture, whose different forms are here presented, classified, and discussed.

Keywords: Visual Perception; Virtual Movement; Kinetic Architecture; Dynamic Architecture; Heinrich Wölfflin; Colin Rowe; Peter Eisenman; Greg Lynn.

Introduction

All buildings move. Although this may seem a paradox for works that are designed to provide people with resistant and long-lasting structures made of inert materials, buildings unperceivably move as a reaction to movements of the earth, to wind pressure or to temperature gaps, eventually leaving traces on the architectural envelope (fig. 1). Moreover, all buildings change. Since the day of their occupation, inhabitants start to customize their internal and external components to enhance or update their performance and even major transformations are required over the years, according to criteria and timescales explored by Frank Duffy (1992) and Stewart Brand (1994).

Corresponding author: Fabio Colonnese (Sapienza University, Rome, Italy);
fabio.colonnese@uniroma1.it; http://orcid.org/0000-0001-7606-8149

Some buildings, or parts of buildings, are properly designed to move. They can rotate to follow the sun, like the Villa Girasole in Marcellise, designed by Angelo Invernizzi and Ettore Fagiuoli and built between 1929 and 1935 or the *Dynamic D*House* designed by David Ben Grünberg and Daniel Woolfson in 2012; they can slide to cover open space, like *The Shed* recently designed by Diller and Scofidio and built in New York; they can close hermetically to protect their inhabitants, like Robert Konieczny's Safe House built in Warsaw, Poland in 2005–2009; they can open and resemble living creatures, like Santiago Calatrava's Milwaukee Art Museum bird-like extension of 2001; they can change their interiors from day to night, like some of Steven Holl's »hinged spaces« or even their envelope to optimize their environmental performance, like the Arab World Institute in Paris, designed by Jean Nouvel and built in the early 1990s.

Conversely, other buildings are forced to move, as victims of urban re-development or spoils of war, colonization, or megalomania, like the Spanish monastery of Miami, Florida (Colonnese/D'Amelio/Grieco 2021).

In the late 1960s, inspired by the results of artistic research by Alexander Calder and other artists, Frank Popper (1968) proposed a classification of the works of art that are dealing with movement. He divided the »plastic arts« into »static« and »kinetic« arts and the movement into »real« and »virtual« movement, which somehow occurs in the eye and mind of the beholder. While architecture can generally be considered as a »static plastic art«, the before-quoted buildings provide proper examples of what Popper defines as »kinetic architecture«.

This article is rather addressed to the »virtual« movement that architecture can produce when it is intended as a representation. While architecture is occasionally represented in motion, from the architects dressed as their buildings at the 1931 Waldorf Astoria Beaux Arts Ball to the city bending in Christopher Nolan's *Inception*, real architecture can be designed to suggest an effect of motion. Architects' interest in virtual movement is revealed not only by some of their drawings – think of the growing importance of diagrams and the envisioning of intangible phenomena (Colonnese 2012) – but also by the terminology and metaphors that architects, critics, and historians of architecture adopt to describe buildings that look absolutely still. This article compares it to the technique of the description of works of art since antiquity, individuating the »dynamization« as a shared approach. In particular, it focuses on the contribution of Heinrich Wölfflin (1864–1945) in stressing the role of architecture in expressing itself as an epiphany of forces fighting each other, eventually denoting the virtual movement of the parts as a deformation resulting from this conflict. At the same time, while describing the different forms of the virtual movement of architecture, it focuses on the contribution of Colin Rowe (1920–1999), Peter Eisenman (*1932), and Greg Lynn (*1964), who are mutually connected in developing Wölfflin's ideas over three generations and in suggesting different interpretations of movement. The article compares the »animated« architecture, whose form is a function of the adaptive motion induced by the context, with the virtual kinetic architecture, in which the observer connotes the motion. It then classifies several types of virtual movement – simple motion, superimposition, transformation, and processual movement – according to Rowe's concept of »phenomenological transparency« (1976: 159–184).

Dynamizing the Description

The process of »temporalization« or »dynamization« is a rhetorical technique that consists in organizing the description or *hypotyposis* of a work of art over time through movement. This attitude is already perceived in Philostratus's *ekphrasis* of ancient, lost artworks (Shaffer 1998), in which, as Mengaldo notes, »the description of the work does not mimic the work but the gaze that runs through the work« (2005: 38, author's translation). In addition to the gaze, the writer can animate the image itself, giving it a virtual movement. For example, in *The Lives*, the historian Giovanni Pietro Bellori describes an annunciation depicted by Federico Barocci like a movie. He wrote that:

> »Pausing in sudden surprise, the Virgin kneels with lowered eyes and opens her right hand in meek wonderment, resting the other on the desk with her book. The angel before her bends one knee and rests his left hand with the lily on the other; and extending his right hand toward her serenely, he reverently announces the divine mystery« (Wohl 2005: 165).

Michele Cometa recalls that:

> »The desire to set the image in motion cannot be limited in the age of cinema, but rather it is a desire (and a fear) that has been addressing the whole anthropology of the image, at least in the West, since its inception« (Cometa 2012: 46, author's translation).

1.
The weaving windows of the second floor of the
Palazzo Borghese in Rome after centuries of pressure and
subsidence. Palazzo Borghese, Rome, end of 16th century.
Photographer: Fabio Colonnese, 2015.

In the »complex iteration between images, gazes that rest on these images, and media devices that make this meeting possible« (ibid.: 44, author's translation), both the reader's media experiences, and the physical ones are fundamental. Often, to convey the *hypotyposis*, the text must induce the reader to collaborate by referring to personal visual experiences. As Umberto Eco proves, this technique »activates not only preexisting cognitive schemes but also preexisting bodily experiences« (Eco 2005: 208).

This seems to be fundamental for architecture, which is designed to welcome, protect, and serve the human body. Moreover, architecture has many points in common with literature. Buildings cannot be perceived instantly but must be observed from various points of view and explored in a linear way, like reading a text (Forty 2004: 39), or rather a hypertext. Large and complex buildings have not only been described following the gaze of a hypothetical beholder along the sequence of their interior rooms or the different levels of elevation, but also by attributing movement to the parts and »animating« the inert bodies of the architecture.

However, this kind of description, which requires an audience able to share the experience and sensations, only emerges in the literature of architecture around the 18th century. It seems that as long as architecture had been conceived as the idea of man as a divine expression, the relationship between the human body and the architectural body, in terms of analogy and proportion, was implicit. This link would be testified to by the Vitruvian tradition (Zöllner 2014); by Antonio Averlino known as Filarete, who defines the client and the architect as the father and mother of the project (Filarete 1972: I, 40); by the anthropomorphic figures Francesco di Giorgio Martini associated with his architectural designs (Millon 1958); and by the many terms borrowed from human and animal anatomy to identify the parts of a building (body, arms, wings, and so on) (Colonnese 2016). After the Renaissance, the development of the idea of man as a biological machine, increasingly oriented toward his physical performance, is accompanied by a mathematical and mechanical conception of the architectural project, which is reduced to a typological scheme of preconfigured shapes to be assembled on a grid. In this passage from the organic paradigm to the industrial paradigm, somehow the *anima* of architecture shifts from a symbolic key to a visual and psychological key, also through the mediation of writing and metaphor.

In his essay »Character and Composition«, Colin Rowe identifies the origin of a new sensitivity toward the topic of movement around the 18th century when, parallel to the emergence of the new aesthetic categories of the picturesque, a debate between »composition« and »character« took place in the academies (Rowe 1976: 59–88). On the one hand, the value of a building was defined by geometric and distributive criteria; on the other, its value resulted from how it affected the beholder. The movement is a key element of the effect. As the picturesque composition of the gardens shapes the architectural interiors, the subject is called to a continuous movement along waving paths and shifted rooms, and somehow this movement pervades the building itself.

Robert Adam is the first to write openly about movement associated with composition, in a footnote in the preface to his *Works in Architecture* (1778), where he states:

> »Movement is meant to express, the rise and fall, the advance and recess, with other diversity of form, in the different parts of a building, so as to add greatly to the picturesque of the composition. For the rising and the falling, advancing and receding, with the convexity and concavity and other forms of the great parts, have the same effect in architecture, that hill and dale, fore-ground and distance, swelling and sinking have in a landscape: that is, they serve to produce an agreeable and diversified contour, that groups and contrasts like a picture, and creates a variety of light and shade, which gives great spirit, beauty and effect to the composition« (Adam, 1980: I, 1, note 1).

As evidenced by Miranda Hausberg (Hausberg 2019: 340), such a definition is reminiscent of Adam's unpublished essay of 1762 »Of the Elevation and its Movement« (Fleming 1962: 315–319), in which the British architect indicated the landscape as a key to regenerate architecture and the landscape paintings as examples for learning about the disposition of forms and the position of the spectator. One could also conjecture that temporalizing the description of a landscape painting was a key to attribute movement to architecture. Anyway, for Adams, virtual movement was a literary device for »animating« the architecture, to give it back an *anima*.

Dynamizing Architecture

Since the second half of the 19th century, art history, aesthetic reflection, the psychology of perception, and the physiology of vision have been sharing subjects and methods, implicitly seeking for mutual legitimacy. By the end of the century, inspired by Robert Vischer's *Theory of Empathy*, which correlates

2.

Francesco Borromini: facade of San Carlino alle Quattro Fontane, Rome, 1644. Photographer: Fabio Colonnese, 2015.

the perceived form with the mood and culture of the subject, the German art historian Heinrich Wölfflin developed his theory of the empathic experience of architecture (Wölfflin 1886). His theory is based on the visibility and judgment that people assign to objects and space not only according to proportions and dimensions, but also in conjunction with their own body and psyche. For example, he argues that the ratios between base and height relate to the characteristics of strength and weight, and effort and rest, whose ideas come from the personal experience of the observers and produce judgments that are analogous to the human and organic. According to Wölfflin »the importance of form is not the shape, but the breath of life that brings frozen forms into dynamic motion« (Wölfflin 1923: 145, in: Jarzombek 1994: 31).

In his studies on Renaissance and Baroque architecture, Wölfflin »was not interested in the actual forces present in the building, but in how the architecture communicates to the observer the sensation of feeling the compression of the columns, the thrust of the vaults, and so on« (Forty 2000: 95). To describe the virtual forces affecting the buildings and their effects, Wölfflin introduced terms such as »effort«, »pressure«, »tension«, »relax«, which thereafter became an integral part of architects' vocabulary up to Colin Rowe – in particular his analysis of Le Corbusier's Convent of Sainte-Marie de la Tourette (Rowe 1976: 185–204), and even further. The integration of these terminologies creates a double effect: on the one hand, they belong to the mechanics of fluids and structures and, by virtue of the distance that scientific disciplines have gradually taken from architecture in the 18th century (Perez-Gomez 1983), they appear capable of clearly illustrating the contents of the architectural experience, eventually attributing a scientific value to the description. On the other hand, as Forty (Forty 2000: 95) recalls, the terms trigger the reader's imagination because they are the same as those that psychology adopts when describing the corresponding emotional states of human beings, who are increasingly associated with the machine (Galimberti 1999).

Wölfflin's interpretation also has the consequence that the architectural form is read as the result of a deformation caused by the acting forces, which promotes the reading of a virtual movement, especially among his followers. According to the Italian historian and architect Paolo Portoghesi, Francesco Borromini saw space as a »rotating vortex, like a tangle of efforts, a tight net« (Pierantoni 1986: 337, author's translation), as exemplified by the facade of the church of San Carlino alle Quattro Fontane (fig. 2):

»Considered as a field of tensions, which can be defined as a function of movement, this space can acquire a variable density through operations based on complex projective geometry. Newton's observation that the study of circles and lines is a task rather of mechanics than of geometry fits perfectly with Borromini's architecture in which the form is always the result of an operation that presupposes a movement and that potentially expresses it. The constant recourse to the curve line derives from the predilection for bent, curved parts; but always referable to original straight parts« (Portoghesi 1964: 27, author's translation).

The decision to refer the curved elements of the facade to their hypothetical primitive rectilinear configurations is based on the possibility of either seeing, in the same building, or knowing, from the experience of other buildings, similar elements in their straight configuration. By considering the straight element to be in a state of rest, the curved ones can be judged as resulting from a deformation. By relating these deformations to the hypothetical force that generated them, other perceptual and psychological aspects emerge that suggest a further classification of this virtual movement which is also concerned with phenomenology, on the individual considerations of the beholder.

In Borromini's case, the deformation seems to be »elastic« because as the forces cease, tympanums, entablatures, and moldings seem to be able to restore their primitive state of rest. In other cases, the definition of »plastic« deformation seems to be more appropriate. Examples may be found in the Max Reinhardt House designed by Peter Eisenman in 1992, some »collapsed« buildings designed by Frank Gehry, or the Turbulence House designed by Steven Holl in New Mexico in 2005. In 1993, Zvi Hecker conceived the Heinz Galinski school in Berlin as a group of aligned parallelepipeds which, subjected to the action of a twister, slide and are deformed in a spiral shape. Borromini's poetic »vortex« becomes here a real vortex, whose metaphorical passage distorts the buildings in a permanent way. Unlike San Carlino's facade, the Berlin school shares no indication that when the cause ceases the effects can vanish. The deformation is plastic, definitive, irreversible, and the reference to movement shifts to an iconographic level, as architecture becomes the index of a violent event, referring with its shape to a movement that has already ceased. This type of reading is indebted to the operational and iconographic contribution of D'Arcy Wentworth Thompson (1917). In *Growth and Form*, the Scottish biologist defined form as the diagram of forces, the result of the simultaneous action of the internal force of inter-molecular cohesion and the external force due to gravity. The irregularities and deformations of the object are considered the organism's response to the environment. In the 1960s, this concept, as well as the potential of diagrams, was assumed by Christopher Alexander to formulate his own definition of form: »If the world were totally regular and homogeneous, there would be no forces, and no forms. Everything would be amorphous. But an irregular world tries to compensate for its own irregularities by fitting itself to them, and thereby takes on form« (Alexander 1964: 15), just like the fish drawn by D'Arcy Wentworth Thompson and deformed according to the underlying grid. Following these suggestions, the American architect Greg Lynn (1999), a pupil of Peter Eisenman, developed the concept of animated design. It is defined by the co-presence of movement and forces at the time of formal definition. This is illustrated in naval engineering, where the shape of a hull is designed by considering water flows, turbulence, and viscosity, or in automotive design, where the body of a car is modeled by studying its aero-dynamics in a wind tunnel.

While Eisenman's language is close to Rowe's and the analyses of archi-tectural pieces he has proposed since his famous dissertation (Eisenman 2006) are full of terms expressing the idea of motion in a metaphorical way, Lynn's language is already shaped by the technical vocabulary of informatics, whose mathematical precision replaces the poetic vagueness of the meta-phors. Anyway, despite Lynn borrowing the term »animate« from anima-tion software terminology (Lynn 1999: 11), it indirectly alludes not only to cartoons – *anime* is the proper Japanese term for animation movies – but also to animals, whose adaptive strategies had been described by D'Arcy Wentworth Thompson, and to the soul, the *anima* of living beings, for move-ment is naturally interpreted as an ancestral sign of life.

A Kind of Motion

Animated architecture emphasizes the frenetic rituals of human beings. It translates the human habitat into a liquid spatiality defined by curved and sloping surfaces that look unable to create traditional places to inhabit, as evidenced by Herman Hertzberger, but rather puts into focus the idea of continuous movement, a sort of Piranesian labyrinth (Hertzberger 2000: 251). Lynn's approach is antithetical to what he calls the »kinematic model«, in which movement does not influence the architectural form, but it is

3.
*Rudolf Schindler's Wolfe House in Avalon, Santa Catalina
Island, California, 1928–31.
Courtesy of the University of California Santa Barbara,
Architecture and Design Collection.*

the beholder who adds the motion, largely negotiated by the experience of cinema, through the multiplication and succession of static still images (Lynn 1999: 11). The kinematic model can be considered a general case of the dynamic model discussed before, in which the »vortex« or an alternative system of forces apparently moves the building or only small parts of it. Gravity is the most significant force architects are supposed to deal with but making its presence evident can require some visual artifice, like Giulio Romano's in Mantua.

Christoph Luitpold Frommel writes that Giulio Romano »always suggests the movement, replacing the static condition with a series of dynamic behaviors« (Frommel 1989: 132, author's translation). Once again, the literary question is closely linked to the perceptual question, which constantly oscillates between iconography and psychology. Among the many different movements detected in Palazzo Te in Mantua, the triglyph on the western front appears to be falling. This triglyph's supposed correct location, evidenced by the position of the triglyphs on other facades of the building, is replaced by an empty void, below which the actual triglyph is positioned. The observers superimpose an image taken from their surroundings or their experience of the element actually seen, whose eccentric location is justified through movement. Sometimes, it may be sufficient to take a shape such as the cube, which is commonly attributed to characteristics of stability and tilt it to induce a sensation of movement, as testified to by the composition research of the artistic vanguard of the 1920s and the plethora of studies around the Gestalt theory.

Sometimes, the disposition of a number of similar figures within a narrow field of vision may induce the beholder to group them together in a series. In this case, they can be interpreted as moments of an ongoing movement, up to reconstructing the intermediate positions and producing an illusion of movement by »superimposition« in pseudo-cinematographic terms. From the hill, Rudolf Schindler's *Wolfe House*, Santa Catalina Island, 1928–31, offered a strong kinetic suggestion (fig. 3). Seen from this exact point of view, the building, which no longer exists, seemed to gradually slide down the slope thanks to the superimposition effect caused by the repetition of the same motif, moved and set back twice. The likeness of the three edges, with the same wall thickness and the vertical windows divided by square frames, is fundamental to inducing the virtual oblique motion along the slope. The eye follows the sequence of the edges, and the gaze moves from the upper to the lower block, giving an effect of movement to the whole structure.

The virtual movement of architecture is linked not only to the change of form, through the concept of deformation, or to the change of place, through superimposition, but also to the change of state and matter, in the form of metamorphosis. In virtue of the reference to nature as a model to imitate, architects often had the ambition to use the inert material of their buildings to stage a geometric, formal, or even material metamorphosis, from the rocky facades of Gian Lorenzo Bernini to the gradual mutation of the architectural order exhibited by Robert Venturi and Denise Scott Brown in the facade of the new wing of the National Gallery in London.

Sometimes, the metamorphosis does not involve nature and its millennial relationship with architecture but emerges from an introspective gaze on the architectural process itself. Sometimes, the architects intend to represent the process that generated the building as movement from some primitive forms to its complex final configuration. This sort of »processional movement« has developed only in the last century, with the introduction of industrial criteria and the methods of scientific research into architectural production, aspiring to a purely deterministic process. The sophisticated graphic devices that have, for many decades, been illustrating the genetic criteria and steps of architectural projects testify to the growing interest in the process, perhaps to compensate for the semantic deficiency of the *International Style* products. The representation of the process is not limited to the drawings but sometimes informs the buildings themselves. Deformations, misalignments, colors, materials, frameworks, and bands are used to leave traces of the operations (translation, rotation, insertion, projection, scaling, multiplication, inversion, substitution, metamorphosis, anamorphosis, and many more) developed through models and drawings, generally onto transparent paper (Colonnese 2021).

This kind of movement, and to some extent all the forms of virtual movements of architecture, can be explored through the concept of »phenomenal transparency« Colin Rowe developed in the 1940s together with Robert Slutzky, a visual theorist (Rowe 1976: 159–184). According to Rowe, who was a hybrid between an architect, an art historian, a theoretician and a critic (Vidler 2012: 9), buildings that possess this quality reveal an aptitude for showing two or more contradictory configurations at the same time, in the sense that no evident reading can explain all the elements. It is therefore an optical stratagem that is useful to activate a mental process and, possibly, to bring movement into play as a possible cause of contradictions. In this sense, phenomenal transparency can be used to illustrate a building in which the final form reveals the traces of the genetic process that generated it.

Although stimulated by the experience of Cubist art, the concept of phenomenal transparency can be properly considered as an attempt to develop and systematize Wölfflin's procedures. Rowe himself recognized his debt to Wölfflin's method (Vidler 2012: 9); yet at the same time, he criticized it for sacrificing the iconography and giving excessive importance to the visual approach, which eventually promoted its success. Rowe limited his work in the literary field, using the phenomenal transparency as a critical filter that exalted the mannerist and contradictory quality of architecture, which was yet to inspire Robert Venturi and Denise Scott Brown's research. On the contrary, his pupil Peter Eisenman expanded these ideas to built architecture, by investigating the design process as a sequence of movements exhibited not only through descriptions and diagrams but also in the built form. As Stan Allen states, »any time we see work that justifies itself by reference to the history of its design process [...] we are in the territory first mapped out by Eisenman in the seventies with his investigations of the index« (Allen 2006: 63). The series of houses he designed as critical research on the methodology of production and representation of architecture, demonstrate the opportunity to translate architecture into a representation of its own evolutionary trajectory. In Eisenman's critical practice, text and drawing, description and representation somehow touch each other. In 1975, referring to his *House IV*, Eisenman wrote: »the building is not an object in the traditional sense, not the end result of a process, but more accurately a record of a process, so that the process itself becomes the object« (Eisenman/Gass/Gutman 1994: 23). Eisenman's approach can also be used for retrospective analyses of previous buildings, of course. In this sense, Schindler's Wolfe House can be interpreted both as an ongoing process and the product of the translation of a figure and the fusion of three specific moments along the way.

Conclusions

The technique of dynamization of the description, through which a virtual movement is applied to the gaze of the beholder and to the figures depicted, was transferred into architecture only around the 18th century, as testified to by Robert Adam's written suggestions coming from the picturesque composition. Inspired by Vischer's emphatic approach, the evolution of visual perception studies, and the power of scientific metaphors, Wölfflin contributed to interpret the architectural form as an expression of real or virtual forces affecting the building and to adopt the deformation as a category to illustrate this phenomenon in an »elastic« sense, like in Borromini's architecture, or in a »plastic« sense, like in the metaphor of the catastrophe adopted by some of the Deconstructivist architects. Wölfflin's approach gives a building a temporal dimension that turns a still object into a sort of show going on. Colin Rowe expanded Wölfflin's approach and vocabulary, providing new conceptual tools that can be used to frame different forms of the virtual movement of architecture. In particular, the phenomenal transparency, which considers the coexistence of alternative configurations in the building, uses the time needed to pass from one to another to denote a different kind of movement. Following this suggestion, Peter Eisenman applied the tools of design analysis to connote the building as representative of its design process, using the phenomenal transparency to stage the progressive definition of the final form. Through the mediation of the scientific studies of D'Arcy Wentworth Thompson and the design environment of engineers, Greg Lynn shaped his »animated« approach according to the original dynamic vision offered by Wölfflin but in a pseudo-scientific vision, somehow closing the circle. Lynn's approach also has the effect of leading the architectural form back to a purely visual perceptive context, in contrast to the centrality of the proactive enquiry and conjecture required by the virtual movement formulas.

Within this chain of references and interpretations, the role of written language is not only fundamental in deciphering the connotative intents of the scholars and architects but also in producing a sort of metatext framing the architectural process and reception while simultaneously promoting an expanded experience of the virtual movement of architecture.

References

Adam, Robert (1980[1778]): *Works in Architecture of Robert and James Adam*, London: Dover.

Alexander, Christopher (1964): *Notes on the Synthesis of Form*, Cambridge, MA: Harvard University Press.

Allen, Stan (2006): »Trace Elements«, in: Cynthia Davidson (ed.), *Tracing Eisenman: Peter Eisenman Complete Works*, New York: Rizzoli, 49–65.

Ansari, Iman/Eisenman, Peter (2013): »Interview«, in: *The Architectural Review*, April 26, 2013, https://www.architectural-review.com/essays/interview-peter-eisenman, acessed July 15, 2021.

Brand, Stewart (1994): *How Buildings Learn*, New York: Viking.

Colonnese, Fabio (2012): *Movimento Percorso Rappresentazione. Fenomenologia e codici dell'architettura in movimento (Movement Path Representation. Phenomenology and Codes of Architecture in Movement)*, Roma: Officina.

Colonnese, Fabio (2016): »Human Figure as a Cultural Mediator in Architectural Drawings«, in: Gülşah Koç/Marie-Therese Claes/Bryan Christiansen (eds.), *Cultural Influences on Architecture*, Hershey, PA: IGI Global, 90–129.

Colonnese, Fabio (2021): »Transparent Paper as a Modernist Architectural Design Environment«, in: Cristina Bartolomei/Alfonso Ippolito/Simone Helena Tanoue Vizioli (eds.), *Digital Modernism Heritage Lexicon*, Cham: Springer, 57–79.

Colonnese, Fabio/D'Amelio, Maria Grazia/Grieco, Lorenzo (2021): »Sum or Total? The Case of the Cistercian Monastery in Miami«, in: *IMG Journal*, 4 (forthcoming).

Cometa, Michele (2012): *La scrittura delle immagini: letteratura e cultura visuale (Writing Images: Literature and Visual Culture)*, Milano: Cortina, 2012.

Duffy, Frank (1992): *The Changing Workplace*. London: Phaidon Press.

Eco, Umberto (2005): *On Literature*, Boston, MA: Houghton Mifflin Harcourt.

Eisenman, Peter/Gass, William/Gutman, Robert (1994). »House VI«, in: Suzanne Frank (ed.), *Peter Eisenman's House VI: The Client's Response*, New York: Whitney Library of Design.

Eisenman, Peter (2006[1963]). *The Formal Basis of Modern Architecture*, Baden: Lars Müller.

Filarete, Antonio Averlino (1972): *Trattato di Architettura (Architecture Treatise)*, vol. 2, Milano: Il Polifilo.

Fleming, John (1962): *Robert Adam and His Circle in Edinburgh and Rome*, Cambridge, MA: Harvard University Press.

Forty, Adrian (2004[2000]): *Words and Buildings. A Vocabulary of Modern Architecture*, London: Thames & Hudson.

Frommel, Christoph Luitpold (1989): »Le opere romane di Giulio« (The Roman works of Julius), in: *Giulio Romano Architetto*, Milano: Electa, 96–133.

Galimberti, Umberto (1999): *Psiche e techne. L'uomo nell'età della tecnica (Psyche and Techne. Man in the Age of Technology)*, Milano: Feltrinelli.

Hausberg, Miranda Jane Routh (2019): *Robert Adam's Revolution in Architecture*. Dissertation, Philadehia, PA: University of Pennsylvania.

Hertzberger, Herman (2000): *Space and the Architect. Lessons in Architecture 2*, Rotterdam: 010 Publishers.

Jarzombek, Mark (1994): »De-Scribing the Language of Looking: Wölfflin and the History of Aesthetic Experientialism«, in: *Assemblage 23*, 28–69.

Lynn, Greg (1999): *Animate Form*, New York: Princeton Architectural Press.

Mengaldo, Pier Vincenzo (2005): *Tra due linguaggi. Arti figurative e critica (Between two languages. Figurative arts and criticism)*, Torino: Bollati Boringhieri.

Millon, Henry (1958): »The Architectural Theory of Francesco Di Giorgio«, in: *The Art Bulletin* 40/3, 257–261.

Pérez-Gómez, Alberto (1983): *Architecture and the Crisis of Modern Science*, Cambridge, MA: The MIT Press.

Pierantoni, Ruggero (1986): *Forma fluens. Il movimento e la sua rappresentazione nella scienza, nell'arte e nella tecnica (Forma Fluens. The Movement and its Representation in Science, Art, and Technology)*, Torino: Bollati Boringhieri.

Popper, Frank (1968): *Origins and Development of Kinetic Art*, New York: Studio Vista and Graphic Society.

Portoghesi, Paolo (1964): *Borromini nella cultura europea (Borromini in European Culture)*, Roma: Officina.

Rowe, Colin (1976): *The Mathematics of the Ideal Villa and Other Essays*. Cambridge, MA: The MIT Press.

Shaffer, Diana (1998): »Ekphrasis and the Rhetoric of Viewing in Philostratus's Imaginary Museum«, in: *Philosophy & Rhetoric* 31/4, 303–316.

Thompson, D'Arcy W. (1917): *On Growth and Form*, Cambridge: Cambridge University Press.

Vidler, Anthony (2012): »Up Against the Wall: Colin Rowe at La Tourette«, in: *Architecture Criticism* 24, 7–17.

Vischer, Robert (1873): *Über das optische Formgefühl: Ein Beitrag zur Ästhetik (On the Optical Sense of Form: A Contribution to Aesthetics)*, Leipzig: Credner.

Wohl, Hellmut (2005): *Giovan Pietro Bellori: The Lives of the Modern Painters, Sculptors and Architects: A New Translation and Critical Edition*, Cambridge: Cambridge University Press.

Wölfflin, Heinrich (1886): *Prolegomena zu einer Psychologie der Architektur. Dissertation (Prolegomena to a Psychology of Architecture. Dissertation)*, Munich: Wolf & Sohn.

Wölfflin, Heinrich (1923[1915]): Kunst-geschichtliche Grundbegriffe, Munich: Hugo Bruckmann.

Zöllner, Frank (2014): »Anthropo-morphism: From Vitruvius to Neufert, from Human Measurement to the Module of Fascism«, in: Kirsten Wagner/Jasper Cepl (eds.), *Images of the Body in Architecture: Anthropology and Built Space*, Tübingen/Berlin: Wasmuth, 47–75.

Dimensions of Architectural Knowledge, 2021-02 ᗭ
https://doi.org/10.14361/dak-2021-0209

Designing Movement, Modulating Mood

Sarah Robinson

Abstract: This article illustrates how the isomorphism between bodily form and emotional expression is manifest in architectural experience through applying research findings in the fields of cognitive science, phenomenology, and psychology to practical examples in the work of Aldo van Eyck, Alvar Aalto, Rosan Bosch, Herman Hertzberger, Steen Eiler-Rasmussen, and Gaston Bachelard. Beginning with the micro-scale movement in facial expressions to larger scale patterns of collective movement and mood, this work understands architecture in its active-verbal form, as a patterning force capable of modulating rhythms and resonances at individual and societal scales of interaction.

Keywords: Resonance; Rhythm; Emotion-Gesture Isomorphism; Entrainment; Counterform; Counter Muscle; Mood Modulation.

> »The gesture does not make me think of anger, it is anger itself.«
> *Maurice Merleau-Ponty (2002: 214)*

Joy is a feeling of levity, buoyancy – an effortless floating on the currents of life. Sadness feels heavy and compressing – a sapping of energy. Joy expands, while sadness contracts. Feeling joy not only enlarges one's sense of pos-sibility, feeling joyful opens the chest and loosens arms and hands. When we are sad, our slumped shoulders and head outwardly express our inter-nalization. Happiness broadens our face and arches our lips upward, while anger tightens the jaw and clenches the fist. The word emotion – e-motion – has motion built into its very name. Emotion and its expression seem to share an isomorphic congruency. Form and feeling match. »It is difficult to feel intimacy while shouting, to rage in a low whisper, to skip and weep at the same time«, wrote the poet Jane Hirschfield (Hirschfield 1997: 54). Indeed, each of these gestures seem to have their own inherent emotional signature. Charles Darwin was the first to conduct experimental research

Corresponding author: Sarah Robinson (Aalborg University, Denmark);
sarah@sarchitect.com; http://orcid.org/0000-0001-6163-1277

on just this question. In his lesser-known work, *The Expression of Emotions in Man and Animals* (Darwin 1872), Darwin argued that emotional gestures are shared not only across cultures but throughout the animal world, and are not exclusive to humans. The basic findings of this early work have since been corroborated and it is now widely accepted among psychologists that certain emotions – such as anger, sadness, fear, surprise, disgust, happiness, and contempt can be considered universal. When the psychologist Paul Ekman and his colleagues studied the facial expressions of these basic emotions, they discovered that each one is linked with a distinct facial expression that was remarkably congruent across widely diverse cultures (Ekman 1993).

What is more, each of these emotions has a gestural corollary that is not asymmetric. That is, not only is the emotion expressed outwardly in a consistent bodily gesture or posture, assuming that specific posture reciprocally evokes that emotion. Smiling is not only the outward expression of feeling happy – engaging the musculature of smiling causes hormonal shifts that relieve pain, reduce stress, and has the same effect as anti-depressants – it also has the physiological signature of feeling happy (Adelmann/Zajonc 1989). Furthermore, the effects of smiling are not limited to the individual – smiling causes others to smile as well (Dimberg/Söderkvist 2011). This facial feedback has been shown to both modulate and initiate emotions for both happiness and anger, and is also involved in the emotions of surprise and disgust (Lewis 2012).

Emotion-Gesture Isomorphism

While the face is the bodily region *sui generis* of this isomorphism between emotion and gesture, this congruency has also been shown to be consistent in bodily postures. Returning to the poetic insight that opened this essay – why is feeling down often accompanied with leaning down? Experimental research indicates that bodily postures do indeed directly impact emotional processes. People who smile while adopting an upright posture are able to remember positive memories more readily (Riskind 1984). Whereas sitting in a stooped position while imagining an event leads people to recall more negative associations (Michalak/Mischnat/Teisman 2014). Assuming a stooped posture is also connected to feeling a diminished sense of pride (Stepper/Strack 1993) and helplessness (Riskind/Gotay 1982). While an upright body posture, on the other hand, enables people to recover quickly from negative feelings and correlates to feelings of empowerment (Carney/Cuddy/Yap 2010) and pride (Oosterwijk et al. 2009).

Posture also plays an important role in recovering from a negative mood and modulates negative feelings (Veenstra/Schneider/Koole 2017). Posture corresponds not only with emotional states but also with cognitive performance. An experiment with Japanese school children found that upright posture increased vitality and pleasure, as well as heart rate, symptomatic of increased vitality, compared with normal posture, and that upright posture also led to significantly higher scores for calculation and listening comprehension tests (Inagaki et al. 2018). This work strongly indicates that assuming an upright posture contributes to maintaining a positive psychological state and improving children's performance in tests.

The isomorphic congruency between emotion and gesture, the very fact that an angry scowl is not a gesture of anger, but anger itself, as Merleau-Ponty insisted, takes us far from traditional theories that understood emotion as a subjective internal state (Merleau-Ponty 2002). According to John Dewey, not only is emotion not the sole possession of the individual – emotion belongs to the broader context in which the individual is situated. So, in a threatening situation, rather than saying that »I am fearful«, it would be more accurate to say that the »situation is fearful« (Johnson 2015: 43). For Dewey, emotions were not »reactions in the head« (Dewey 1934: 72), but a kind of shared situated resonance. Fear, in this case, is an emergent response to an actual situation – an eruption in the fluid dynamic in which both organism and event are embedded. The »concrete whole« of emotional experience is comprised of the internally experienced neural and physiological responses together with the situational processes in their complex interaction. Far from being confused thoughts that needed to be suppressed, Dewey argued that emotion is the basis of rational thought and meaningful action and that its healthy expression is critical to individual and cultural creation and equilibrium.

Counterforms

Taking emotion out of the head and into the body and world must be a welcome development for designers – it proves that what we make matters. In creating the concrete situations of daily life, we mold the posture, invite gestures, and orchestrate the movement of countless bodies. And in doing so, we have the power to shift the emotional state and influence the mental outlook and cognitive abilities of those who inhabit the places we make. Yet to fully appreciate these possibilities requires a thorough rethinking of form. Form, as I have insisted elsewhere (Robinson 2021), must be considered in its verbal sense. Form *forms*. Instead of thinking about design in terms of what it looks like in a passive sense, one must develop the knowledge of what design can do in an active sense. What actions, thoughts, and feelings might design activate?

This understanding resonates with the way in which Aldo van Eyck understood form. He insisted that the architect's task is to build the counterform to human action – and imagined this relationship as the shell is to the mollusk. The shell, while apparently solid is extruded from the force, pressure, and movement of the body. He referred to this innate reciprocity between body/form/action as a perpetual homecoming. What if we imagine this dynamic interaction as analogous to the way that a smile is the counterform to happiness, or a whisper is the counterform to intimacy, or the actions of skipping and laughing are the counterforms to joy? Perhaps we might find a way to create forms that share this same isomorphic congruency. Smiling, whispering, skipping, and laughing not only express happiness, intimacy, and joy – they also loop back to generate those particular emotions and feelings.

One example to consider in this direction is Alvar Aalto's iconic chair for the Paimio Sanatorium, a hospital dedicated to those who suffered from tuberculosis. While, at the time of its construction in 1930, sunlight and fresh air were the only known cures, the Paimio chairs' sinuous curves were not designed for how they looked, but for what they *did*. The curves were specifically designed to open the chest and ease breathing. Aalto was inspired by Marcel Breuer's Wassily chair, but intentionally eschewed tubular steel because it conducts heat away from the body. Instead, Aalto pioneered curved plywood – a most humane material that is porous and breathes like human skin. The chair is gorgeously sensuous, but its aesthetic appeal was not its main objective but a consequence of its success as a counterform that affords the healing process. The chair is not an object, but an instrument for healing, and its form is an outward expression of relaxed breathing, just as the smile is an outward expression of happiness. The chair was intended to be an instrument of healing nested within in a larger series of instruments: the chairs were assembled in a sunlit room with fellow patients, the sunlit room was nested in a strategically positioned building, which was in turn nested in a forest for an integrated curative whole.

While the Paimio chair was designed for a specific purpose – Aldo van Eyck insisted on designing counterforms that were at once specific and open-ended. He was particularly sensitive to the shifting needs of children's developing bodies and the entire orphanage complex he designed in Amsterdam exemplifies his remarkable sense of care and accommodation for the changing physical and psychological needs of children. Each age group had its own space structured according to their emerging capacities and skills. At the center of the area for infants to two year olds, for example, sat a three-tiered raised platform that echoed the shape of the circular room in which it was placed. A railing encircled the outer edge of this area and the whole was crowned with a single dome. The central »hilltop« provided an opportunity for very young children to crawl up and practice standing, while the adjacent railing served as an ideal support for their first tentative steps. The building itself became an active partner in the adventure of learning how to walk and concretely empowered the children's newfound sense of verticality.

From this room, the circular sandpit for the two to four year olds is visible in the courtyard. Four benches are situated in a pinwheel pattern so that adults can observe the children without impinging on their exploratory activities. From their position within the sandpit, the children can see the play hill from which they recently graduated. These visual relationships lend a reassuring sense of continuity and security. The sandpit for four to six year olds was set in a smaller raised platform whose bowl-shaped circular recesses collected rainwater to become splash pools and mirrors reflecting the sky, and because children desire more independence at this age, the encompassing benches were intentionally left out. Van Eyck's celebrated »play pool alias seat« as he called it (McCarter 2015: 110), is located at the seam between the indoor and outdoor spaces. On one side, the children felt a sense of shelter, while on the other, a sense of openness – which subtly appeals to the oscillating tension between the need for adventure and the need for retreat. The shallow pool is filled with water and encircled by a bench so that the children can dangle their legs and splash their feet with a sense of abandon. The bench has concrete backrests interspersed with pink glass. In the sunlight, bright pink reflections shimmer simultaneously on the surface of the water and on the ceiling above. This multi-dimensional dance of light and color is a counterform to the magical act of play in a place perfectly fit for the needs of the children, at once a place of protection, mischief, and delight.

1.
Frank Lloyd Wright: Taliesin West, 1937.
Stairs to Dining / Theater Pavilion. Photographer: Sarah Robinson.

The designer Rosan Bosch has also developed learning situations for young people with great care and consideration. Understanding the need for a variety of postures and gestures, her designs offer diverse experiences within a single space. These configurations: the mountaintop, campfire, cave, and water hole emphasize hands-on movement. The mountaintop establishes a place for individuals to express themselves before a group, in an elevated position that allows thoughts and ideas to flow from one person to many. The cave situation offers a protected place for individuals and very small groups to concentrate and reflect. The campfire is a space for group learning with attention directed centripetally and the water hole is situated along a circulation route, attracting a flow of passer-by to gather here. In this situation, students learn through spontaneous encounters, disruptions, and surprises. Movement in, and between, these situations emphasize the non-verbal dimension of communication and continually renew energy to keep learning fresh.

Countermuscles

Gaston Bachelard was also fond of using the image of the mollusk and the shell to evoke the deep reciprocity between the body and form and, in another provocative analogy, he called the road or path on which one walks a countermuscle to our muscles, »it is as though the road itself had muscles – or should I say counter muscles.« (Bachelard 1964: 11). Here too, the surfaces that support our footsteps are not passive and inert but actively resisting the force of our movements in an act of reciprocity and these repeated interactions are the way in which the places we inhabit work their way into our nerves and tissues – into our muscular consciousness. He goes on to say:

> »The house we were born in is physically inscribed in us. It is a group of organic habits. After twenty years, in spite of all the other anonymous stairways, we would recapture the reflexes of the first stairway, we would not stumble on that rather high step. The house's entire being would open up, faithful to our own being. We would push the door that creaks with the same gesture, we would find our way in the dark in the distant attic. The feel of the tiny latch has remained in our hands.« (Bachelard 1964: 14).

What he is suggesting here is that our bodily capabilities were exercised by the doors, stairs, and latches of our earliest years – that our bodies grew and

2.
Frank Lloyd Wright: Taliesin West, 1937.
Breezeway and Stairs. Photographer: Sarah Robinson.

were shaped in correspondence with the possibilities and affordances of our environments, and given what we now know about the emotional import and cognitive consequences of certain gestures and postures, it would be difficult to overestimate the importance of careful design through all passages of life – but most importantly in our earliest, most vulnerable years.

Stairs are perhaps the most powerful »countermuscles« to shape our movements. The most sensitive attention to the rise and run ratio of stairs very concretely slows one's movements down or speeds them up. At Frank Lloyd Wright's Taliesin West where I lived for years, the treads were broad and the risers were shallow, forcing one to assume a slower gait. Walking at this pace and rhythm felt as though one were wearing a gown. Running on stairs of this proportion causes the most awkward movement, lacking in all elegance. Alvar Aalto employed the same strategy in his Viipuri library, where the supple linoleum stairs that lead to the reading room cushion the step while slowing one's gait, as is befitting of the quiet, reflective character of the activities meant to take place there. In both of these cases, calibrating individual movements in such specific concrete ways impacts the collective mood. In the first case, the stairs lead to the theater where festive formal events regularly occur. The stairs ever so subtly force one to assume a formal posture, priming one's mood for the social role that the theater was meant to fulfill. While in the latter case, the hushed and slowed walking extends a sense of courtesy to the atmosphere of quiet study collectively taking place in the space.

Again, while both Aalto and Wright were specific in the gestures the wanted to configure, like Aldo van Eyck, Herman Herzberger emphasizes the polyvalent use and meaning of his work. In his extended school in Arnhem, the Netherlands, for example, he designed a large set of wooden stairs with varying rises and runs to invite multiple uses and interpretations. In this way the stairs fulfill their utilitarian purpose, while going beyond it. The children study, read, play, and perform on these risers, as they are broad enough in places to lay and work upon. The open risers open myriad ways to crawl through and around them, the places below become intriguing hiding places, and their slightly offset diagonal layering subtly shifts and eases the need to march from one place to the next without noticing the possibilities of the in-between. And, like Bachelard's evocation of the »first stair« that lies dormant in the muscles, Herzberger remembers the pleasure of sitting on the softly rounded cornerstones in Amsterdam that he played on 78 years ago. The careful attention that went into making and placing those sculpted

3. + 4.
Alvar Aalto: Viipuri Library, 1935.
Stairs to Reading Area and Detail.
Photographer: Sarah Robinson.

cornerstones remains in his muscular consciousness and no doubt shapes his designs to this day.

From Emotion to Mood

As we have seen with these various stairs, shifting our movements shifts our mood. While postures and gestures have very concrete physiological and psychological effects, larger scale movements can shift collective moods. While the words emotion and mood are often used interchangeably, the difference between them points to the way that moods can tend toward the collective more than emotions can. The primary difference is that emotions are sudden and tend to be fleeting, while moods tend to linger over longer periods of time. Emotions are discrete and readily expressed, while moods are vague and often difficult to name. Emotions are responses to specific situations, while moods are pervasive and slow – and while also situated, can linger beyond spatial boundaries. Emotion is closely tied with movement both etymologically and physiologically, while mood is a more diffuse affective state spread out over time. Mood is also closely tied to movement, but movement understood in a more subtle way. Rhythm is the kind of movement more clearly related to mood.

Rhythm was a central concern for John Dewey, who understood it to be a deep pattern in »the world of physical material and energies« (Dewey 1934: 151). He considered architecture to be as much of a rhythmic art as music and insisted that »denial of rhythm to pictures, edifices, and statues, or the assertion that it is found in them metaphorically, rests upon ignorance of the inherent nature of every perception« (Dewey 1934: 180). Dewey anticipated what we now know about perception by five decades: perception is rhythmic. Not only does the auditory system operate according to rhythmic vibrations – visual, touch, taste, and proprioceptive systems are rhythmic as well. They sample the world in quanta or packets like the saccadic movements of vision, and because the brain is rhythmic, repetitive patterns of neural activity can be measured and understood in terms of resonance and oscillating waves. We live in a sea of rhythm from the human heartbeat to the circadian rhythms that connect us to the cycles of light on a rotating planet. All of our experience is rhythmic and these movements from micro to macro scale introduce a critical, if little understood, temporal dimension into architectural experience.

In his classic *Experiencing Architecture*, Steen Eiler Rasmussen dedicated a chapter to rhythm, and like Dewey, understood rhythm as a feature of the natural world – of oscillating energy between tension and release. In terms of architecture, he understood rhythm to be »subtle variations within strict regularity« (Rasmussen 1959: 127). Yet he also discusses rhythm in terms of bodily movement and mood. Physical work, for example, becomes more enjoyable and easier when the movements involved are regularly alternated:

> »There is something mysterious about the stimulating effect of rhythm. You can explain what it is that creates rhythm but you have to experience it yourself to know what it is like. [...] A man who moves rhythmically starts the motion himself and feels that he controls it. But very shortly, the rhythm controls him; he is possessed by it. It carries him along. Rhythmic motion gives a feeling of heightened energy« (ibid.: 134).

Rasmussen also points out that those who move in the same way collectively share rhythms. Clothing from earlier eras that now seems cumbersome and limiting was once worn with great ease because the people in those cultural milieus moved to different rhythms. Architecture in various periods can also be understood in terms of the expression of changing rhythms. Here, the Spanish Steps in Rome provide a classic example. The functional role of the staircase was to connect the low-lying *Piazza di Spagna* with the *Piazza della Trinità* above and the more obvious solution would have been to build long, straight monumental stairs, such as those that lead to the *Piazza del Campidoglio*. The Spanish Steps however, with their rhythmic bends and curves, were not only designed to walk upon, as much as they were made to dance upon. They were built during the period when the Baroque waltz, the *Polonaise*, was in high fashion. In the choreography for the *Polonaise*, the dancers advance four by four in a line and then divide, two going to the right and two to the left, then turning, curtsying, and meeting back on the large landing, then repeating these movements. Imagine gradually waltzing one's way up to the uppermost terrace and elegantly turning to face the panorama of Rome lying at one's feet. The Spanish Steps concretize an altogether different rhythm than the contemporary rhythms to which we have now grown accustomed: »We can see a petrification of the dancing rhythm of a period of gallantry; it gives an inkling of something that was, something our generation will never know« (Rasmussen 1959: 136). Moving together engages shared rhythms that coincide with shared moods. We know from research in the psychology of musical experience that people who move together during a live musical performance experience higher levels of interpersonal coordination and cooperation (Dotov et al. 2021). Neuroscientists at the University of Parma also found that audience members in a concert experience cardiac synchrony regardless of whether they are strangers or not (Ardizzi et al. 2020). We entrain with movements whether or not their source is living or non-living. Entrainment is a process where the frequency of energy, from two or more systems, tends to synchronize through a process of mutual influence as one adapts to the other. The closely related phenomenon of resonance refers to the transfer of energy from systems vibrating at the same or similar frequencies. A familiar example is when a tuning fork transfers its vibration to a string on a musical instrument tuned to the same frequency, or when a vocalist shatters a glass by matching the frequency of the crystal from which it is made. Yet, as it was mentioned earlier with rhythm, resonance and entrainment apply to non-sonic phenomena as well. Non-linear couplings between the brain, body, and environmental oscillations have been studied in terms of cognitive, perceptual, autonomic, physiological, motor, and social entrainment (Trost/Vuilleumier 2013; Vara Sánchez 2021). The tendency toward entrainment is shared across cultures, taxonomies, and species, and because the processes of entrainment and resonance are features of the animate and inanimate material world they point to a way to understand the potentials of architecture and human interaction.

The complex and daunting mandate to provide »perpetual homecoming« is overwhelming in its complexity. Yet, when we begin this task by taking the capacities and potentials of the body seriously, new horizons of possibility begin to present themselves. Everything we make has untold dimensions – and starting with the movements of the body is far from mundane. An entire cosmology is contained in the words, »stand up straight!« as Pierre Bourdieu insisted (Bell 1992: 141). When we consider that every gesture elicits a cascade of oscillatory, hormonal, muscular, psychological, and cognitive effects, one can begin to get an inkling of what is meant by those words. Our movements and the very expressive possibilities of our bodies are always conditioned by, and respond to, a specific context. The contexts that designers and architects are responsible for creating, exercise the muscular repertoire, reinforce and modulate moods and emotions, and instill cultural habits and attitudes for generations of people who inhabit our work.

References

Adelmann, Pamela K./Zajonc, Robert B. (1989): »Facial Efference and the Experience of Emotion«, in: *Annual Review of Psychology* 40, 249–280.

Ardizzi, Martina/Calbi, Marta/Tavaglione, Simona/Umiltà, Maria Alessandra/Gallese, Vittorio (2020): »Audience Spontaneous Entrainment During the Collective Enjoyment of Live Performances: Physiological and Behavioral Measurements«, in: *Nature Scientific Reports* 10, 3813.

Bachelard, Gaston [1958]: *La Poétique de l'Espace*, Paris: Presses Universitaires de France – English translation *The Poetics of Space*, New York: Orion, 1964.

Bell, Catherine (1992): *Ritual Theory, Ritual Practice*, Oxford: Oxford University Press.

Carney, Dana R./Cuddy, Amy J./Yap, Andy J. (2010): »Power Posing: Brief Nonverbal Displays Affect Neuroendocrine Levels and Risk Tolerance«, in: *Psychological Science* 10/21, 1363–1368.

Darwin, Charles (1872): *The Expression of Emotions in Man and Animals*, London: John Murray.

Dewey, John (1934): *Art as Experience*, New York: Minton, Balch & Company.

Dimberg, Ulf/Söderkvist, Sven (2011): »Facial Feedback«, in: *Journal of Nonverbal Behavior* 35, 17–33.

Dotov, Dobromir/Bosnyak, Daniel/Trainor, Laurel J. (2021): »Collective Music Listening: Movement Energy is Enhanced by Groove and Visual Social Cues«, in: *Experimental Psychology* 6/74, 1037–1053.

Ekman, Paul/Davidson, Richard (1993): »Voluntary Smiling Changes Regional Brain Activity«, in: *Psychological Science* 4/5, 342–345.

Hirshfield, Jane (1997): *Nine Gates: Entering the Mind of Poetry*, New York: Harper Collins.

Inagaki, Kazuki/Takeshi, Shimizu/Yosuke, Sakairi (2018): »Effects of Posture Regulation on Mood States, Heart Rate and Test Performance in Children«, in: *Educational Psychology* 38/9, 1129–1146.

Johnson, Mark (2015): »The Embodied Meaning of Architecture«, in Sarah Robinson and Juhani Pallasmaa, (eds.), *Mind in Architecture: Neuroscience, Embodiment and the Future of Design*, Cambridge, MA: The MIT Press.

Lewis, Michael B. (2012): »Exploring the Positive and Negative Implications of Facial Feedback«, in: *Emotion* 12/4, 852–859.

McCarter, Robert (2015): Aldo Van Eyck, New Haven: Yale University Press.

Merleau-Ponty, Maurice [1945]: *Phénoménologie de la perception.* – English translation [1962]: *Phenomenology of Perception*, London: Routledge, 2002.

Michalak, Johannes/Mischnat, Judith/Teismann, Tobias (2014): »Sitting Posture Makes a Difference-Embodiment Effects on Depressive Memory Bias«, in: *Clinical Psychology and Psychotherapy* 21/6, 519–524.

Oosterwijk, Suzanne/Rotteveel, Mark/Fischer, Agneta H./Hess, Ursula (2009): «Embodied Emotion Concepts: How Generating Words about Pride and Disappointment Influences Posture«, in: *European Journal of Social Psychology* 39, 457–466.

Rasmussen, Steen Eiler (1959): *Experiencing Architecture*, Cambridge, MA: The MIT Press.

Riskind, John H./Gotay, Carolyn C. (1982): »Physical Posture: Could It Have Regulatory or Feedback Effects on Motivation and Emotion«, in: *Motivation and Emotion* 6, 273–298.

Riskind, John H. (1984): »They Stoop to Conquer: Guiding and Self-Regulatory Functions of Physical Posture after Success and Failure«, in: *Journal of Personality and Social Psychology* 47/3, 479–493.

Robinson, Sarah (2021): *Architecture is a Verb*, London: Routledge.

Stepper, Sabine/Strack, Fritz (1993): »Proprioceptive Determinants of Emotional and Nonemotional Feelings«, in: *Journal of Personality and Social Psychology* 64/2, 211–220.

Trost, Wiebke Johanne/Vuilleumier, Patrick (2013): »Rhythmic Entrainment as a Mechanism for Emotion Induction by Music«,: in Tom Cochrane/Bernadino Fantini/ Klaus R. Scherer, *The Emotional Power of Music: Multidisciplinary Perspectives on Musical Arousal, Expression, and Social Control*, Oxford: Oxford University Press.

Vara Sánchez, Carlos (2021): »Enacting the Aesthetic: A Model for Raw Cognitive Dynamics«, in: *Phenomenology and the Cognitive Sciences*, doi: 10.1007/s11097-021-09737-y

Veenstra, Lotte/Schneider, Iris/ Koole, Sander L. (2017): »Embodied Mood Regulation: The Impact of Body Posture on Mood Recovery, Negative Thoughts, and Mood-Congruent Recall«, in: *Cognition and Emotion* 31/7, 1361–1376.

Assemblage

»Consider movement, consider through movement.

I experience availability in thought, in the organic tissues that also become the body, I listen to the pulse of being/doing aligned with this availability.

I learn how to learn.«

Sophia Neuparth 2014: 8–9.

Neuparth, Sophia (2014): *Movimento*. Escrito em Estado de Dança, Lisboa: c.e.m. Centro em Movimento. – English translation by the editors, 2021.

Dimensions of Architectural Knowledge, 2021-02 ᴓ
https://doi.org/10.14361/dak-2021-0211

Seeking Experience in Architecture:
Corporeal Attempts at Perception and Conception

Katharina Voigt and Virginie Roy

Abstract: This contribution presents the proceedings from a series of transversal university projects, addressing bodily forms of knowledge concerning the perception, inquiry, and conception of architecture. It retraces the phases of different manners of investigation over a three-semester teaching cycle, addressing perceptions and experiences of architectural spaces. The proceedings of, and results from the seminar cycle are documented and framed with an introduction to the applied methods and ways of working as well as their reflection and evaluation. These varying approaches all center around the questions of how to bring body-based and incorporated knowledge concerning architectural space to awareness and how attention to sensual and corporeal ways of perception can be increased. Thus, it investigates how the spectrum of design methods in architecture can be extended in order to actively include bodily forms of knowledge in the anticipation of spatial experience in the design process. The article introduces a concept of »Architecture Imagery« as a way to include bodily ways of knowing and body-based practices in the perception and memory of lived experience and the process of architectural design.

Keywords: Corporeal Experience; Architecture Imagery; Body-Knowledge; Sensory Perception; Embodied Phenomenology; Transdisciplinary Practice-Related Approach.

Prologue

Essential to this investigation is the question of *how* an elaborate consciousness for multisensory, sensorimotor, and sensual architecture perception can provide more refined access to the incorporated knowledge gained through experience, in order to actively implement it in the process of architectural design. Such analysis is pertinent, as it allows for the anticipation of future experience already present in the associative, and inventive processes of imagination and creation – reaching beyond the visual senses of the imaginary.

Corresponding authors: Katharina Voigt (Technical University of Munich, Germany);
katharina.voigt@tum.de; http://orcid.org/0000-0002-2547-8292; Virginie Roy (Music and Arts University
of the City of Vienna, Austria); v.roy@muk.ac.at; http://orcid.org/0000-0003-2879-1839.

In the following text, the thematic field of bodily knowledge, corporeal and sensual experience, and body-based perception of architecture is unfolded using various means: It opens with an introduction to the project's phases, centered around the discourse and investigation of sensual, perceptual, and corporeal dimensions of experiencing architecture. Moreover, the investigation presents an assembly of reports on encounters with a broad variety of different buildings and the corresponding evoked sensations. These seek to replicate the sensual and poetic qualities of the encounter through writing, visual documentation in photographs and sketches, as well as through corporeal forms of conveyance. Physical gesture is explored as a tool to retrace incorporated knowledge and to express lived experiences and impressions in bodily ways. Finally, the process and proceedings of the working cycle are reflected with specific focus on their potential to form a basis of knowledge as well as an extension of the methodological approaches to architectural design.

Exploring Experience

The seeking of experience in architecture is based on raising awareness of diverse modes of perception. At the center of this exploration lie sensory and bodily approaches to investigate the efficacy of architecture. The principle research question guiding transversal exchange over a three-semester-long university project examined how lived experience, sensuality, and movement in architecture can be accessed, collected, and articulated. Starting from this acquired knowledge base with respect to experience, we are concerned with the question of how we as designers – in architecture, but also in other disciplines – can draw from conscious experience and the knowledge gained from it: our own experience forms the impulse and basis for our own creative process and design. This interest created the framework for open-ended research in collaboration with master students in the Technical University of Munich's Department of Architecture under the supervision of the authors. The experience of architectural space was investigated in a transdisciplinary practice-related approach.

Architecture and movement have a complementary effect on each other: The spatiality of a building is only revealed to the recipient by moving through it, while the architectural form has a decisive influence on the type and expression of movement carried out within it (Janson/Tigges 2014: 118–120). Our bodily constitution and the bodily knowledge gathered from previous spatial experiences of architectural space suggests that architecture has a direct effect on us – one that we literally feel in our own bodies. The human and the architectural body encounter each other as related and yet distinct bodily forms and resonate with each other regarding their respective impact, expression, and gestures. Accordingly, both can be defined as spacious, spatial, and material. They are reciprocally interdependent, as the spatial sphere of the human body is affected by the architectural form itself and responds to it in gesture and movement. The spatiality of architecture is only revealed in movement. By walking through it, the spatial sequence is comprehended and thus inscribed by the body (Noë 2004; Janson/Tigges 2014: 118–120; 144–146).

The sensory perception of architecture is complex. It is a synesthetic experience. Upon entering an architectural construct, one is absorbed into the immersive experience of the surrounding setting. When diving into the exploration of a building, a sequence of rooms or urban spaces, moving within the spatial layout and being moved by its impetus and sensual impact, reciprocally condition each another. As we move in space, we are moved by the space; it attracts our attention, invites specific movements, and influences the types of movements conducted within it. Movement gives access to experience. Deeper layers of understanding and experience emerge in the contingency of moving in space. Investigating movement and the sensation of being moved promotes the inclusion of this bodily knowledge in research. The body here is regarded as an all-encompassing sensory entirety, which grants access to sensual perception and mediates perceptual sensations. Aspects like being surrounded, being included, and being enclosed in an immersive spatiotemporal situation are addressed in the investigation of architecture experience. In relation to the physical presence of a building, an individual interacts with it corporeally, through resonance and dialogue between the body and the architectural space. Architectural space, here, is understood as enclosed and containing space, as a context within which an individual immerses themselves and moves, and which, respectively, only unfolds its entire complexity upon its exploration in movement. It can be a sequence of rooms, a series of inner spaces, but also an affiliation of spaces in cities – such as alleys, streets, and squares. All spatial typologies – be they transitory spaces, places of rest, interstices or thresholds – evoke an all-encompassing holistic and immersive feeling. The entirety of an experience cannot easily be dissected into its individual facets of experience; rather, it is an overall impression that we gain by experiencing a situation. Sight and hearing, sensory experiences to which we have heightened tangible access and which are often perceived to be predominant, overshadow the complex correlation of all senses, whose influence we experience as implicit knowledge beyond conscious access.

Thus, the project of experiencing architectural space in a body-based context examines the spatiality of the body and its movements. The individual lived experience of the participants forms the essential basis upon which the knowledge of perception builds, while reflective and superordinate texts from various disciplines – such as architecture and art studies, phenomenological philosophy, theories of perception, psychology and cognitive sciences – broaden the spectrum of perspectives discussed. Initiated by the question of how architecture affects the experiencer, special focus was placed on observing individual perceptions and sharpening awareness of one's own sensations. Furthermore, it is not only important to perceive these observations, but to also make them accessible to oneself through different means of expression, and, in an additional step, to make them comprehensible and legible to others. In this sense, this inquiry concerns reconnecting to the sensuality of experience, as well as about seeking ways to communicate and transmit it.

Acquainting Body-Knowledge

In the first step, each participant was asked to visit a chosen architectural site and pay particular attention to their initial perception as well as how their process of exploration revealed the site to them. The exploration was to be non-evaluative, guided by the senses, and allow for the emergence of whatever came up, without any pre-conceived focus set beforehand. In order to increase the ways in which the building can be perceived, the sensations and observations gained upon its exploration were refined in descriptive essays which portrayed the individual, subjective, and situational lived experience of the place and which were supplemented with photographs that reflected the individual's personal perspective. The individual experience of architecture is examined with particular regard to the method of approaching the building, to thresholds and transitions of the architectural tissue, as well as to the spatial structure. In dialogue with the body, the focus centers on the impulses of movement and the sensual impact evoked by the structure.

In the following semester, the initial task remained the same as in the first. However, in order to uncover the substance of the observations, the participants did not only draw from within themselves but were interviewed by another participant, who asked questions to refine their descriptions. Meanwhile a third person was asked to witness the gestures and movements which emerge, while trying to find the right words to express lived sensual and tacit qualities. In the search for words before verbalization, somatic and body-based practices enabled expression through gestures and movement.[1] Therefore, in the subsequent work process, particular attention and vigilance were paid to the body and the involvement of gesture and movement. Just as it is difficult to differentiate between different aspects of experience, it is difficult to put sensory and multisensory experience precisely into words and expression. Beyond verbalization, corporeal forms of expression allow for instant responses to the lived experience.

Movement and gesture allow one to reconsider, retrace, narrate, or mediate the immediate impression perceived and to express it by corporeal means. Therewith, the verbal translation of the experienced sensation becomes obsolete. What affects the body is articulated through the body. The body remains the medium of expression that brings forth an immediate description of the experience. Working manners from contemporary dance, and particularly improvisation, choreographic methods, and somatic practices, were introduced as methods to exploit and apply bodily forms of knowledge and to bring the body as medium a of perception, conveyance, and expression into the discourse.

Collecting Sensual Experience

As the research cycle progressed, the focus increasingly shifted from the dominance of visual observations to attuned awareness of multi-sensory, complex, and experiences, emphasizing the sensual, sensorimotor, corporeal, and body-based dimensions of lived experience. In the last phase of the cycle, this shift was encouraged by omitting the visual sense through blindfolded, tactile exploration of a building: In teams of two, the participants explored the space of the building. The blindfolded person explored

---

1   In the chapter »Poetics of Movement« Laurence Louppe states: »It could be also be said that ›movement‹ concerns the whole body, and that ›gesture‹ is more fragmentary, visibly at least, making movement more global, closer to posture and thus to an unconscious charge which is more interesting poetically than a segmentary gesture which is ›decided‹ and clearly ›emitted‹« (Louppe 2010: 72).

the building and was free to find their way through tactile exploration, while the second person observed and accompanied the exploration to create a safe space and to witness the process. In this activity, the blindfolded person actively guided the exploration of the space, with the protection given by the second participant creating the freedom to fully discover. Starting with slow movements of palpating and touching the surfaces of the architecture, after a while the blindfolded explorers gained more and more freedom to let go of the support of touch, and began to move around and to sense different aspects of the bodily discovery of space. Also during this activity, the lived experience was recapped and unraveled in dialogue between the partnering participants in order to deepen the consciousness of the lived experience.

However, in contrast to the previous phase, movement and gesture did not only unintentionally occur during the conversation, but the whole body was brought to the fore and actively involved in movement. While the two prior phases explored how sensual experience affects and involves the body, the moving body became the center of attention in this final phase: It was analyzed as a medium to explore, a channel to provide access to sensuality, movement, and gesture, and as a tool for the discovery and examination of place. As movement and gesture had been essential for the exploration itself, they were investigated as integral parts of the exploratory experience. Along with the recall and reflection of these sensations that emerged during the interviews came the refinement of gestural expressions, which were then elaborated upon as an embodied essence of these key moments of experience.

The impressions gathered in this process assemble a variety of sensations, which can be retraced in gestures and movements. Recalling these sensations, an individual's memory of the experience sets the participants in motion. They either embody the sensation or reenact the actual movement of exploration or its associated imagery. In the empty space of the central counter hall of the main customs office in Munich, where the investigation took place, this collection of sensations was recalled and retraced in an act of improvisation, – as a performative intervention through the body in the space –, to allow the key moments of the experience to spontaneously emerge in movement and gesture. The choice of place was also essential to the experience, as the qualities of the building impacted the movement. The actual impressions are retraced in the lived moving experience.

Assemblage of Observations

The following collection of works – descriptive observations and gestures – presents proceedings from the process of investigation. It includes excerpts from essays and photographs of gestures to document the various facets of individual architectural experience. The diversity of forms and styles of representation is explored, as the works are arranged in a complementary manner, without attempting to align them with one another. Corporeal and somatic observations are put into words and narrated in detailed descriptions, emphasizing the sensations assembled throughout the exploration of a building or a sequence of rooms. They are traced in tangible discovery and recaptured in gestures and movements.

Gathered from several selected places, the following narrations convene the individual observations and lived experiences that occurred during the encounters with such buildings. Upon these subjective, situational, and often distinctly sensual and body-relating contemplations, emerging thoughts and attentive observations are brought together as fragments, bits and pieces taken from the complex, synesthetic overall experience.

The following contributions are excerpts from seminar works by master's students from the following courses:

- »**Architectural Perception**«
  Seminar held by Katharina Voigt in Winter 2018/19 at the Technical University of Munich, Chair for Architectural Design and Conception.

- »**Phenomenology of Architecture**«
  Seminar held by Katharina Voigt in Summer 2019 at the Technical University of Munich, Chair for Architectural Design and Conception.

- »**Architecture Experience**«
  Seminar held by Katharina Voigt and Virginie Roy in Winter 2019/20 at the Technical University of Munich, Lecture Position, *Questions from Science and Society in Architecture and Urban Planning*.

Quirin Goßlau: Cabin, Tegernsee

»From a great distance, the visitor is able to view the hut's surroundings, such as the forest in the background; at a closer distance, however, the dark wooden material surrounding the structure becomes the main focus. Only increasing proximity and finally entering the hut enable the visitor to become aware of the more subtle details. Yet closer examination and conscious perception in turn, require selecting and focusing one's field of vision.«

»The first glimpse into the main room shows a dark expanse countered by faint rays of sunlight, which create small crevices in the closed shutters on the opposite side of the room, appearing to cast strikes of light in the haze. Opening them requires loosening numerous wing screws on each window by hand and thus moving through the inside of the building, as well as moving around the outside of the cabin, to individually remove the counterparts of each screw.«

»The successive action of opening all seven windows and the recurring entry and exit between the inside and outside make active movement an obligatory ritual upon arrival, even for a recurring visitor. Only with the opening of all shutters and the sequentially established connection between the inside and the outside of each opening is the visitor finally able to enter the cabin. Each view from the windows increasingly locates the structure between the contrasting sides of valley and slope, lake and mountain, as well as between two forest edges on the side of the gable.«

»The mental distance and perspective of the surrounding landscape are reinforced by the feeling of refuge that the hut provides, an escape from the hustle and bustle of the big city. The ascent to the cabin, which is small and inconspicuous in color, is barely visible from the lake and reinforces this perceived distance. Ultimately, the visitor looks back into the valley and across the lake as an uninvolved, neutral observer, thus keeping their surroundings at a safe distance.«

»Situated in the surroundings yet shielded, the shutters open like outstretched arms: In its appropriated state, the cabin represents an intelligible and assured relationship between inside and outside, and is thus an ideal environment for the visitor and their self-reflection.«

Matthias Peterseim: *Domus Aurea*, Rome

»The first section near the entrance looks like a utilitarian corridor. From here on we follow a sequence of rooms arranged in a polygonal manner. It is difficult to orient oneself within them without visual references to the outside. We quickly pass through several of the brick-vaulted rooms or corridors. In other, better preserved halls, we pause. We detect places that, simply due to their character, prompt us to stop. The respective purpose or use of the rooms eludes our attention. Instead, we concentrate on exploring the very character of the place.«

»It is astonishing that by using the same means, such different shapes and geometries have been created in the very same complex. The rigor that often comes from symmetrical layouts and axes is not noticeable here. While the individual room is symmetrical, the sequence of rooms is not. Thus, the structure of the underground Domus Aurea does not tell us much about its spatial arrangement. It is only revealed as we walk through it.«

»While passing through, the building resembles a pulsating, organic body. As it has no exterior, I have no choice but to enter inside it. The subterranean structure affects my body immediately upon entry by making me attune to a new atmosphere. While my eyes adjust to an enormous change in contrast and only slowly get used to the darkness, I become aware of other sensory impressions. The hot dryness of the outside gives way to the cool dampness of the interior. In this way, it is immediately clear that I have moved right into a different environment without hesitation. A glance behind alone would not be enough to verify this change; it is my body that really experiences the sudden adjustment. However, as quickly as the change comes, my body has the ability to adapt to new circumstances just as quickly.«

»My eyes move rapidly back and forth from the earthy floor below my feet to the vault above my head, to the side toward the prohibited spaces. Using my visual sense, I explore the spatial structure. In some directions, the further extensions of the space – which include not only the corporeal, but also the visually grasped – run into the void. In a floor plan, there would be open ends here, without specific frontiers. In the depth of the aisles the spaces fade into a blur. They resemble black holes: They are immaterial and inevitably attract glances, generate curiosity, and almost physically repel and resist the visitor.«

»In this place, we as knowers encounter much more than the solely visible; in this way, we additionally enter into dialogue with different layers of history. We recognize the construction method and connect it to the Roman Empire. We know that the walls were once covered with marble and stucco. Today, we see a porous brick surface. We begin to wonder if we might like this brick texture – which seems almost monolithic – better than the original plaster and fresco decoration. But who can tell?«

»Every place we visit is trivial in its own way; we can always rationally break it down into its distinct components and describe them. Humans possess this characteristic as well, in particular those that exist within the context of Enlightenment ›modernity‹. We strive to get to the bottom of things and to explain them, yet we lose the imaginative access to space and things.«

Viktoria Kelderer: *Warrior Memorial*, Munich

»Despite the lack of a door, the first step inside is a very special experience. Before I take my first step, I always ask myself which of the twelve staircases is the right one to take this time. It becomes a kind of game to choose a different way into the space each time and, in turn, to take another one on the way out.«

»The inscription ›To Our Fallen‹ triggers certain uneasiness; associations with death or tombs come to mind. The steps become slower, more hesitant. My head is submerged under the ceiling tile at the next step and suddenly the obscurity vanishes. The light of the sun no longer blinds my eyes. They adjust rapidly to the new environment and I pause for a moment to appreciate what is revealed to me.«

»After a long time of looking at the architectural sculpture from the outside – from a distance, so to speak – the scale of the space finally becomes clear upon entering it. It encompasses an unexpected space, the stairs turn into normal steps, and the openings appear as entrances of a familiar size. In the center, however, lies another sculpture: the representation of a fallen soldier, carved from gleaming stone. Here again, my sense of scale becomes confused. This soldier of stone resting in the center of the room appears to be disproportionately large and makes his surroundings seem much smaller than they actually are.«

»The architecture is structured by the massive stone ashlars. Deep, massive barriers to the outside world alternate with similarly wide openings. The rhythmic character of movement makes me speed up. Where is the right place to pause?

»As I pass along, I run my hand over the surface of the stones. Contrary to my expectation, they are less cold than I thought. It seems that their warm color is more than just the chromaticity. My fingers glide from the precise edge over the broad surface to the other edge and finally fall into the void until the game begins anew.«

»The surfaces turn out to be smoother than I had suspected, the strong grain is only striking in terms of color; it cannot actually be tangibly detected.

The striking pattern of the grain reminds me of old trees. Thick deforested trunks that reveal a glimpse of their age in the form of countless annual rings. Thoughts begin to wander: Rings for years, rings for days, and rings for human lives. And again I shiver.«

»The oppressive effect of the large block of stone towering above me makes me abruptly aware of my own physicality. The cover plate presses heavily on one's shoulders. The grain of the stones, reminiscent of annual rings, immediately guides one's own thoughts in new directions: ›physically, as anatomy and skin, as mass, membrane, as fabric or sheath, cloth, velvet, silk and shiny steel‹ (Zumthor 2006: 31). The monument exerts its effect on the visitor through its skillful interplay of material and form.«

»If I did not know that this is a monument to fallen soldiers, I would assess the gravity of the place in a different way. Is this kind of perception now less true than a perception that occurs solely through the body and the senses? It would not have been possible to grasp the significance of the place only through the senses. Of course, the architecture in itself has the gravity necessary to express that it is a special, contemplative place, but wouldn't the monument be meaningless if perception stopped here? The explanatory component of the pictorial symbols on the stone blocks and the soldier inside are necessary elements of this architectural structure.«

»I continue to climb the stairs, but the redeeming arrival outside does not yet occur. I am still much deeper in the ground than the park's other visitors. I continue to work my way up. From the gravel court, up the stairs, past the hedges, to the very top, where the trees and individuals visiting the *Hofgarten* finally appear and immediately absorb me, creating a distance from what I have just experienced. Once again, the anonymity of the city engulfs me.«

»I turn around one last time. It is only now – looking back and against the background of what I have just experienced – that the abstract structure of stone blocks reveals itself to me as a symbol: broad-shouldered soldiers standing side by side, holding a protective shield over a fallen comrade.«

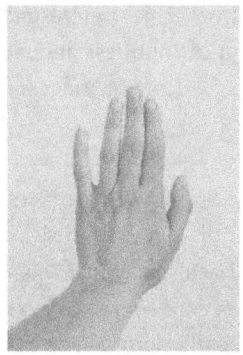
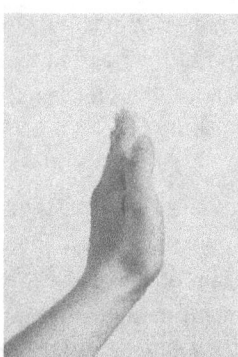

»confrontation«   *»linearity«*

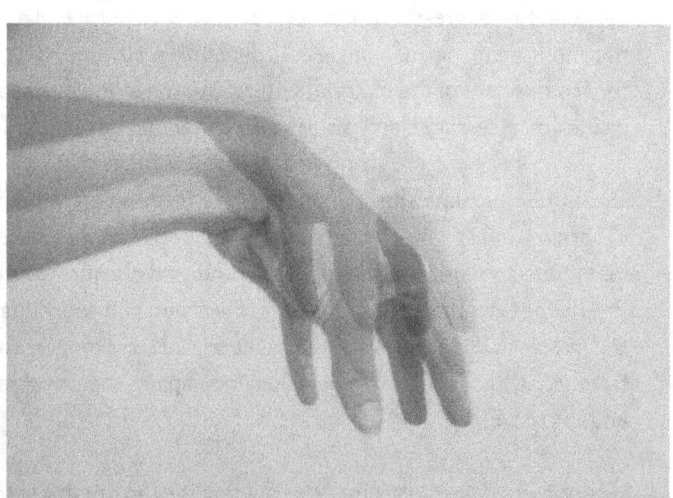

»placement«

Melanie Sommerfeld: Museum *La Congiunta*, Giornico, Ticino

»Through the growing feeling of proximity that engulfs me, I begin to feel a connection with the architecture, the proportions of which I perceive as coherent in relation to my body. At the same time, I recognize details in the materiality, such as the horizontal division of the surfaces through a form-work pattern in the concrete, which emphasize the linear movement.«

»I hear the space's sounds in a muffled manner – the chirping of birds, the murmur of the river, and the church bells – create another reference to the outside world. Thus, the structure provides protection and conveys a feeling of being enclosed without excluding the external environment. Reverberation is characteristic of the sound in the rooms and I become aware that I whisper when talking to other visitors.«

»The movement in the interior, which is initially linear and finally bends in the direction of the adjoining space, finds its counterpart in the exterior space, in which I walk linearly along the museum until I alter direction toward the entrance door. These two figures of movement intertwine and must be retraced back in the same way when leaving the place.«

»As I contemplate the landscape, I become aware of my own size, and in com-parison to the expanse of the landscape, I perceive my own spatial sphere to be pushed back to the contours of my body. The dimension of the spatial sphere depends on the sensory perception and occasionally corresponds with the boundaries of space. Thus, I perceive the expansion of my spatial sphere during the widening of the walkways around the building in one way, but sense its minimal expansion in the face of the landscape space in another. At the same time, my perception extends beyond the limits of my body, and I can clearly perceive the building at my back, even though it is not in my field of vision. I feel the protection of the canopy and simultaneously, in contrast, the exposure to wind and weather.«

»While architecture leaves an impression on me, generates memories, and shapes my experiences, I express myself through my movements in spaces.«

Lisa Schröter: Public Pool *Müller'sches Volksbad*, Munich

»I climb a stone staircase and perceive distinct sounds. I hear echoing voices and the water. I see the lockers. In the background, a spectacular view emerges: I see the bright blue of the water and hear noise from a throng of people. I get closer to the parapet. I can overlook the entire hall. A moment of astonishment! I look down and, for a while, observe how people behave, where they put their towels. I continue walking to my locker. I open the wooden door and put down my things. What do I need, what do I take with me, what is important? From up here I feel safe, unobserved. Here, I am in the position of an observer. The thought of going down and becoming someone to be observed makes me feel insecure.«

»After I get out of the shower, I want to descend the big stone stairs into the pool. I step down into the water. The water is cold. I dive in and stand for quite a while watching the others use the free lanes. I think about how best to blend in. I move from a vertical body position to a horizontal one and begin to swim. It is a different pace at which I now glide through space, a different sensation. I feel the water flowing between my fingers and the effort of resistance. Meter by meter I work my way onward. I look around the room, marvel at the vault. I watch the sun graze the plaster and illuminate the upper dressing rooms. Over and over I travel the same distance. My line of sight alternates back and forth.«

»After several laps, I pause. I hold on to the edge of the pool and look around. I notice that I have once again become an observer. In contrast, while swimming, the faster I became, the more I strained, the more my attention was focused on myself. I swim one last lane and climb the cold stone steps again and leave the water. I now perceive my body in a completely different way. My legs have become tired and heavy.«

»Now I enter a smaller hall. It is much more intimate than the first. I no longer feel exposed. I slowly and carefully enter the water by walking down the large stone steps that lead into the pool. The water is very warm. Only now do I realize how cold I was when I was walking alongside the pool. The water in this small pool feels very pleasant. In this basin I can linger, there is no need to draw lanes. There is no compulsion to swim in an orderly and speedy manner. I am disturbed by the echoing noises, by the numerous voices.«

»For the first time, I submerge into the water. Silence. Murmurs. Listening to my own heartbeat. I let myself drift, swim slowly at my own pace. I take a good look around the room. Here, I feel safety and security in the room. Through the window I see that it is windy outside and slowly getting dark. I am in a fortress, in a protected space. There are only a few glimpses of the outside world. Only the here and now exists in this space, everything else is shielded and unimportant. I feel secure in the space, firmly located despite my floating state in the water. I perceive the volume of space in a completely different way because I am carried and surrounded by water, my feet not touching the ground. I can perceive and sense the volume of space beneath my body through my movements. The darker it gets outside, the quieter it becomes in this space, making me feel more safe and secure.«

»While my movements in the elongated pool's water are directed and brisk, I can let myself drift in the smaller pool. The space is smaller and seems more intimate. My gaze is caught again and again in the oval dome, visually retracing its curved shape, while floating in the water in a circular motion. In this pool my movement is undirected. I constantly vary my directions of movement, diving my head underwater. Sometimes I let the water move me and I lie almost motionless on its surface. My body is relaxed. In the big hall, on the other hand, I constantly keep my muscles tense, always in motion.«

»The moment of entering the water is a tactile experience. The texture and temperature of the stone can be felt with bare feet. The coldness of the water initially presents a barrier, but it is hesitantly overcome. The surface of the water can be clearly felt, like a line enveloping the body.«

»When leaving the water, the breeze becomes noticeable on the skin. The moment of touching the cold, rough stone of the stairs contrasts sharply with the warm water in the smaller bathing hall. It now becomes a memorable impression to stand firmly on the ground in the room again. The awareness of the body changes significantly. One's own corporeality is brought to attention.«

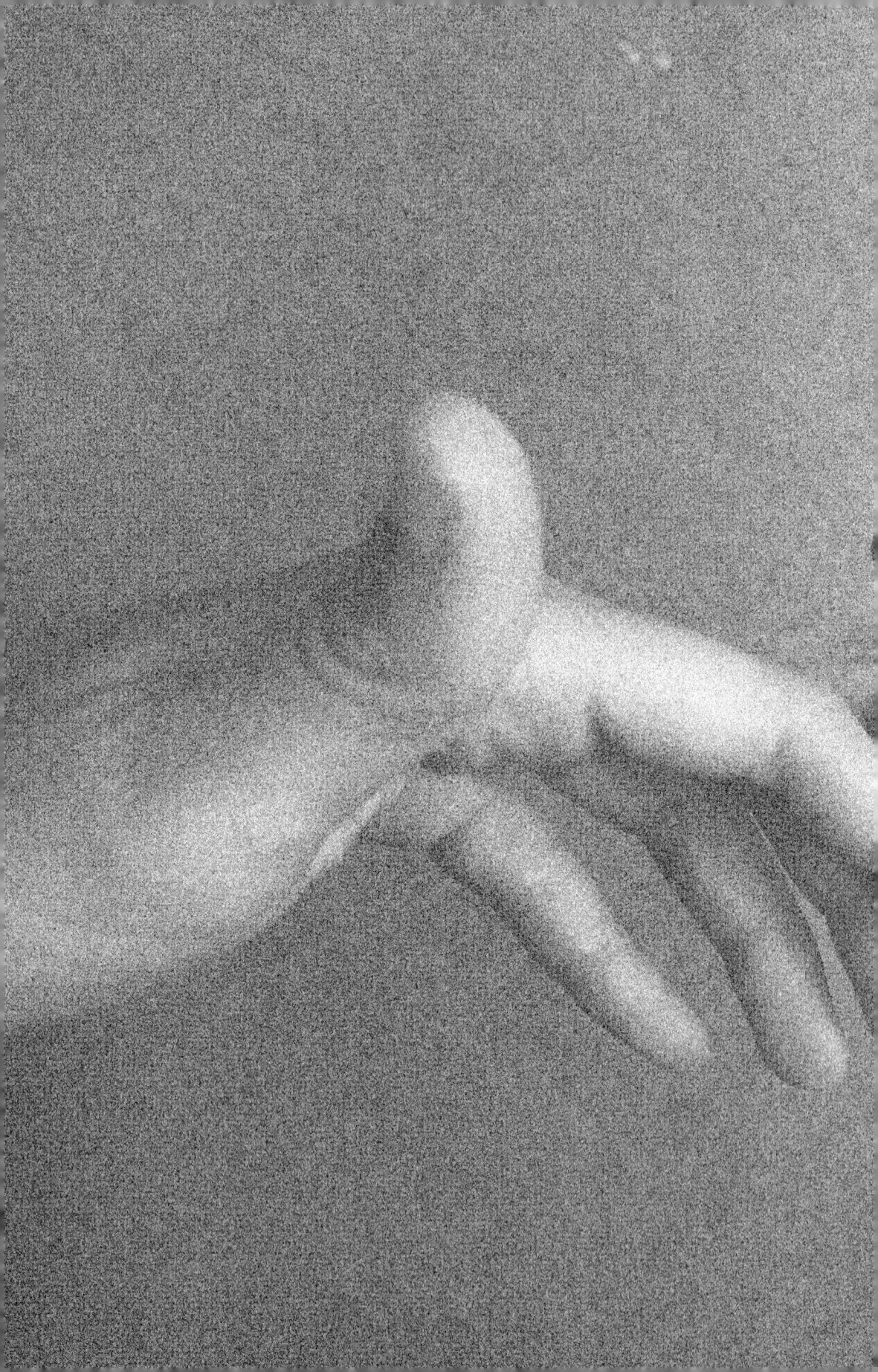

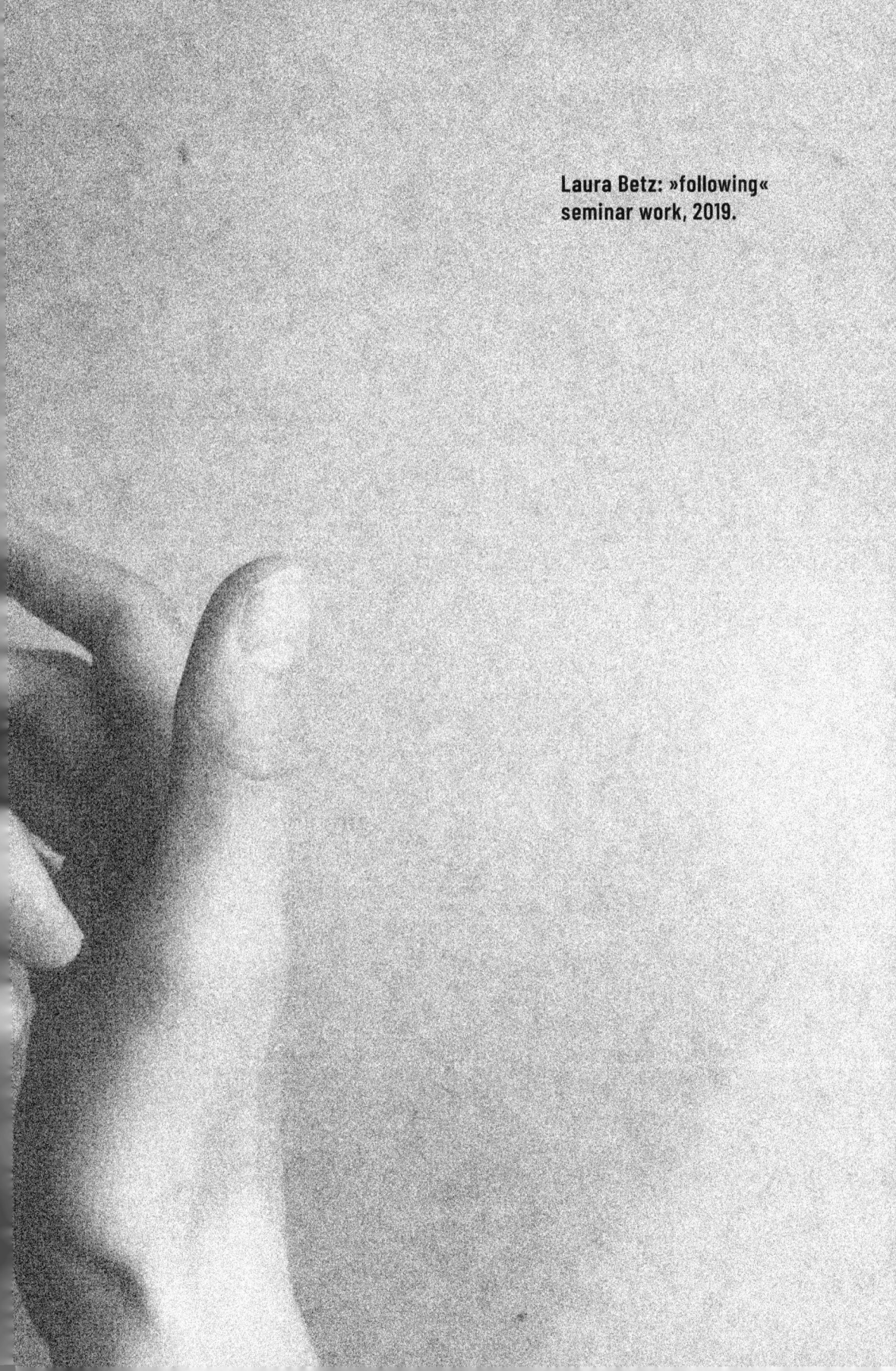

Laura Betz: »following«
seminar work, 2019.

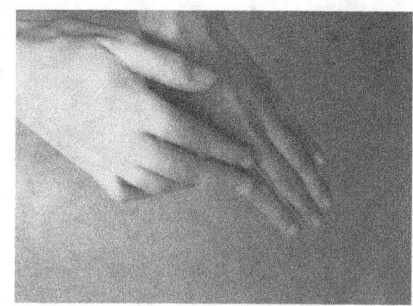

»sensing«

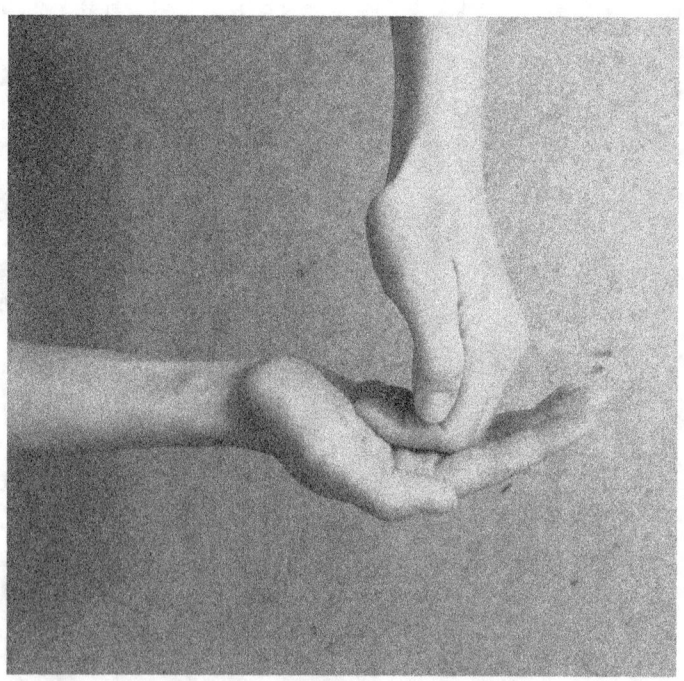

»immersing«

Laura Betz: A Sense of Indulgence and Belonging

»My initial timidity gives way to an urge to discover. My fingers explore my immediate surroundings. I shimmy along railings and balustrades, always striving to be in close contact with the elements that surround me. Free in space, I have no chance of orienting myself in the building.«

»The noise of the city penetrates dully through the walls of the building. While shortly before I had delicately wiped the dust from the radiators with attached stone cornices as I passed along, the temperature has changed now and it has become a little chillier. My premonition is confirmed when I arrive at the end of the stairs. The soles of my feet plunge into a soft material. I feel my body slightly sinking into a material, which, to a certain degree gives way under my load. It feels as though I am walking in a surface itself. I am carving my way through the space instead of treading on a hard surface and pushing off as I did before. But can I be sure that I am on a doormat? If so, the entrance door should appear right away. I continue shuffling my feet across the mat until I reach the rubber edge where I stop abruptly, arms outstretched. Where is the door? There should be three doormats in a row and I should experience a halting, pausing reaction to the supposed end of each mat. I feel amazement and annoyance. At the same time, I feel my partner's warm, reassuring palm on my right shoulder. With the opening of a heavy wooden door, the tension is released. I step out into a rush of fresh air. «

»The theme here is transition, movement, stepping through and out of something familiar into a vague spatial memory. Whereas before I only saw a sequence of large, clearly proportioned rooms, I now perceive a branched system of spaces, the beginning of a labyrinth or perhaps a system of tunnels or channels.«

»Finally, apart from the individual experience of a situation, I would like to record the scenario of the entire, collectively experienced spectacle. Unexposed to the gaze of others, a collection of individuals roam an unfamiliar building in search of the unknown. What we share in the end is emotional information, the breakthrough to hidden spheres of perception. This information cannot be described as an increase in knowledge of building data, but arises from a unique event in a unique constellation. We have become accomplices, witnessing a common experience.«

Melanie Sommerfeld: Envisioning the Invisible

»My concentration is intensified and shifts to my own body, which gains presence and comes strongly to my attention. At the same time, the relationship between my body and my environment becomes tangible, my body developing a more sensitive awareness of the space – seeming to reach out into it. I perceive the space, which, to me, is without dimension when I stand still, as something enclosing and surrounding me. This space turns into a space of action that I explore for sensory stimuli of various kinds, evoking a constant focused vigilance that is present in me.«

»In movement, sensory perceptions multiply and acquire a spatial dimension. Through the contact of my feet with the ground, which seems to me a strong point of reference since it is the only point of contact between my body and my environment, I feel the resistance and can differentiate between a yielding and a rigid ground. In addition, the movement produces sounds that evoke associations and memories of previous experiences, and I imagine a wooden or a stone floor. The visual stimuli I absorbed immediately before the blindfolded architectural experience also influence my perception. For me, a particularly memorable moment of perceiving the floor is when I step over a threshold that stands out in comparison to the flat floor and forms a clearly perceptible linear elevation, which can be experienced by pressing it firmly against the lower side of my foot.«

»My hands, in addition to scanning the surfaces for which I am in constant search, also serve as a point of reference to grasp the dimensionality of the space. I stretch my arms out in all directions, until I meet the resistance of the material withstand of a surface or on the contraty, I have a sensation of being lost in the perceived infinity of space. Here, my body to me resembles the center of the surrounding space. Through this expansion of my body, I feel the relaxation of my body, which enables me to move freely in space.«

»During my experience, the haptic stimuli not only represent the only direct contact with my environment – already initiating the awareness of the point of contact between my feet and the floor, – but are also reflected in my change of behavior as I try to understand the architecture through haptic sensations. My altered approach to space thus manifests itself in touching the materials, listening to the space, and actively perceiving scents.«

»For certain situations, our memory is oriented more towards bodily experience, simply because a specific movement – those associated with ascending a staircase, grasping a handrail, or opening a heavy door – have been imprinted in memory incisively as a *figure of movement*‹ (Janson/Tigges 2014: 198). I experience this in particular at the moment of climbing the stairs, where, without seeing the steps, I can retrieve the necessary movement from my body memory and conduct it. Through the movement of the body, which is strained when climbing the stairs, a space of tension is thus created which stands in contrast to the free and loose movement in the large hall. Here, the body also provides me with orientation and allows me to envision the dimension by letting my foot travel along the stairs in order to grasp, with the help of my imagination, where I am on the stairs – when they begin, when I am on the last step, and what the measures of the steps are.«

»When recalling the memory from the architectural experience while experiencing other spaces, the experiences become interconnected, so that spaces no longer form separate entities, but are interdependent. Ultimately stemming from the interweaving of all previously experienced places and spaces, my imaginary space and view of the world emerges.«

Pauline Wessel: Experiencing the Imagery

»A hand, resting on my shoulder, directs me through the room and pro-
tects me from obstacles of any kind. At the beginning of the exploration
with closed eyes, I see myself moving in the imagined coordinate system
and my position in relation to the individual components and the objects
in the room. However, the more I engage in perceiving the space without a
visual background, the more I lose my orientation and sense of security.
Slowly, groping with my feet, I move through the room, taking one uncertain
step after the next. We climb several smooth steps to a landing and move
to the wall enclosing the room, which I explore with my fingers. I grasp cool
panes and realize that they are windows. Again, we descend a few steps, back
onto the smooth stone floor of the hall. Although I know that I am now back
on level ground and that no more steps are to be expected, I tentatively move
my foot forward, expecting to find another step. The feeling of potentially
falling down the imagined stairs with the next step prevails over me for a certain
period of time that I cannot define more precisely. I continue to move through
the room, putting one foot in front of the other with a dragging motion, while
the sensation of the possibility of falling down a staircase slowly fades.«

»Paying attention to my slow progress with dragging steps, feet barely lifting
off the ground, it becomes clear how the smooth, stone floor is perceived
and how the body reacts to it. The architectural body – its spacial void as well
as its material outline – and the sensing human body are in direct exchange
with each other and create a space of movement for me, in which I walk and
seek my way. As a gestural element, the steps of the stairs, among others,
should be mentioned. As a movement-leading material shapes, they provoke
differentiated behaviors: While climbind the stairs, the foot bumps against
the first step and recognizes it as such. Carefully, the foot is lifted and placed
on the elevated level, tracing the second, again inching forward to recognize
the following step. This process is repeated until the landing is recognized by
the lack of resistance to the foot. The staircase as a spatial gesture produces
uncertainty in the steps and the exploring movements of the feet. Through
this movement, it becomes clear that the bodily sensing is decisively addressed by architectural means.«

»Without vision, the space is grasped, palpated with the hands, feet, and arms, thus attempting to recognize objects and architectural elements. On one hand, the suggestion of movement is directly perceived, since bodily communication involves the interplay of the request for movement emanating from the given object and the associated action. The perception of objects implies an act of incorporation (cf. Schmitz 2005: 100). As the hand feels the surface, its material and thermal nature, understands it as a wall, recognizes stairs with the tips of the toes and the sole of the shoe, takes one step after the other on the smooth and even surface of the previously climbed platform, it becomes clear once again that the ›suggestion of movement […] belongs directly to the object […], without it, it cannot be realized‹ (Schmitz 1999: 45, author's translation). A concrete movement must be executed in order to constitute or confirm the idea of the sensed object.«

»Here, it is evident that the perception of architecture is always based on a process of memory, since individually perceived spatial sequences must be put together in a temporal sequence to form a whole in order to obtain a complete image of the built space. The individual spatial sequences must first be recognized, as already described, through palpation and incorporation, in order to connect the supposedly recognized spatial situation to the previous one in an act of memory. The subject tries to find orientation in space by matching the perceived spatial situation with the stored coordinates of the building in memory. The architectural space serves here on the one hand as an object and at the same time as a generator of memory at the respective point in time (Havik 2006: 190).«

»Like gestural space, poetic space suggests certain attitudes can deviate from the reality of things, as this example also shows. The bodily relationship to architectural space is manipulated (cf. Jäkel 2013: 50) in that the suggestion of movement actually emanating from the level ground – the steady progress – cannot be executed without the component of sensory memory determining existence. The suggestion of movement results here rather from the remembered architectural space, which at this point seems to be present as stairs. In the state of reverie, the associated sensory impressions determine the perception of the actual space, and the levels of memory interfere.«

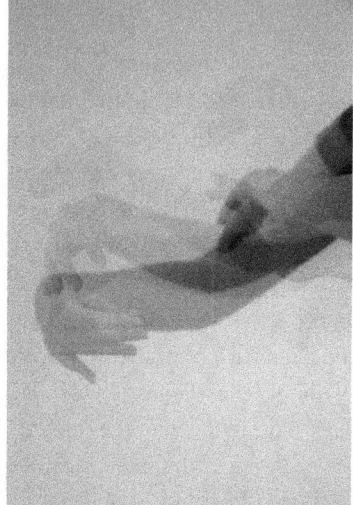

»adjusting«

»against the wall«

Friederike Drewes: Expansion and Resistances

>*Against the Wall*. The tips of my right toes feel the first resistance. This is followed by my two palms, which I hold protectively in front of my body throughout the experience. Springy and less hard than my toes, my palms meet a surface. This is where the movement of my whole body almost comes to a halt. The abruptness of this moment remains strongly in my memory.«

>*Running.* My steps become longer and faster. The cool air around me and the sounds of my footsteps make me suspect that I am in a large, oversized room. The quickening of my steps urges me to just go for *it*. For *what*? To make as far a distance as possible in a short time? I run and I don't feel the need to stop. There seems to be nothing around me and I have the impression of expanding. My steps are so large that the time of contact with the ground becomes smaller and smaller. I feel a rush and air on the skin of my face. I hear the brief tread of my shoes and the echoing in the space. There is room for me.«

>*Adjusting.* I experienced a different tension in my body during the last moment, which was impactful, as I have never felt the sensation of warmth or cold in the surrounding space so consciously. With every step I take, I feel a difference – gradually, and especially in relation to my initial situation, in which I generally felt comfortable. This sensation of comfort and ease is re-established again with every step – but therefore a brief phase of adjustment is needed. With each step I felt as if I was stepping over a boundary and into something new.«

>I became aware that with all the above mentioned experiences I perceive a change in my body. But I wonder, how exactly do I feel this change? Something happens around me, to which I resonate and which I perceive in myself, in my body – inevitablly bringing all of my senses to awareness. As I envision this sequence of event, a liniar image emerges in my mind: It is an arc of tension, a diagrammatic representation, which breaks through a boundary at any moment of shifting focus and attention. In the beginning, there are distinct words for this sensation of the change of state, which I note in an associative manner: They are frontiers, bordering situations, moments of surprise, affect, and change, they are crossings or thresholds, entrances or exits.«

Epilogue: Toward an Architecture Imagery

This reflection aims to investigate what underlies these exploratory studies and evaluates how they can reveal ways of knowing; furthermore, it analyzes how they can be versatile for the creative process in the architectural design. As already explored in the introduction to this contribution, the experience of architecture – both the spatial and space-related dimensions of experience – are examined with particular care. The experience of space is addressed in regard to its corporeal effects and the spatiality of perceiving the body itself. While throughout the history of architecture the body has often been set in relation to architecture as its mold, its reference of scale, or its resemblance in proportion and structural arrangement (i.e. Le Corbusier's *Modulor*, or the personification of columns in Caryatides), here, the body is investigated in regard to its relation to space and the ways in which it engages in dialogue with its surroundings. In this sense, the body is understood as the starting point for sensory experience and as a medium and tool for exploratory move-ment in space. The body's corporeality is regarded in a phenomenological manner, aiming to develop an awareness of the experience and construction of knowledge that arises from it. As such, body-knowledge is brought to the fore and its objective is to unravel its capacities to interlink perception to conception.

With the intention of bringing the body into architectural discourse and addressing body-knowledge as an integral tool to provide tacit knowledge, the three following questions are essential:

- How can the body and movement – as media of experience and archive of memory – be opened up in such a way that the body's own reservoir of knowledge can be made accessible to the discipline of architecture?

- How can bodily-knowledge – gained with the (moving) body and anchored in it – be made available to nurture the architectural design and creative process of conception, as the core of the discipline and essential part of architectural education?

- Which methods can be introduced to access body-knowledge and to attune awareness to the sensual, corporeal, and somatic experience of architecture?

Discovering (with) the Moving Body

Bringing body-knowledge into architectural discourse does not only demand reflection on how the moving body is involved in perceptual and creative processes, but also – in order to reveal a stable basis – seeks to address the discovery of the moving body as such and to foster the closely linked relation of perception and conception as an essential element of the design process. On this basis, it is then possible to invent a method that includes the body in both research and design in architecture.

Awakening the sense of creation through and with movement and bringing somatic practices and contemporary dance to the discourse on architecture experience provides possibilities to explore sensual creative architectural experience and the moving body in space. Therefore, pre-conscious, tacit, and implicit forms of knowing are brought to attention and the bodily ways of knowing, here, serve as tools to access them. All associative and imaginative processes draw from this embodied information. They (re-)create ideas and conceptions from prior experience and memory. It is the aim then to develop body-based ways of inviting designing architects to deepen their awareness of their body-knowledge.

In order to address the creative potential of the body – as a container of memory and experience, as a medium of expression, and as a sensory precondition to sensual perception – it needs to be asked, how the senses can be expanded to a broader sensitivity and how they can be relied upon, and furthermore, how the body – particularly the moving body – enables us to engage the senses more intensively. For this, the body needs to be acknowledged as an indispensable prerequisite for sensual and multi-sensory perception. As a medium, the body allows access to the experience and creation of space. These bodily gained and embodied sensations themselves are of crucial importance, as they form the incorporated basis of experience and memory, which creative imagination and thought draw upon and from which ideas and conceptions are preceded. Furthermore, this cultivates the notion of trusting the bodily forms of knowledge which are subconsciously already applied in intuitive procedures of the design process. As lived experience – in its manifold facets of sensual and multisensory complexity – reveals the origin of creative thought and imagination, its refinement improves the basis upon which creative processes are built.

Creating access to the experiencer's physicality results in active access to knowledge intrinsic to the body. Consciously getting into motion, perceiving with the body, and perceiving the body in motion offers a fertile extension of the existing methodologies in the discipline of architecture. The transfer of working methods from contemporary dance and somatic practice to architecture allows for the involvement of the body. It raises awareness of bodily and sensual perceptions and allows for the resolution of their complexity with distinct observation and analysis of its detailed aspects. In this respect, it is interesting to address it as a specific disposition in creation and to consider how it can be applied to the conception of architectural design to let ideas emerge through physical practice and consciously lived moments of bodily, sensual experience.

Based on the feedback of the participants in the three phases of the cycle, it became clear that the introduced working method would benefit their further studies – especially in the context of architectural design. The example of Free Master's Theses[2] revealed how the students applied and adapted procedures of this working method to their own design practice and self-assigned tasks. For instance, designing a hospice for the dying, one student chose to exploit the extraordinary sensual and corporeal condition of the body in the terminal phase of life as inspiration for her design process. From the sensual particularities of the restrained body – the lying body, the vulnerable body, the body troubled by insecurity, fear, and unease – she invented spaces to counter these experiences, providing protection with thresholds to achieve varying degrees of intimacy. Changing proprioceptive sensations resulted in new space designs which allowed for multi-directional experiences –horizontally and vertically. Another student set herself the task of designing a shelter for recreation and relaxation in the English Gardens in Munich. She addressed different modes and qualities of movement that initiated the design of corresponding architectural counterparts of spatial typologies. She then composed such typologies into a perpetual sequence of spaces in a circular building, inviting the ambulating exploration of ever-changing spatial experience composed in a choreographic manner. Furthermore, another student introduced subjective, sensual, and descriptive narration – which was introduced as a way to preserve and mediate

---

2 The format of *Free Master's Theses* allows students to complete their studies working on an individual task, the assignment of which they invent themselves and which they elaborate upon during a period of six months under the supervision of a professor, in this case Prof. Uta Graff, Head of the Chair for Architectural Design and Conception at the Technical University of Munich.

observations from lived experience – as a method for the design process. She therein discovered a tool for anticipating the intended experience in verbalized narrations of imaginary architecture. Starting from the description of her first encounter with the site and the sensual experience of the place, she then continued to elaborate upon her intentions and ideas for the architectural design in a consecutive continuation of this narration. Lastly, the work of a different student made observations on movement, gesture, and touch as a starting point to investigate different stages of spatial framing for sensual ambiances under the overarching notion of *poiesis*, in relation to the poetics of architecture and the making.

These approaches encourage us to continue and deepen this direction of working in order to be able to develop a methodology from it, thus contributing to the canon of design methodologies. Accordingly, human centered design accordingly not only requires human needs to be satisfied by the design, but also entails the development of architecture in correspondence to sensual, multisensory, and sensorimotor experiences of and with the body.

The integration of bodily awareness and somatic practices with the teaching of architecture and the discipline's discourse is rather rare. One example of addressing body-knowledge in the conveyance of architectural studies has been explored in the architecture department of the Alanus University of Arts and Social Sciences. Here, first year students are introduced to different working methods which encourage implementing bodily ways of knowing into architectural design, starting from perception. With the aim to increase the awareness for the bodily sensory, tacit, and sensual experience, somatic practice is introduced to architecture teaching. Proprioceptive knowledge is emphasized, in order to form a reliable basis upon which the design of the built environment and the architectural encasing of the body can be developed. Relating to an understanding of architecture as »indivisible«, which »includes us as humans«, self- and body-awareness are essential to the training of attuned awareness as a prerequisite for perceiving and conceiving architecture (Beeren 2020: 22–29). Within Alanus' architecture education, body-based and somatic practices, which are thereafter intended to infuse the creative and conceptual process, are integrated as part of the curriculum.

According to the proceedings of the completed three-phase cycle, we propose an enactive approach in which the *moving* body as sensorium, container of knowledge, and medium of impression and expression is attributed a central role in the teaching of architecture, fostering its capacity to initiate the investigation and creation of architectural space. In order to allow architecture students to achieve access to the potential of their moving bodies and to bring attention to their body-knowledge in perception, reflection, and creativity, the implementation of somatic practices and the conscientization of the body – its movements, its sensations, and its knowledge – would be a fertile addition to teaching architecture. The integration of body-based practices into the curriculum of architecture schools could be a way to accentuate its relevance and to provide access to body-knowledge in order to actively integrate it into the repertoire of design methodologies.

Attuning Awareness to Bodily Sensations

This contribution retraces the journey we took, seeking to let knowledge emerge from experience, bringing the body and the incorporated sensuality of perception to the fore of the investigation. The contribution aims to find ways to make explicit how implicit knowledge is acquainted with the process of encountering and experiencing architecture. Memory and experience don't always come to conscious attention, but often go unnoticed. The investigation and active realization of experience gained in a pre-reflected, sensual manner brings the plurality and complexity of perceptual sensations to awareness and increases their accessibility – both with regard to their attentive assembly and their influential integration into the creative process.

Anchored in our memory and incorporated into our repository of experience, the sensations gathered while exploring architectural spaces stay with us as sensual and bodily felt experiences. They predict our knowledge, association, and imagination on spatial situations and constitute the individual's body-based knowledge on architecture and space incorporated into our bodies. As experience is situational, subjective, and very personal, the assemblage of memories – and respectively the basis upon which imagination, creativity, and inventory draw on – is individual to each person. Furthermore, perception does not only depend on prior experience but constitutes a complex, creative, and associative act that brings all counterparts of the lived situation together in a seemingly complete and harmonious entirety.

As Juhani Pallasmaa points out, »experiencing, memorizing, and imagining spatial settings, situations, and events, engage our imaginative skills«

(Pallasmaa 2014: 34). Furthermore, he continues that »even the acts of experiencing and memorizing are embodied acts, in which lived embodied imagery evokes an imaginative reality that feels similar to actual experience« (ibid.). Herein lies the tremendous potential of introducing body-knowledge and corporeal forms of expression into the discourse and the design process of architecture: As architectural design relies heavily on anticipating future (sensual) experience in the creative process, it can benefit from an increase in awareness of its corporeal, sensual, and somatic efficacy. Increasing awareness of the embodied, inner world of prior experience enables us to broaden the spectrum of design methodologies in architecture; bodily ways of knowing enable a more sensual envisioning of the process of conception and the anticipation of future corporeal, sensual experience in the design process.

Taking the Moving Body into Account

The awareness of the body in motion forms the anchoring point from which the exploring body reaches out to the surrounding (architectural) world context. By opening a new spatial and imaginary dimension, the exploration with the body allows relation to the space, reaching out into the space, and incorporating the perceived. The sensations collected upon its discovery evoke an internalized world of experience. The stimuli of the external environment initiate inner spaces of experience, the impression of which are then expressed in movement and gestures. In the complexity of this synthetic experience of the interplay of different stimuli, some moments of the experience stand out more clearly than others as moments for particular attention.

Including the body and its sensuality in architecture is to understand experience as a reserve of knowledge for one's own design practice. As José Mateus states in the opening to Mariabruna Fabrizi's and Fosco Lucarelli's publication *Inner Space:*

> »Creativity in architecture is the capacity to consider the given constraints in order to bring together information from different universes and then generate concrete and potentially innovative solutions that may hitherto not have existed« (Mateus 2019: 2).

Accordingly, creative, associative, and anticipatory acts of architectural design and conception are based on this very foundation of assembled experience, because as Mateus continues, »creative imagination draws on experience, memory and all the information and know-how accumulated over time« (ibid.). Furthermore, he emphasizes that creative imagination »lives off – and is totally subject to – the quality of perception with which the creator studies, learns about and relates to the world« (ibid.). Therefore, one could argue that the more aware we are of our sensations and experience, the more refined the collection of experiential knowledge is to fuel the creative process and constitute a stable and reliable base of creative imagination and conceptual invention.

In intuitive, subconscious dimensions of decision-making, the knowledge from the body is already taken into account and relied upon. But as an implicit, tacit form of knowledge, it merely goes unnoticed. Hitherto, it is the claim of this text that the more we become aware of how we perceive – meaning how we experience and remember, associate, and imagine – the more we will be willing to actively include our perceptual sensation and experiences in the creative process of conception.

The creative process of searching, creating, and innovating demands a particular specific physical and psychological disposition, an »openness to experience« (Kaufman et al., in: Abraham 2018: 4), a state of internal resonance in which the idea remains a sensation at first, an impulse before a movement. Through movement, the body tends to encompass the essence and develop the idea by making it perceptible and letting it emerge on the surface. Through the corporeal nature of the human body, it relates to the presence of the things that surround it, generating attentive awareness of their physical presence through corporeal resonance. Accordingly, every sensual perception is based on engagement and openness to the experience of presence: »Perceiving is a way of acting« (Noë 2004: 1). As Alva Noë points out, however, perception is by no means to be understood as a mere display of the world; the world and its perception is only revealed to the percipients, as soon as they discover its experience. In this sense, perception is neither something that occurs to us, nor something that happens within us, but something one *does* and is *actively involved in* (Noë 2004; 2012).

When the body is brought into the design process of architecture, the experiencer is again attributed an enactive role, as the way in which prior experience is gained determines the wealth of memory we rely upon as the basis of the creative process. Physical movement and corporeal exploration constitute sensations, which result in incorporated experiences and memories. Contained within the body, they are retraceable upon their recalling and reconsideration. Embedded in the cultural context of collective memories and narratives, as well as the individual, subjective impressions and sensations gained in experience, as well as manifold dimensions of knowledge are layered to form the basis that we access in mental processes of remembrance, association, and creative thought. Mental processes themselves are inner movements relating to the mind and body. Retracing mental processes with the body allows us to not only reconnect to memories, but to actually relive them. When attention is focused on these inner movements, the spontaneous expression of very vivid impressions is able to emerge. They demand a certain vigilance, implying high receptivity, both internally and externally in order to capture the whole expression. A combination of focus, awareness, and letting go allows the creative process to reach a deeper level.

Before being formulated, these moments emerge in our senses within the dialogue between the body and mind. They initiate the elaboration of creative processes and the inception of artistic statements. Taking into account the ability to consciously live these moments of particular attention enables access to a further creative process, a creative practice that invites the architect to open new perspectives and sensual spaces for creation. In architecture, different divisions of mental processes – intellectual and creative thought – are at play, which contribute to varying attempts to the creative process (cf. Abraham 2018: 4).

Emphasizing the manifoldness of experience and its ability to bring forth imagination and creativity results in the revelation of particularly sensual ways of anticipation.

Bringing Tacit Knowledge to Consciousness

Architectural design is embedded within a context – topographically, culturally, and in regard to the genius loci of the place – and therefore requires an initial phase of discovery and familiarization with the given circumstances. Perceiving what is there, wondering what to relate to, exploring and investigating the place are perceptual and experiential processes that precede the design. Prior to the process of architectural design, a distinct process of contextual, spatial, and cultural observation creates a basis of knowledge, to which the designing architect returns over and over again in order to testify and verify the decisions, choices, and proceedings in the ensuing process of architectural design and conception:

»The most significant time is the one preceding the design [...] It is the time when you approach a context, most of the time as a stranger, and you start a journey literally, walking along the landscapes, streets and houses, or through the words and images of books, the sounds of songs or unknown languages, the refrains of popular tales and traditions. This ›time of the traveller‹ collects hints of the culture of a place and traces an open map where many other different information lay and rest – such as the brief of an assignment, the budget, local building regulations and construction technique and materials available – somehow alike the pebbles and shells brought to the shore from the sea that appear and disappear at every new wave« (Torzo 2019: 109–110).

Just as the »pebbles and shells« that emerge and vanish, reappear and dissolve with the ocean's tide or the sprawl of sand, memories and sensations from experience and observation often go unnoticed, or only briefly emerge before they are blurred again with ever-changing, indulging recall and the loss of memories. While exploring the terrain of the architectural task, – both physically and in a figurative sense – various dimensions of »experience and know-how, accumulated over time« (Mateus 2019: 2) are taken into account. In order to be able to achieve these more decisively, we need to ask: where are these memories contained and how can they best be accessed?

Here, we argue that they are incorporated into the body, inscribed into the sensual and corporeal experience, embodied in the body-knowledge. And although such memories might lie unnoticed beyond the surface of conscious comprehensibility, they can be brought to attention – in particular through bodily means. As we retrieve bodily sensation with the body, we omit their translation into conscious thought and verbalized expression. Rather, the tacit knowledge from sensual, bodily experience emerges through the body in pre-reflected ways of expression, through movement and gesture, in corporeal and somatic articulations.

Dedicating Vigilance to Movement, Gesture, and Touch

Movement is an inevitable prerequisite for the experience of space. Only through shifting perspectives can a space be perceived as such. The complexity of a building only reveals itself upon its exploration (Merleau-Ponty 2003[1945]). The figure of movement, initiated by the layout and sequence of spaces, and spatial experience reciprocally condition one another (Janson/Tigges 2014: 118–120). Gesture is an articulate movement of expression, indicating a specific quality, character, or even significance. Bodily gesture finds an equivalent in architectural and spatial gesture (Janson/Tigges 2014: 144–146). Furthermore, the appropriation and use of architectural structures require gestural movements to react and refer to them: The hesitant step on a threshold, the turning of the wrist to open a door handle, the welcoming gesture of opening a door, or the caressing of a hand rail. Gestures conducted in relation to architecture, often go unnoticed in the recalling or envisioning of impressions of architectural experience.

Beyond the movement and gesture conducted in space and time, touch indulges beyond the sensory response to the architecture and addresses the sensual, tangible dimensions of physical encounter. Materiality and texture, tactility and haptic come into play and amplify the sensorial engagement even further. Not only does touch involve immediate contact with the physicality of a building, but it also refers to the sensation of being touched and moved by this encounter.

All dimensions of movement, gesture, and touch are inherent parts of the experience of architecture and are thus anticipated in the design. In a lecture on her design for the Belgian design brand *Maniera*, architect Francesca Torzo explored how gesture and movement form the initiation into the design process – both for architectural space and for objects of quotidian use – and how in response to the respective space or object, we relate to the world:

> »The way in that we move, touch, use, or better said, live objects and spaces, speaks about who we are – and who we are is a layered certification of time« (Torzo 2020).

Observations on quotidian gestures formed the basis from which Francesca Torzo examined movement patterns that her furniture and quotidian objects respond to. To her, these quotidian objects are embedded in the context of what she calls the domestic landscape, defined as: »the domestic landscape is a scene where we find intimacy. It is also a setting, a place. A place where we can relieve our mind, and travel with the mind« (ibid.). From her studies of movement, gesture, and touch within this setting, she explores how to complement this landscape with elements that respond to the elaborate characteristics of movement, either providing them with an initiation, continuity, or counterpart, each embodying the awareness of the intimacy and sensuality of the realm of quotidian domestic life. Objects, furniture, and clothes – just like architectural spaces – are designed to incorporate the movements attributed to their playful exploration, use, and appropriation. They respond to them, guide them, or create the freedom to discover them.

Francesca Torzo explores the gestures and movements evoked in correspondence with places, spaces, and objects. Investigating the notion of corporeal needs, she creates objects made for enactive encounters and invites one to engage with them physically, sensually, and through movement. She emphasizes the need to study how people move in particular situations and in relation to specific objects in order to be able to design along with the requirements of these movements as well as to create components that interact with and reciprocally respond to them. Movement and sensual engagement are not only stimulated in sensual and perceptual experiences of objects, furniture, and architectural spaces, but are anticipated in the design process and therefore become inherent to it.

The architect Nicolai Bo Andersen explores the relevance of physical architectural models as a tool and technique to implement sensual and sensory experience in the design process. He emphasizes their capacity to invite physical encounter and bodily engagement, including the full sensory spectrum, because, as he states »the architectural model is – in contrast to the computer rendered image – a physical, three-dimensional thing that I can touch, walk around, and maybe lift and hold in my hand«. This is of particular value, because, as he continues, »perceiving an architectural model involves all the senses of the human body as well as the motor system, not only sight« (Andersen 2021: 26). Accordingly, he argues that by involving all the senses and their complex synesthetic interplay, the encounter with the physical architectural model »is richer and more nuanced than the perception of the two-dimensional image« (ibid.). Under the superordinate question of how exactly it is different to the perception of the plain image and how we, as perceivers, relate to it and experience it differently, Anderson introduces a variety of modes to look at the image, aligned with Husserl's phenomenological observations on »physical image«, »mental image«, »image object«, and »image subject« (ibid.: 28). Beyond two-dimensional representations – however physical their presence or how sensual their perception may be – Andersen emphasizes the qualities of the models as relating to all senses and allowing for movement, touch, and an actual opportunity to relate to it spatially and through movement. Other than the gaze at an image or the perception of an object, the physical model allows for corporeal, sensorimotor involvement:

»I don't just look at the architectural model with my eyes. I perceive the three-dimensional totality involving my whole body. In the model of the city, I perceive each building volume as individual bodies, like playful figures I can grab and hold in my hand. [...] What I perceive is not simply the formal pictorial qualities of a flat image, but rather physical properties closer to a real work of architecture, for example weight, solidity, consistency, thermal conductivity, textural effects, gravitational impact and changing light conditions« (Andersen 2020: 30).

The great benefit of architectural models rests in their interactivity: As they cultivate engagement through movement, gesture, and touch, they intrigue sensual and bodily investigation. According to their particular degree of abstraction – through different scales, miniatures, and replication in different material – they allow for association and invite the observer to embark on an associative and creative sensual encounter through movement. In this way, the architectural model enables an all-encompassing, holistic approach to experience which engages the entire body and all of its senses. It is a tool and medium in the anticipatory and creational processes of architectural design and it prompts the experiencer to engage with it physically, sensually, and through movement.

Architecture Imagery

In the sense of inter-subjective conviviality and exchange, the subjective experience – although highly individual, situational, and temporary – thus relates to others. The subjective approach makes it possible to develop knowledge starting from oneself, to include the sensuality of one's own body and to draw conclusions from this for the creative and research process – especially in the context of architectural design. It is the familiarity with previously unprecedented spaces that reveals that an experience of the not-yet-present is possible in its imagination. Although imagination or visualization is literally linked to the visual, the impression of having already passed through the architectural edifice in the imagination reveals that not only is the dominant visual perception anticipated in architectural design, but that multi-sensory, sensual experience as a holistic process of encountering space is as well.

This inventive imagination of future realities is linked to highly complex processes that call into question the chronology of temporal sequences.

Memory and present experience are integrated into the conception and design process of what is yet to come, as well as initiating it. In this sense, they thus stand for themselves and yet reach beyond themselves in equal measure.

In architectural design, pre-reflexive intuitive knowledge and analytical, reflective concern converge. In this process, however, it is far easier to deal with rational parts than vague, working ones from one's own sensibilities. Nevertheless, the latter are a necessary and integral part of the design process, because »if I allow the factual course of the design process to be repeatedly confused by subjective and unreflected ideas, I acknowledge the importance of personal feelings in designing« (Zumthor 2010: 21, author's translation). An increased engagement with pre-reflective perceptions facilitates recourse to the same memory and thus makes it possible to integrate them more intensively into the design process:

> »The process of designing is based on a constant interplay between feeling and reason. The feelings, the preferences, longings, and desires that arise and want to take shape are to be examined with a critical mind. Feelings tell us whether abstract considerations are coherent.« (Ibid.)

This interdependent nature of rational and pre-reflective knowledge requires an equal approach to both, with abstract, analytical, and considered knowledge being more easily learned, communicable, and more established as a form of knowledge. Accordingly, we argue that the body – and body-relating, corporeal, and somatic practices in particular – possess the opportunity to make immanent tacit and pre-reflective knowledge explicit and accessible. The aim is to negotiate the predominance of vision in imagination processes and to include an enlarged polyphony of senses to do justice to the complexity of multisensory sensual experience. In order to do so, in conjunction with the notion of »Dance Imagery« in contemporary dance – and dance in general – we introduce the concept of a sensual »Architecture Imagery«.

In contemporary dance, kinesthetic forms of creativity (Abraham 2018) that have been introduced to the architectural experience in exercises from which the presented proceedings of the latest phase of the cycle were derived are explored. Bodily-kinesthetic intelligence, as psychologist Howard Gardner frames body-knowledge, is thereby fused with architecture and made explicit through bodily means (Gardner 1983). Therefore, recent findings from neuroscience on embodied cognition are introduced to applied forms of working.

As a »mental practice of movement« »Dance Imagery« forms a working method to anticipate and observe dance in imagination. Through the visualization of dance movements, the actual movement and its multi-sensory experience are mentally recreated. All senses are engaged to invent or recreate the actual dance experience mentally. Imagined movements result in inner movements, which allow for the study of actual physical movement as a sole mental-sensual procedure (cf. Liu et al. 2004). The reconsideration of former movements in the mind enables us to recreate information stored in our memory and create and invent new information through imagination. The perception finds an immediate continuation in associations and further implementations.

Learning from the actual physical exploration and taking into account the manifold sensual and perceptual dimensions involved in it, it becomes possible to relate to it again only through mental processes. Working with »Dance Imagery« includes the principles of visualization: envisioning oneself while dancing and tracing the sensations and feelings evoked by this dance. As a technique applied in training, teaching, and production work, »Dance Imagery« grants access to the inner world of experience, memory, and the senses.

Creative and inventory processes in architecture are usually visualized using architectural means and various mediums of representation, such as sketches, plans, models, mock-ups, and images. Visualization here usually entails the act of finding ways to convey ideas to others and making them visible. The subjective process of envisioning is rather secondary. Learning from the working methodologies attributed to »Dance Imagery«, this concept could be translated into a visualization technique that incorporates polysensory imagery, using the physicality of all the senses to enable one to *feel* the imagery. Accordingly, a few guiding questions would arise: How do you envision yourself in the architectural space? Do you feel the sensual effects of it and how does your body relate to them?

It is the a great achievement for lively imagery when »vivid images are realistic, detailed, and clear and include all of the requisite, senses, thoughts, and emotions« (Taylor/Taylor 1995: 88). In regard to their constitution, Jim and Cice Taylor explain that »vivid images replicate actual experience, increasing the likelihood of proper performance in the future« (ibid.). Beyond the recalling and replication of actual experience, the notion of vivid images as sensual »Architecture Imagery« can therefore provide the opportunity to »live« an envisioned scenario during the anticipating course of architectural design. If the sensations of envisioned experience are precisely observed, they can provide direct information. From feelings like calm or ease, serenity or vastness, confinement or oppression, associations between relating spaces can occur immediately. Spatial typologies, characteristics, and the ambiance of a place are evoked by these space-relating sensations and allow for the emergence of envisioned architectural designs as complements and counterparts to the »Architecture Imagery«.

Movement- and motion-relating practices of any kind provide increased awareness of the sensual and corporeal polysensory experience in architecture and increase the designing architects' capacity to anticipate future experiences of architectural spaces throughout the design process. In addition, the practice of contemporary dance provides greater access to movement, with particular focus on the plurality of characters, qualities, and patterns of movement that have an attentive awareness to the perceptual and expressive modes of the body. Beyond the field of contemporary dance, here, the moving and sensing body is an integral part of a cultural and artistic practice: Dance has a different relationship to the body insofar as it reflects the *poiesis* and poetics of movement. In this sense, movement is not purposeful and utilitarian, but rather of an aesthetic nature, e.g. emotional, abstract, formalistic, imaginary, sensual, creative, and conceptual. The dancer is an actor in an artistic event and in this sense, introducing somatic practices and ways of working from contemporary dance to the discipline of architecture means translating aesthetic, creational, and investigative procedures from one creative and artistic process to another.

References

Abraham, Anna (2018): *The Neuroscience of Creativity*, Cambridge University Press, doi: 10.1017/9781316816981

Andersen, Nicolai Bo (2021): »Architecture Enactment. Understanding the Architectural Model as Embodied Participation«, in: Alberto Calderoni/Carlo Gandolfi/Jacopo Leveratto/Antonio Nitti (eds.), *STOÀ 01 I.1/2*, Naples: Thymos Books, 26–43.

Beeren, Willem-Jan: » ›that Architecture is Something Indivisible‹. The Perception of People and Architecture«, in: Perceiving Architecture, *Mensch + Architektur 02/2020*, 22–29.

Gardner, Howard (1983): *Frames of Mind. The Theory of Multiple Intelligences*, New York: Basic Books, https://www.academia.edu/36707975/Frames_of_mind_the_theory_of_multiple_inteligences, accessed July 20, 2021.

Havik, Klaske (2006): »Lived Experience, Places Read: Toward an Urban Literacy«, in: Grafe, Christoph/Maaskant, Madeleine/Havik, Klaske (eds.): *OASE 70*, 10/2006, 37–44.

Jäkel, Angelika (2013): *Gestik des Raumes. Zur leiblichen Kommunikation zwischen Benutzer und Raum in der Architektur (Gestures of Space. On the Bodily Communication Between User and Space in Architecture)*, Berlin: Wasmuth & Zohlen.

Janson, Alban/Tigges, Florian [2013]: *Grundbegriffe der Architektur. Über das Vokabular räumlicher Situationen.* – English translation by Ian Pepper: *Fundamental Concepts of Architecture. The Vocabulary of Spatial Situations*, Basel: Birkhäuser, 2014.

Kaufman, Scott Barry (2016): *Openness to Experience and Creative Archivement in the Arts and the Sciences*, https://scottbarrykaufman.com///wp-content/uploads/2013/11/Kaufman-2013.pdf, accessed July 20, 2021.

Liu, Karen P./Chan, Chetwyn C./Lee, Tatia M./Hui-Chan, Christina W. (2004): »Mental imagery for promoting relearning for people after stroke: a randomized controlled trial«, in: *Archives of Physical Medicine and Rehabilitation 85*, 1403–1408, doi: 10.1016/j.apmr.2003.12.035

Louppe, Laurence [1997]: *Poétique de la danse contemporaine*, Brussels: Contredanse. – English translation by Sally Gardner: *Poetics of Contemporary Dance*, Alton, Dance Books, 2010.

Mateus, José (2019): »Imagination«, in Mariabruna Fabrizi, Fosco Lucarelli: *Inner Space. Triennal de Arquitectura de Lisboa*, Barcelona: Polígrafe.

Merleau-Ponty, Maurice [1945]: *Phénoménologie de la perception.* – English translation: *Phenomenology of Perception*, transl. by Colin Smith (2003[1962]), London/New York: Routledge & Kegan Paul.

Noë, Alva: (2004): *Perception in Action*, Cambridge, MA: The MIT Press.

Noë, Alva: (2012): *Varieties of Presence*, Cambridge, MA: The MIT Press.

Pallasmaa, Juhani (2014): »Space, Place, and Atmospheres«, in: Christian Borch (ed.): *Architectural Atmospheres. On the Experience and Politics of Architecture*, Basel: Birkhäuser.

Schmitz, Herrmann (1999): *System der Philosophie, Bd. III: Der Raum, 5. Teil: Die Wahrnehmung (System of Philosophy, Vol. III: Space, Part 5: Perception)*, Bonn.

Schmitz, Herrmann (2005): *Situationen und Konstellationen: Wider die Ideologie totaler Vernetzung (Situations and constellations: Against the Ideology of Complete Interconnectedness)*, Freiburg: Herder.

Taylor, Jim/Taylor, Ceci (1995): *Psychology of Dance*, Champaign, IL: Human Kinetics Publishers.

Torzo, Francesca (2019): »Relation and Memory«, in: Uta Graff/Katleen Nagel/ Felix Zeitler, *Schwarze Räume/Black Spaces*, 99–113.

Torzo, Francesca (2020): »Gestures. These Are Only Hints and Guesses. A Project for Maniera«, Lecture, August 12, 2021, *The Architecture Foundation, 100 Days Studio*, https://www.youtube.com/ watch?v=AiePloB25BM, accessed July 20, 2021.

Zumthor, Peter (2006): *Atmosphären (Atmospheres)*, in: Archplus 178, 06/2006, 30–37.

Zumthor, Peter (2010[2006]): *Atmosphären (Atmospheres)*. Basel: Birkhäuser.

Friederike Drewes: »running«
seminar work, 2019.

Extension

»In a Landscape

Sense what is around you ... in every direction ... behind ... above ... below
What is close to? ... What is far away?
What is the furthest you can see/sense?
Breathe ... listen ... to close ... and distant ... sounds
Sense the movements ... of weather ... land ... sky ... light

What calls to you in this landscape?
Feel your connection with it
Move to explore its qualities
Make something in response«

Miranda Tufnell and Chris Crickmay 2011: 245.

Tufnell, Miranda/Crickmay, Chris
(2011[2004]): *A Widening Field. Journeys in
Body and Imagination*, 3rd edition, Alton,
Hampshire: Dance Books.

Dimensions of Architectural Knowledge, 2021-02 ∂
https://doi.org/10.14361/dak-2021-0213

Discovering Weedy Landscapes as Sensory Commons

Inkeri Aula

Abstract: Environmental relationships need to be understood as crucial in contemporary social research. This article explores relating with nature in urban contexts and its diverse temporalities. How do people relate to the more-than-human natural environments in the city? How does urban nature appear through sensory memories and perceptions? To answer these questions, this research analyzes sensobiographic walks conducted with young (15–30 years of age) and old (70+ years of age) city dwellers in Turku, southwest Finland. Via transgenerational sensobiographic walks (Järviluoma 2021), less controlled urban green spaces such as parks, riversides, margins, and pathways are discovered as weedy landscapes, where encounters between the human and the non-human take place. These weedy landscapes allow the sharing of sensory experiences and memories of transformation, following that sensing itself can be grasped as a collective endeavor. This article asserts that urban biodiverse sites maintain their interrelations with other forms of life. The multi-sensorial atmospheres they provide – smells, sounds, silences, views, moisture, shadow, feeling – could be cherished as sensory commons. The findings presented in this article contribute to current discussions in several research fields from urban planning to mobile ethnography, landscape architecture, spatial design, and the anthropology of the senses.

Keywords: Sensory Commons; Weedy Landscapes; Environmental Relationships; Anthropology of the Senses; Sensobiography.

Introduction[1]

Environmental relationships formed in everyday lives can prove crucial in fighting for a more sustainable future. Also, the COVID-19 pandemic surged partly due to loss of biodiversity (Platto et al. 2021). As the concurrent wave of mass extinction becomes aggravated by the unstable conditions of a changing climate, social and human sciences are increasingly turning toward ways of knowing that seriously consider more-than-human

---

1 The research for this paper has received funding from European Research Council (ERC) in the SENSOTRA project (GA 694893).

Corresponding author: Inkeri Aula (University of Eastern Finland);
inkeri.aula@gmail.com; http://orcid.org/0000-0002-5781-7965

interactions. Wilderness and non-human forms of life affect not only our daily atmospheres and health, but also fundamentally participate in the constitution of our living spaces and our very being – also in urban environments (Schliephake 2015; Aula, forthcoming). Nevertheless, not much is known about sensorially mediated relationships with the more-than-human environment in cities, nor about how they have changed in recent decades.

This article asks how urban wilderness is experienced through the senses, and explores spaces that often go unnoticed as »weedy landscapes« by combining anthropologist Anna L. Tsing's thinking about attunement to multi-species ecologies (Tsing 2015: 22, 33; 2017) with landscape geography of urban wildscapes (Jorgensen/Keenan 2012). Environmental relationships are explored through multisensory ethnography produced on transgenerational sensobiographic walks, as coined by Helmi Järviluoma (Järviluoma 2021), in the seaside city of Turku in southwest Finland. The research design is set to multisensorially discover less controlled spaces of urban nature such as parks, riversides, margins, and pathways. In these weedy landscapes, multisensory encounters of human and non-human participants take place, and sensing itself can be grasped as a collective endeavor.

A plethora of research exists on the beneficial health effects of urban green areas (e.g. Roslund et al. 2020). This article focuses on the often overlooked mixed spaces of weedy landscapes, with particular focus on their experiencing, namely investigating how they are experienced, remembered, and sensed by people from different age groups living in Turku. The question emerges of how these transforming spaces could be understood as points of encounter for personal and social convergence of the present moment, the not-yet, and the ghostly presences of the past:

> »The winds of the Anthropocene carry ghosts – the vestiges and signs of past ways of life still charges in the present. […] Our ghosts are the traces of more-than-human histories through which ecologies are made and unmade« (Tsing et al. 2017, G1).

Sensobiographic Walks into Urban Nature

Multisensory ethnography enables researching forms of diversity, collaboration, transformation, and particularities that often remain covered up by the master stories of progress and urban development. However, accounting for both the more-than-human elements of shared space and people's personal experiences as formative parts of urban environmental relationships poses methodological and epistemological challenges. A response is offered in the methodology of sensobiographic walking formulated by soundscape scholar Helmi Järviluoma (Järviluoma 2021; 2017) and developed in the ERC Horizon 2020-funded, transdisciplinary research project SENSOTRA in 2016–2021[2]. In the application of this method, younger participants of 15–30 years of age and older participants born before the 1950s were asked to pick a route that has been significant to them at some point in their lives. On these walks, conversations about sensory perceptions and memories are filmed and recorded.

This article is based on 64 walks conducted in Turku from 2018–2020 with a pair of research participants of different ages, and one or two researchers of a team of seven (the author participating as a researcher in 34 of the mentioned walks). Three walks have been chosen for a closer reading. These transgenerational group walks tackle different temporalities, where the sensations and memories evoked intermingle with a conversational and embodied interaction between the participants (Murray/Järviluoma 2020). For instance, when walking over bridges, the interlocutors vividly how terribly the River Aura smelled in the 1960s when it was still used as a public drain, but they also recalled the »wonderful smell of the trees in the spring«[3] (Ylva, age group born in 1945–49).

Personal routes trigger sensory memories. Here, biographic research reaches beyond individual life courses: sensobiographic walking acknowledges the particular, unique, and situated nature of the sensobiographic narration in a shared experience of walking, where the interaction between all participant components and their relations influence both sensing and remembering (Järviluoma 2017; Karjalainen 2009). The very landscape itself has agency in triggering and mediating narration and remembrance (Järviluoma/Vikman 2013; Kantonen/Kantonen 2017). Ways of sensing in urban surroundings include different material and imagined relations that become actualized when moving in space on the walks, while the dialogue moves back and forth, also in time. This situated collective on a sensobiographic walk brings sensing into awareness as a mutual act (for more

---

2 See uef.fi/sensotra.

3 Interviewees are referred to with pseudonyms and approximate birth years to protect their identity.

elaborate discussion on the co-constitutive nature of the walks, see Tiainen et al. 2019).

When moving in space and sensing together is understood relationally, the nature of urban nature needs to be rethought as well.[4] Relational epistemology focuses on the co-constitutive entanglement of human and non-human agencies in constant change. This mixed diversity implies transformative encounters: not self-contained units thrown into an empty space, but the coming together of different life forms in co-constitutive existence. Knowledge is formed in relation to different others.

Natural phenomena such as fires and floods, as well as plant and animal life – domesticated or wild – have always had their part to play in urban ecologies (Schliephake 2015). The climate crisis and aggravating loss of multi-species ecologies has evoked growing interest in post-humanist approaches across disciplines. Natural forces and other species are also being analyzed as entangled in the social, cultural, material, and political life of contemporary cities (e.g. Franklin 2017). By following Anna Tsing's suggestion for noticing weedy configurations and particular encounters, it is possible to perceive an alternate life in the city landscape. In landscape geography, similar observations have been made about urban wildscapes, defined as sites »where the city's normal forces of control have not shaped how we perceive, use, and occupy them« (Sheridan 2012: 201; Jorgensen/Keenan 2012: 1).

Where multi-species diversity is present, human and non-human routes and developments gather together forming entanglements of different modes of being in the world, encounters of different aspirations (Tsing 2017: 7, 17) – not necessarily all harmonious. These relations are perceived and mediated by multiple senses and their interactions (Howes 2011). Culturally informed ways and routines of sensing can be tackled with multisensory ethnographic data, such as the archive produced in Turku with 64 different sensobiographic walks, from which sensorial accounts of »weedy landscapes« on five different walks have been chosen for analysis.

Sensing Ghostly Temporalities with the More-than-Human

Many of the walks in Turku were taken on sites of urban green, in forests, and on shores, especially in the case of routes chosen by the younger participants (Aula, forthcoming). Non-human forms of life, including bodies of water,

---

4 For discussion on the different notions of nature in anthropology, see Descola 2012.

are in many ways connected to the sense of belonging and social experience of places. One of the walks, led by a teenage girl, Sanni (2000–05), took us up the River Aura to the nature reserve at Halinen rapids, just three kilometers from the center on foot. The rapids were mentioned by some of the older interviewees in remembering a seasonal event historically recognized by the dwellers of Turku. That is, the springtime flood from Halinen, when ice breaks at the dam and the glaciers forcefully rush down the River Aura, through the city center all the way to the sea. This noisy cracking ice mass is known locally as the »Old Men of Halinen« (»*Halisten ukot*«). Somehow, the term refers to old names of folk religion deities (the god of sky is called »*Ukko*«, the »*Old Man*«), and of rune spells about sacred places (verses such as »the high masters of Mount Koli«, »*Kolin korkeat isännät*«)[5].

We walk past the dam and the rapids running down from it. Once we enter the reserved park area, the sound of traffic disappears and the scent of pines in spring sunlight fills the air. For Sanni, the place is a favorite among the riverside paths in Turku she has explored widely with her father to enjoy the peace and quiet. When the icy path becomes extremely slippery, almost impossible to walk on, we slow down and stop at a cultural heritage sign pointing at Iron Age cup-marked stones. In Finland, stones with natural or carved holes, »cups«, supposedly functioned as placements for sacrificial gifts to connect with the invisible world of the dead (Ahlqvist 2020). To our surprise, we notice that someone has left a modern gift in one of the cups: a mandarin opened into a round mandala form, shining amid snow and ice. Looking at the stones, a distant past converges with the present, together with the hint of a wish, hope or prayer oriented toward the not-yet. Landscapes as overlaid arrangements of human and non-human living spaces (Tsing et al. 2017: G1) enable the sensing of ghostly temporalities and traces of an invisible past (fig. 1).

This ancient grove and its open meadows in between big old trees can be experienced as carrying an aura of the sacred. Anthropologists Pirjo Kristiina Virtanen, Marja-Liisa Honkasalo, and Eleonora Lundell have discussed the way that landscapes are populated by diverse human and non-human agencies that assemble and transmutate in co-constitutive relations to form ritual landscapes (Virtanen/Lundell/Honkasalo 2017). Here, while the »Old Men of Halinen« are preparing for the spring, Neolithic sacrificial

---

5 Several rune verses of these topics are found in the Finnish folklore archives, such as SKVR VII2: 1463 in www.skvr.fi.

»Maderine arranged in a clearing in the snow.«
SENSOTRA research project / Inkeri Aula
Photographer: Inkeri Aula.

stones bear gifts of orange tropical fruit left not long ago. This place is not untouched nature, but walked and felt by generations before us who now color our steps. The walk evoked reflections on the concept of »nature«. The oldest participant in the walk, Markku (age group 1945–49), had a daily habit of long walks along the riverside and through the urban parks. Yet he claimed to hate nature, as the following excerpt from a conversation with the author illustrates:

> Markku: »It's funny how nature, the way nature is. All my life I've been against nature, and against sport, but I've always practiced sport [laughs]. And here you notice how there's suddenly a swift, suddenly you walk like this here. It has a huge effect, on the longer run, it influences the general state of one's psyche, it's immensely effective, no matter what you, think of nature.«

> Inkeri Aula: »How do you mean you've been against nature?«

> Markku: »Well it's so repulsive to me, all that kind of promoting a thing real hard, anything, say all the fuzz about healthy living, or say, that now we are ›nature-loving people‹ or whatever-something people, this way you lose the core of it.«

This passage expresses a dislike of common representations of nature, even of nature as a representation. For the speaker, the practice of walking in green sites and its effects are something that the idea of nature does not capture. There are trees, there is wind, there are the sounds of birds and of snow under the shoes as bodies move in a landscape, which is also in constant and seasonal transformation. Markku goes on to compare the ancient magical practices of sacrifice to modern human activities: to him, both are based on ignorance, the little we actually know about the world or about ourselves.

Thus, the sensory perceptions of the non-human world are not about interacting with »nature« as a separate realm but as something we are part of. Ghosts of the past, the not-yet, and the perceptions of the present surroundings are entangled with personal history and life experiences. This plural, co-constitutive way of being enables diverse ways of sensing.

Diverse Weeds in Common Sensescape

Standing ashore in a seaside neighborhood of Uittamo evokes memories in two research interlocutors, Mirja and Katja. They both reminisce about swimming adventures as children and skiing or skating on ice in the winter. The experiences with the waterfront have molded the selfhood of the participants and some of their affective memories are brought to consciousness by the conversation on the walk. Entanglement with the landscape in these walking interviews can be understood as a becoming, where particular sensations and memories emerge together.

Mirja (age group 1945–49) describes her feeling of wilderness in the little forest area in Uittamo, when she encountered a wild beast in the dark, suddenly standing eye to eye with a fox. Laughing, she recalls thinking to herself: should I play dead in front of one of those? But the fox was as wary of her as she was of the fox, so they just »parted ways«. As in many cities, city foxes are common in Turku. They have their own life in the shadows of the human world, like the many forms of wildlife at home in urban surroundings, from common rats to snakes, seagulls and rabbits. Many research interlocutors mentioned having seen foxes; even some Turku-born foxes' caves in Luolavuori Park were known to some. Although foxes and other wild animals in the city are mainly treated as a public hygiene problem in the interviews, they had a positive connection to natural forests even in urban surroundings.

Natural sounds from water and wind to birdsong, and the green visual scenery are often brought up on the sensobiographic walks. Here, other senses also became present: the tactile experience of water, the affects in animal encounters, the proprioseptic perceptions of one's own body movements in freezing when crossing paths with a fox or in the pleasurable found in moving on ice. This way, the more-than-human weedy landscapes in Turku form a significant common resource for the senses. As inclusive spaces free to use, they afford particular sensory experiences appreciated by the city's inhabitants.

The refuges for diversity, which make these encounters possible, could be thought of as a *commons*, not a form of a private, but of a shared resource. Cultural studies scholar Juhana Venäläinen has proposed that the sensory can also be analyzed as commons. Sensory commons could be understood as what we sense and what we can bring about to be sensed by others, in the way that producing noise takes the silence away from others sharing the same space (Venäläinen 2020).

Close to the shore there is a painting of barnacle geese that, as Katja points out, refers to the often aggressive flocks of birds that invade the beach in the summertime, leaving a mess on the ground – in a way, contesting the recreational human space. Multispecies encounters enabled by the site are not necessarily harmonious. Rewilding forms of life may constitute an aggressive invasion of space and a particular coordination of »weeds« may effectively block other weeds, other types of coordination that constitute a local environment (Tsing 2017: 14). Growing flocks of wild barnacle geese, unlike the declining native geese, are protected under Finnish hunting laws and cause much debate in the country due to the serious harm they cause farming. However, the overall number of birds has declined globally, and the accelerating extinction of bird species indicates a bigger loss of bio-diversity, oftentimes caused by farming (Birdlife International 2006). »Geese on beach« signs signal changing ecological circumstances, in which resolving multi-species cohabitation can become crucial for maintaining diversity.

Geographer David Harvey asserts that the freedom to make and remake our cities is a human right (Harvey 2003). To go further, public space can be understood as commons, where more-than-human forces also claim their agency. The question of who controls the ongoing transformations, and how, is crucial for experiences of belonging, but also for the sensory, by defining what kind of sensescapes are available. That means how, where, and by whom the environment is sensed – in short, how life is lived. This exercise of power is revealed in observations by Siiri (age group 1990–94):

Siiri: »For instance the place where I live, there's a forest and sometimes, well, I don't know where it came from, this request, that the kids would not bring sticks to the yard. And we were all like, huh, there really is no reason, [laughs] why should we implement this! There are things that, you can understand somehow, why is it forbidden or requested not to do [...] Like, some of us parents think that – [Her baby stumbles on playground stairs] Climb down backwards, Aino!«

Inkeri Aula: »A bit demanding these stairs.«

Ylva: »Oh but she can do it alright.«

> Siiri: »I think that trees can be climbed too. And then the janitor thinks trees should not be climbed too. Somehow, I don't know, it supposedly ruins the tree. Well, why is it that they want to control that, this somehow wild part in the yard, and in the children, in people? And how come it is okay to make it into a rule, like, whom does it harm really?«

What Siiri refers to as wilderness controlled both in the environment and in people or their behavior, especially in the case of children, relates a lot to the culturally constituted ways of haptically interacting with one's surroundings and with the body. Choice of routes is controlled by planned structures, sometimes in vain: people walk on grass and cross the railways when they benefit from the shortcut. When thinking of urban space as common and shared, the sensory perceptions and memories experienced on weedy landscapes could also belong to the sphere of urban commons: something not private, but shared among many (Stavrides 2016). In anthropology, the idea of *politics of sensing together* proposes a parallel approach to sensory commoning (Laplantine 2015[2002]). The sensory experiences afforded by weedy landscapes and routes can defeat order imposed by the few, and afford communally initiated ways of sensing together. Routes and ways to interact with the environment do not need be harmful to others or to other ways of interacting with the surroundings.

The Smell of the Railway

Sensobiographic accounts in Turku bring up the success of the authorities in cleansing undefined spaces from the city center. Between the 1950s and the 1970s, the River Aura was still used as a drain and the riverside was dark with few lamp posts. Trucks loaded products in the backstreets next to the river and industries resided in the center. Older walkers repeatedly mentioned how homeless alcoholics literally lived in cardboard boxes on the riverside and under the bridges.

The horrendous odor of the water has now gone. The polished riverside has become a well-appreciated living room and a preferred walking route for locals and visitors alike. The river bank is furnished with benches, flower beds, and pieces of art, and the water bounces with restaurant ships. Here, some of the old and even medieval cityscape is preserved unlike in many other central sites of Turku, where collaborations between municipal authorities, construction companies and media known as the »Turku disease« led to the demolition of many traditional buildings in the 1960–70s (Lahtinen 2018; Le Galès 2002: 190–91).

This facelift received praises from several of the research interlocutors. However, there were different opinions about the riverside's atmosphere. It has become clean and commercialized with no space for wilderness. Some of the older participants savor memories of lost liveliness including art, political activism, fishing boats and small industrial activities. On the walk with retired architect Ylva, coming from the river bank, to the university campus, to a street where there used to be a civil activist center with the cooperative Emmaus that offered free meals:

> »Here, there was a bike repair workshop and everything. And I suppose all that served well those people who moved about in here, in this so-called, border zone. Where there are no new buildings yet, but they are already being planned. These are, to me, terribly interesting areas in a city, those that are in a process of transformation. Something new is coming in, and the old will be gone, but how it will be gone and what is preserved? It brings up a lot of emotions too. There's also the history of the people, there was this and that and suddenly it's not there anymore, landmarks are gone, and such.«

Site-related memories are connected to the physical surroundings: where demolished old buildings are replaced with modern ones, it becomes more difficult to recall what used to be and happen there (on sensory remembering on site, see Järviluoma 2002; 2017). The demolishing of weedy landscapes takes away a wide array of personal and collective sensory experiences, memories, and possibilities of encounter. Geographer Tim Edensor (2005: 829) has criticized the modernity of oblivion: »because of imperatives to bury the past too swiftly in search of the new, modernity is haunted in a particularly urgent fashion by that which has been consigned to irrelevance but which demands recognition of its historical impact.« The weedy spaces cleared for construction still haunt the city space through the memories that older interviewees shared on the walk. This sharing also makes their memories become part of the walk's other participants' experience of the place (cf. Tiainen et al. 2019).

Upstream, only a few steps from the city center, the riverside continues framed with bushes and wild growth. A railway bridge connects other neighborhoods to the university across the river. Students who have still managed to find flats for rent in the gentrifying historical area of Raunistula will have a rather short walk to the campus, if they cross the railway and use the pedestrian side of the railway bridge. An overgrown shortcut over the rails passes by signs warnings against trespassing, but it continues to be used anyway as it offers a straight route on foot or by bike. The wild growth and the warning signs signal that stepping on the path takes one away from the ordered city.

The railway margins also have a sensescape of their own. With Ylva and Siiri (born 1990–94) we listened to the whistle of a train passing, and I asked how they experience the sound:

> Ylva: »Somehow, it's related only to pleasant things, the sound of the train. To traveling, to leaving, and furthermore there's of course what is represented by the sound.«

> Siiri: »Railway smells really good to me. Here, it's a weird smell too, somehow, I don't know what it is. But it can be sensed here as well, just next to the railway.«

> Inkeri Aula: »The smell of trains.«

> Siiri: »No! It's the, I don't know if it's in the — in the rails themselves, or it's what's between the rails.«

> Ylva: »It's the iron, and oil, and then these, well, saturated wooden parts, and the rocky soil, and all that there is — I was just about to say that it's what's in these borderline areas, like, some spaces that have not yet been taken into, so called, better use. These places also relate to such odors. Like, the relation with them is not so protective, so hysterical, so there all this life that is becoming, the diversity. Just all that.«

These very analytically rich accounts of sensory perceptions and their meaningful connotations inspire the whole walking group (Ylva, Siiri, and the author-researcher) attuned to the contaminated diversity present in the weedy landscapes of railway margins. In the central area of Turku, this kind of less-defined space, partly abandoned by the city's efforts to ensure order can be found in the unofficial shortcuts, upper riverside, and rocky hills with wilder growth. On a smaller scale, weeds crack through the pavements, however, attention to weedy landscapes entails attention to the non-scalable (Tsing 2015). Immensely powerful thought systems such as neoclassical economics, population genetics, and Social Darwinism onto-logically rely their premises on self-contained units that strive toward their own interests. Weedy landscapes bring forth mixture and transformative entanglement where neatly packed monads melt into a bubbling diversity of co-constitutive existence.

Weedy landscapes are contaminated by previous uses, polluted by urban traffic, litter, and microplastics. The dirt, the smells, the uneven stepping ground on weedy pathways is something that rebels against the order inherent in dominant notions of development. There is danger in waste, as elaborated in Mary Douglas' conceptualization of purity, dirt is something out of place that threatens the order of things (Douglas 1966). Yet, despite its apparent scarcity, a small patch of green, between gray blocks of flats, can sustain a gathering site and lifeline for differing forms of life. Wilderness is not always purposeful for human intentions in the city, nor pleasant for everyone.

Nevertheless, there is something about wild growth and uncontrolled diversity that touches on the classic Spinozan concept of *natura naturans*. Nature is there, »naturing« for itself (Descola 2012). Let us return to the smell of the railway. What is revealed by this particular experience of a weedy land-scape is an almost intangible atmosphere of breaching order. Contamination is something that enters your sphere of life, crossing (imaginary) boundaries of self and other:

Inkeri Aula: »What is it then, that wasteland smell?«

Ylva: »It's just that! Like, someone has spilled oil on the soil, and, there's decomposing and rotting, wood, wood and leaves and.«

Siiri: »Yeah. Perhaps that's what it is, a kind of contrast that appears. That somehow, something is in a way, dirty, and not made for anyone. It's not made for, like, so that it should please anybody. The way a railroad is not, it's not meant to be, it's not having a pleasurable smell so that it would be some-how nice to me! [Laughs.]«

Ylva: »No but you're such a freak that you need to go there to smell it! [sniffs air inwards, both laugh.]«

Siiri: »But that's what is interesting, this, how something else enters your sphere of life. Maybe the appeal is, that it's not so clinical, not so constructed and ready-made.«

Wilderness is there, a bursting life of its own. As Siiri eloquently points out: it is something else, an affective alterity that is encountered in a way that is potentially transformative: something that makes one feel, sense, or think differently in the moment. Weedy landscapes, thus, lead us to grasp a politics of the sensible (Laplantine 2015[2002]) that takes into account the multi-faceted and sometime inharmonious qualities of contemporary environments.

Weedy Spaces Maintain Diversity and Sensory Commons in Urban Environments

This article has elaborated on the idea of weedy landscapes as spaces of »contaminated diversity« by analyzing how they are sensorially co-constituted among a temporary collective moving through space, together with more-than-human forces and life forms. In recent decades, the development of the center of Turku has turned idle lands into buildings, pavements, commercial venues, and streets. This transformation affects the sensory environmental relationships of the people who move through the urban landscape in their daily lives. The central riverside is well appreciated by the city dwellers as a common space. Some research participants, however, long for the ambience of freedom, community, and self-agency in the previously less ordered riverside.

Encounters with wildlife and the atmospheres experienced on walking paths relate to multiple senses. These kinds of experiences could be difficult to capture in formal interviews at a desk. The multisensorial method of sensobiographic walks provides a tool for noticing local ways of relating to the more-than-human, and for bringing these particular encounters into social scientific knowledge practices. Thus, sensobiographic walking in weedy landscapes can function as a grassroots takeover of urban experience. Simultaneously, it enables the sharing of sensory memories between participants from different age groups, and the following overlap of different temporalities in narration and focus, which affect the sense and perception of place for the walkers. Sensing can thus be perceived as something relational that happens together between the participants. In the same vein, biodiversity in landscapes contaminated by encounter is formed in inter-relations with other forms of life.

The spaces of urban nature that have here been called »weedy land-scapes« are experienced and remembered by the multisensorial percep-tions they provide – smells, sounds, silences, views, moisture, shadow, and feeling. The perceptions related in this article suggest that, together with urban parks and other formal recreational spaces, the weedy landscapes could be approached as a form of *sensory commons*. This multiplicity could be cherished as a common, an important property not to be privatized but shared.

Ethnographic reflection on the walks in Turku has demonstrated that weedy landscapes of virtually unnoticed sites can emerge and bloom with diverse forms of life that remain in people's memories, after they are also demolished. Even small-scale sites between the formal lines of urban routes and the discovery of these weedy areas can prove valuable. An important assertion for environmental planning and policies that emerges from this sensobiographic analysis is that urban wilderness plays a fundamental part in sustaining possibilities for different forms of life and their encounters.

The findings of this article demonstrate that natural areas left without formal maintenance are also significant for sensory environmental exper-iences in an urban context. After the data was produced, the COVID-19 pandemic further increased the use of urban green areas. Urban wilder-ness, from forest parks to small stretches of weedy greens that cross-cut formally planned areas, is significant for the environmental relationships of the city dwellers in Turku. In the contestation over public space and sensory experience, domesticated and regulated life does not have the final say over the wild.

Data

Sensobiographic Walks, SENSOTRA Archive: *TP2WYSanni, TP1WYKatjaB, TP23WOYlva*. Sensobiographic Walking Interviews, conducted in Turku from autumn 2017 to autumn 2018, duration: 60 – 90 minutes. Interviewers: Inkeri Aula, Sonja Pöllänen, Milla Tiainen.

References

Ahlqvist, Arja (2020): »Läpikiven kautta tuonpuoleiseen« (Through Stone, to Beyond), in: Ulla Piela/Petja Kauppi (eds.), *Tuolla puolen, siellä jossakin: käsityksiä kuvitelluista maailmoista (Beyond, Somewhere: Conceptions of Imagined Worlds)*, Helsinki: SKS.

Aula, Inkeri (forthcoming 2022): »Urban Nature and Digital Media Technologies Entangled: Sensobiographies of Young People in Turku, Finland«, in: Helmi Järviluoma/Lesley Murray (eds.), *Sensory Transformations: Environments, Technologies, Sensobiographies*, London: Routledge.

BirdLife International (2006): »Agricultural Intensification has Caused the Decline of Many Common Bird Species in Europe« http://www.birdlife.org, accessed May 07, 2021.

Descola, Philippe (2012): *The Ecology of Others: Anthropology and the Question of Nature*, Chicago: Prickly Paradigm Press.

Douglas, Mary (1966): *Purity and Danger: An Analysis of Concepts of Pollution and Taboo*, New York: Praeger Publishers.

Edensor, Tim (2005): »The Ghosts of Industrial Ruins: Ordering and Disordering Memory in Excessive Space«, in: *Environment and Planning D: Society and Space 23/6*, 829–849.

Franklin, Adrian (2017): »The More-than-Human City«, in: *The Sociological Review 65/2*, 202–217.

Harvey, David (2003): »The Right to the City«, in: *International Journal of Urban and Regional Research 27/4*, 939–941.

Howes, David (2011): »The Senses – Polysensoriality«, in: Francis E. Mascia-Lees (ed.), *A Companion to the Anthropology of the Body and Embodiment*, Malden, MA: Wiley Blackwell, 435–450.

Järviluoma, Helmi (2002): »Memory and Acoustic Environments: Five European Villages Revisited«, in: Ellen Waterman (ed.), *Sonic Geography Remembered and Imagined*, Toronto: Penumbra Press.

Järviluoma, Helmi (2017): »The Art and Science of Sensory Memory Walking«, in: Marcel Cobussen/Vincent Meelberg/Barry Truax (eds.), *The Routledge Companion to Sounding Art*, New York: Taylor & Francis, 191–204.

Järviluoma, Helmi (2021): »Sensobiographic Walking and Ethnographic Approach of the Finnish School of Soundscape Studies«, in: Geoff Stahl /Mark Percival (eds.), *The Bloomsbury Handbook of Popular Music and Place*, London: Bloomsbury.

Järviluoma, Helmi/Vikman, Noora (2013): »On Soundscape Methods and Audiovisual Sensibility«, in: *The Oxford Handbook of New Audiovisual Aesthetics*. Oxford: Oxford University Press.

Jorgensen, Anna/Richard Keenan, eds. (2012): *Urban Wildscapes*, Abingdon/New York: Routledge.

Kantonen, Lea/Kantonen, Pekka (2017): »The Living Camera in the Ritual Landscape: The Teachers of the Tatuutsi Maxakwaxi School, the Wixárika Ancestors, and the Teiwari Negotiate Videography«, in: *Journal of Ethnology and Folkloristics 11/1*, 39–64.

Karjalainen, Pauli T. (2009): »Topobiography – Remembrance of Places Past«, in: *Nordia Geographical Publications 38/5*, 31–34.

Lahtinen, Rauno (2018): *Turun puretut talot 1–5.* – English translation: *The Demolished Houses of Turku 1–5*, Turku: Sammakko.

Laplantine, François [2002]: *Le social et le sensible. Introduction à une anthropologie modale, Paris: Téraèdre.* – English translation: *The Life of the Senses: Introduction to a Modal Anthropology,* London/New York: Bloomsbury Academic, 2015.

Le Galès, Patrick (2002): *European Cities: Social Conflicts and Governance,* Oxford: Oxford University Press.

Murray, Lesley/Järviluoma, Helmi (2020): »Walking as Transgenerational Methodology«, in: *Qualitative Research* 20/2, 229–238.

Platto, Sara/Jinfeng, Zhou/Yanqing, Wang/Huo, Wang/Carafoli, Ernesto (2021): »Biodiversity Loss and COVID-19 Pandemic: The Role of Bats in the Origin and the Spreading of the Disease«, in: *Biochemical and Biophysical Research Communications* 538, 2–13.

Roslund, Marja I. et al. (2020): »Biodiversity Intervention Enhances Immune Regulation and Health-associated Commensal Microbiota among Daycare Children«, in: *Science Advances* 14, doi: 10.1126/sciadv.aba2578

Schliephake, Christopher (2015): *Urban Ecologies: City Space, Material Agency, and Environmental Politics in Contemporary Culture,* London: Rowman & Littlefield.

Sheridan, Dougal (2012): »Disordering Public Space: Urban Wildscape Processes in Practice«, in: Anna Jorgensen/ Richard Keenan (eds.), *Urban Wildscapes,* Abingdon/ New York: Routledge, 201–220.

Stavrides, Stavros (2016): Common Space: The City as Commons, London: Zed Books.

Tiainen, Milla/Aula, Inkeri/Järviluoma, Helmi (2019): «Transformations in Mediations of Lived Sonic Experience: A Sensobiographic Approach«, in: Friedlind Riedel/Juha Torvinen (eds.), *Music as Atmosphere: Collective Feelings and Affective Sounds,* New York: Routledge.

Tsing, Anna L. (2015): *The Mushroom at the End of the World: On the Possibility of Life in Capitalist Ruins,* Princeton, NJ: Princeton University Press.

Tsing, Anna L. (2017): »The Buck, the Bull, and the Dream of the Stag: Some Unexpected Weeds of the Anthropocene«, in: *Suomen Antropologi: Journal of the Finnish Anthropological Society* 42/1, 3–21.

Tsing, Anna L./Swanson, H.A./Gan, E./ Bubandt, N., (eds.) (2017): Arts of Living on a Damaged Planet: Ghosts and Monsters of the Anthropocene. Minneapolis: University of Minnesota Press.

Venäläinen, Juhana (2020): »Aural Commons without an Aural Community? On the Difficulties of Living Together in a City with Sound«, in: *Etnologia Fennica* 47/1, 57–80.

Virtanen, Pirjo Kristiina/Honkasalo, Marja-Liisa /Lundell, Eleonora (2017): «Introduction: Enquiries into Contemporary Ritual Landscapes«, in: *Journal of Ethnology and Folkloristics* 11/1, 5–17.

Dimensions of Architectural Knowledge, 2021-02 ∂
https://doi.org/10.14361/dak-2021-0214

»Reclaiming« the City: A Collective Endeavor

Sergiy Ilchenko

Abstract: This contribution elaborates upon the appropriation of urban space in spatiotemporal and procedural interventions in the example of the city of Kharkiv, as well as the impact of urban space on the process of how various groups rediscover and use various parts of the city. Being moved during collective actions – in the sense of feeling urged to move along – goes beyond routine practices by influencing the city and its perception. It seems that these general processions, celebrations, and festive activities of the residents are their contributions to the process of »urban renaissance« – the rebirth of interest in the urban way of life. Since public spaces reflect the historical inheritance of local communities, joint transformative actions such as, »appropriation«, »production«, and »governance« of urban spaces are considered. This article advocates for the practice of domestication of urban space by the local community, as well as the need for the existence of »urban lagoons« – free (unregulated) areas of the city used as resources for urban development and interaction of citizens.

Keywords: Urban Environment; Public Space; Urban Communing; Collective Action; Space Domestication.

Introduction

The transformation of urban landscapes can be instigated by the actions of authorities, business activities, or urban communities, where each actor has their own interest and levers of influence. If we focus on the activities of citizens (collective action) and their impact on urban space – we notice that they do not necessarily result in physical improvements (Koch/Latham 2013: 10). To a large degree it is a transformation in the mental attitude toward the ownership of urban space by the wider community, and inclusion of the latter into daily life (sometimes through temporary use, and through the increased activity of the residents).

Releasing the »abstract« urban space (Lefebvre 1996[1968]) from objectification is a step-by-step process of the adaptation of the cityscape by its residents. This domestication (Koch/Latham 2013: 10) of abstract space by means

Corresponding author: Sergiy Ilchenko (Kharkiv State Academy of Design and Fine Arts);
ilchenkostudio@gmail.com; https://orcid.org/0000-0001-5275-155X

of communal action: festive processions, urban »occupation«, artistic practice and public expression within the city environment, creates a complex pattern of relationships, claims, and appeals by varying residential groups as to their particular rights to the city (Lefebvre 1996; Harvey 2012). Collective actions by the residents are rather more of a temporal nature; and such interventions in the urban space are limited in time. At the same time, these short-term influences affect the perception (or acceptance) of certain urban spaces, not always leading to physical changes in the latter, but influencing their further development.

This article is based on continuous long-term, active, participant observation of the communal activities of residents and the transformation (over time) of their perception of public spaces of Kharkiv, and the observation of the gradual inclusion of the latter into the daily practice of local society, which took place in the period from 2021 until recently. It is safe to say that not all public spaces and open environments can be classified as *civil* (Douglass 2007: 49). In order to discuss this aspect of inclusivity of communal space the researcher defines the latter as: open to a wide range of *civil use*, whether in private or state ownership, with equal rights for everyone to enter it and initiate contact with each other (cf. Goffman 2008). In this way we can define the aspect of *inclusivity* in urban space as an intangible manifestation of disputes and power struggles between civil society and the state, where civil space is not only a place but also a process similar to a physical or computer network (Douglass 2007: 49). Long-term observation of collective actions and their choice of venues (locations), inadvertently draws our attention to »urban lagoons« – abandoned (overlooked during urban planning) fragments of the urban fabric, and to the significance of »urban lagoons« in the life of local communities. This new term is different from the urban voids that emerge between a public and private space. On the one hand, these are plots that are privately owned (not used for various reasons), on the other, these are the territories of public institutions that have limited access, due to specifics of the local area.

Theoretical and Conceptual Framework

Coming back to the concept of the »domestication« of urban space, it is worth pointing out that it is considered by Koch and Latham (2013: 9) from the stance of providing »domestic« qualities (a sense of trust, comfort, or amenity). At the same time, academic and urban rhetoric in the context of encroachment on the democratic mood of public space, translates the term »domestication« in a negative way, reducing the contemporary definition of communal environments to control, pacification, disciplining, and commercialization (Jackson 1998, Allen 2006; Zukin 2009). The criticism directed toward aspects of authority and global cultural structure appears reasonable in the case of the *production* of spaces by either the government (De Certeau/ Mayol 1998[1980]), or the administration (Lefebvre 1996[1968]). Nevertheless, a lithe (from a certain perspective) system of »government/bureaucratic – civil society«, where one predominantly *produces* spaces while others *consume* (or interpret) them does not, in the full sense, carry the colorful assortment of specific disputes and shifts in the power balance in relation to communal spaces. The researcher proposes a model of development where the strategies of polarized social groups become a resource for further urban development and human interaction. Here, communal endeavors take center stage, and the right to the city is understood as an inclusive freedom of the broader urban community that is integrated into its daily existence (Harvey 2012).

Sharing the concern that cities are gradually losing the democratic nature of public space and the authentic forms of public life that have historically defined them, Koch and Latham (2013: 9) consider the latter to be exaggerated, believing that the term *domestication* can, and should be, understood differently – as a process of adjustment and adaptation to *others* as part of routine practice (ibid.: 17). Communal actions in particular develop into unanimous practices and become a »laboratory« in which to develop a different (reinvented) public sphere (Vaiou/Kalandides 2016: 461).

The cooperation of city inhabitants is realized through everyday spatial practices of urban communing and collective endeavors (Bresnihan/Byrne 2015: 36) including forms of *appropriation, ownership, and governance*. It should be noted that the majority of these collective actions are a targeted response to the challenges and limitations of various dimensions of social and cultural life (ibid.: 40).

The processes of urban development (in each specific case) cannot be reduced to only the influence of government or business. We should take into account that inclusive public spaces with a high degree of independence from state and corporate economies exist as well. Both the state-led and independent processes link to the complexity of urban development processes. They are created through implicit and explicit negotiation, as well as the broadening sphere of social privilege and opportunity (Douglass 2007: 19).

They are crucial to the exchange of ideas, cooperation, and the involvement of corporate and governmental actors in the active development of cities (ibid.: 19). Under these circumstances, we can consider the perspective that:

> »views domestication as a process through which big political and social projects – largely the ideas of politicians, experts and social institutions – become enmeshed within everyday practices and processes of social reproduction« (Koch/Latham 2013: 13-14).

In this study, the influence of joint (collective) endeavors upon both, the material (and immaterial) components of *civil* spaces and the development of urban culture, is of central interest. It should be noted that the analysis of public spaces is not limited to parks, squares, plazas and public transportation hubs. Urban streets (and courtyards) are also considered, regardless of their function as conduits of movement, but as social and public spaces as well (von Schönfeld/Bertolini 2017: 49). Initial data for the study were obtained by participant observation, the secondary data were obtained by chronological reconstruction of archival materials and unstructured interviews with the organizers of the campaigns with further interpretation of the obtained materials. The main issue of this study is the impact of collective action on the formation of attachment to a place. This issue led to the question of the impact of collective processions (movements) on the expansion of the public space of the city. The influence of such collective actions on the emergence of inclusive public spaces with a high degree of independence from the state and corporate economy was investigated.

Results

Context

Kharkiv is the second largest city in Ukraine in terms of population (over 1.43 million), a large industrial, scientific and educational center located near the border with Russia. It's a multicultural city (with large Vietnamese and Afghan communities), the diversity of which is complemented by about 20,000 foreign students studying at the city universities. The city is gradually joining the European integration processes. The processes of civil society formation (accelerated after the »Revolution of Dignity«) are a characteristic of countries with transition economies. The civil society reaction to

Russian aggression in 2014 intensified the consolidation process of various groups. The collective influence of European integration processes and the growth of civil consciousness accelerated the pace of various public organizations formation. Also, the attention of local residents to the processes of urban development is increasing and, as a result, a sense of responsibility for the city is on the rise too. In the process of including citizens in urban planning, Kharkiv is distinguished by a much more variegated configuration of various groups, movements, and associations all claiming their rights to public space.

Resumption of Collective Action Practices

Since public space is a reflection of the cultural heritage of local residents, let us take a quick trip to the year 2012 to seemingly insignificant (at first sight) events. It seems that these events heavily influenced the perception of collective practices by the local residents. Three processions of Dutch fans (who came to Kharkiv to support their national team playing at the local stadium), which took place before the matches on June 9, 13 and 17, 2012, demonstrated to local residents an unusual practice of temporal appropriation of street space. It was a different practice from the routine method of moving around the city. Similar processions had been organized by the communist authorities until the period of independence, but the participation of the townspeople was rather compulsory. The format of a self-organized march (not tied to political protests) was not typical for Kharkiv. The function of public space is revealed by its critical function – which: »allows people to linger, interact with one another, ignore each other, read, sit, stand or even lie down« (von Schönfeld/Bertolini 2017: 49). Furthermore, the final parade included a large number of local residents. In the first procession, – the overwhelming majority were Dutch, Danish, and German fans, accompanied by traffic police, while local residents were more likely to be spectators. A grand show was presented with orange uniforms, a double decker bus, the »Orange Club«, Dutch patriotic hymns were sung by the attendants, and ribbon streamers were shot into the air overhead (Tarasova 2012a). The city welcomed over 10,000 Dutch football fans, for the accommodation of which the »Orange Camp« was erected on the grounds of the Zhuravlivs'kiy River Park, housing several thousand people (Tarasova 2012b). The closing parade was different. It was composed of a large number of local residents, much fewer traffic police, and with about 50 local cyclists at the head of the procession. What changed in those eight days? It seems it was the perception of urban environment and the understanding of one's own right to claim the space for one's own means, which is mentioned by David Harvey (2012). These processions were choreographed by Dutch activists and were lined up around the »orange bus« opening the procession, and there were musicians (among the fans) in different parts of the column:

> »Kharkiv residents reacted to Dutch ›fans'‹ requests to support their team and wore the colors of the Dutch national team, and participated in the march alongside them. Many locals also cheered the Dutch fans along the streets, waving from windows and balconies, holding Dutch flags and posters, wishing the Netherlands victory and shouting ›Holland‹. In turn, the Dutch carried banners with the words ›Thank you, Kharkiv!‹, while also repeatedly chanting ›Ukraine‹« (Tarasova 2012c).

This small event seems to have somewhat changed the local community's perception of urban space. Manifestations of collective action in the city center should be considered in two respects. The first concerns the resulting sum activity of cultural and educational institutions, local communities, and city administration. The significance and influence of local institutions on the urban activity of the residents should be considered in the context of compelling changes (the participation of the city in global projects). Thus, in 2010, the city was connected with the world wide event »The Night of Museums«.[1] Kharkiv's Museum of Literature was the first of the four city museums to join the event. The key aim of this format is to bring forth an interconnection between the museum and urban space, in order to bring the internal world of the museums out onto the streets and to the inhabitants of the city, creating new points of contact and encouraging easy access to art exhibitions and cultural events. In 2012, 14 museums and galleries joined »The Night of Museums«, with the majority of events taking place in the open, unconfined by museum walls.[2]

---

1   »Ukrainian museums are joinining an international action ›Museums night‹«, in: NOVOSTI N, May 14, 2010, 15:45, https://novosti-n.org/ukraine/Ukraynskye-muzey-prysoedynyatsya-k-mezhdunarodnoj-akczyy-Noch-muzeev--21581, accessed July 15, 2021.

2   »14 Kharkiv Museums and Galleries welcome to the ›Museums night‹«, in: Official Site of Kharkov City Council, Mayor, Executive Committee, May 9, 2012, 11:52, https://www.city. kharkov.ua/ru/news/14-muzeyiv-i-galerey-harkova-zaproshuyut-na-nich-muzeyiv-13556. htm, accessed July 15, 2021.

The museum courtyards and surroundings became sites for exhibitions, installations, concerts, literary evenings, theatre performances, fire shows, and even telescopic observations of the Moon and Saturn. Over time, more and more organizations embraced this open format event, and in 2013, a total of 18 organizations joined, and the city administration decided to extend the operational hours of public transport.[3] Similarly, collective festivals (which take place annually) are important to the evolution of new practices of adapting space. Over time, the activities of the Kharkiv Literary Museum expanded beyond the initial event and the space around the museum is now purposefully utilized almost every week. A street library[4] appears on Bagaliya Street, near the Museum, and the inner courtyard of the museum becomes a platform for numerous exhibitions,[5] film screenings,[6] and concerts.[7] Soon Kharkiv Academy of Design and Arts also joined »The Night of Museums« festival, and later, »Street Day Fest«,[8] which lets artists, musicians, and actors showcase their work in outside spaces.[9] A temporary food court is set up on the campus of the Academy and space is provided for a vintage car show.

3 »18 Kharkiv Museums and Galleries welcome to the ›Museums night‹«, in: Official Site of Kharkov City Council, Mayor, Executive Committee, May 13, 2013, 14:54, https://www.city.kharkov.ua/ru/news/18-muzeyiv-ta-galerey-harkova-zaproshuyut-na-nich-muzeyiv-19245.html, accessed July 15, 2021.

4 »›Knyzhkova cljumba‹ starts with the bookcrossing with wrighteress Julia Iljuha«, in: Facebook group ›Kharkov – kuda b shodit‹, April 11, 2018, https://www.facebook.com/kharkovgo/posts/1018688328280178, accessed July 15, 2021.

5 »Portrait Exhibition of Ukrainian writers ›Polychka‹ at the Literary Museum Garden«, in: Litme.com.ua, http://litme.com.ua/vystavka-portretiv-ukrayinskyh-pysmennykiv-polychka-u-sadku-litmuzeyu, accessed July 15, 2021.

6 »Openair Cinema at the Literary Museum«, in: Facebook group ›Kharkov – kuda b shodit‹, August 14, 2017, https://www.facebook.com/kharkovgo/posts/893992134083132?comment_tracking=%7B%22tn%22%3A%22O%22%7D, accessed July 15, 2021.

7 »Literary Museum Will Hold a Book Swapping and Ukulele Concert«, in: Newsroom, August 2, 2017, 11:23, https://www.newsroom.kh.ua/ua/node/17575, accessed July 15, 2021.

8 »›One Street Day‹ Festival will be held in Kharkiv on September 19«, in: Stroy Obzor, September 17, 2015, https://stroyobzor.ua/ru/kharkov/news-city/19-sentyabrya-v-kharkove-proydet-festival-den-odnoy-ulicy, accessed July 15, 2021.

9 »One Street Day in Kharkiv – Iskusstv Street«, in: DOZOR.UA, April 18, 2016, 09:40, https://dozor.com.ua/news/tabloid/1205571.html, accessed July 15, 2021.

1.
*The pro-Ukrainian rally – a line of the local
cycling community, March 09, 2014.
Photographer: Sergiy Ilchenko.*

2.
*The fire show on Mystetstv Street during the »Night of Museums«,
2017. Photographer: Sergiy Ilchenko.*

The suspension of car traffic, as in the case of regular sporting events or the Kharkiv International Marathon (held since 2014)[10] or Kharkiv's Cyclist Day (held since 2006),[11] helps the streets of Downtown reclaim their essential status as a public space (Von Schönfeld/Bertolini 2017). Even the temporary adjournment of car traffic can encourage communication and change spatial function – communication replaces mobility (fig. 1 and 2).

At the beginning of the 20th century, Anastasia Bozhenko described the events taking place at Chamomile Day, a local Ukrainian holiday:

> »Notably, concerning organized charity events, one of them was inter-national Chamomile Day, dedicated to raising awareness and fighting tuber-culosis. Furthermore, the urban space, even public transportation was trans-formed by the festivities, as we can see from the pictures of the event, trams were decorated with wreaths and flowers, which means public transport was also included in the celebration. Buildings were decorated with garlands of white flowers and signs prompting support for the resolution« (Bozhenko 2018: 165).

Inclusion of Urban Spaces

Collective events that are not connected to a particular place or neighborhood but are held each time in different places, can be attributed to the second type of collective action in public space. Collective action is composed of a myriad of repercussions and unfortunately, dissatisfaction expressed by certain groups can overshadow the understandable feeling that the problem can be solved collectively; so social movements seek a common ground – »positions where social coalitions unite to achieve collective goals (Martin 2003).

In this respect, with the example of Kharkiv's gastro-enthusiast community it can be shown, how they established their claim to use urban space and created the basis for cooperation and communication. This community appeared in Kharkiv in 2013 with the introduction of the first

---

10 »Kharkiv Marathon has Entered the International Organization Events Calendar«, in: Official Site of Kharkov City Council, Mayor, Executive Committee, January 21, 2014, 09:28, https://www.city.kharkov.ua/uk/news/harkivskiy-marafon-uviyshov-do-kalendarya-za-hodiv-mizhnarodnoyi-sportivnoyi-organizatsiyi-22844.html, accessed July 15, 2021.

11 »Bike Day-2019 Took Place in Kharkiv«, in: Official Site of Kharkov City Council, Mayor, Executive Committee, May 19, 2019, 13:24, https://www.city.kharkov.ua/uk/news/-41702.html, accessed July 15, 2021.

food festival held here, »Day of the Restaurant«. The concept behind the festival is that anyone can open their own restaurant, café, or bar for 24 hours.

The goal of this kind of communal action is to bring people together through the enjoyment of food culture and the social event of eating together.[12] It is thus a certain rediscovery of the texture of local culture, where urban space is perceived as a platform for bringing together different social groups, and renewing urban enthusiasm, or »renaissance« (Latham 2003). In addition, these collective actions reveal the role of local cultural entrepreneurs, who, as Sharon Zukin says, shift the trend toward the authentic consumption of tangible products and spaces and thereby promote diversity and justice (Zukin 2009).

The new urban culture eventually materializes within these »open spaces«[13] geared towards active initiatives and creating connections between residents. There is also a revival in the »second line« of urban space – in outdated state grocery stores, once displaced by trading stands. These new open spaces, anti-cafes and small coworking hubs become places of collective action, where urban culture is rediscovered.

Outdated public premises that have lingered for years are now becoming platforms for common development. For example, the urban public association »Critical Thinking«,[14] located on the premises of the club for children and youth »Rassvet« at 6, Maximilianovskaya Street, which used to be a base for »DASH«[15] (school for young architects) and »Kharkiv Dom Aktera, Lesya Serdyuka«[16] on Manizerom Street 3, which became home to some 30 independent theaters. As well as becoming the venue for the local branch of

---

12 »Restaurant Day in Kharkiv«, in: Robinzon TV, May 23, 2014, https://www.youtube.com/watch?v=5tOJIVIIsLk, accessed July 15, 2021.

13 »Small Photo Report from Restaurant Day in Tsyferblat on February 21«, in: Facebook group ›Restoranny den v Kharkove‹, February 24, 2016, https://www.facebook.com/permalink.php?story_fbid=451018038356393&id=344482849009913, accessed July 15, 2021.

14 »Public Organization ›Krytychne myslennja‹ Presents Projects for Architectural Urban Space Development«, in: ART UKRAINE, October 27, 2014, https://artukraine.com.ua/n/go-kritichne-mislennya-prezentuye-proekti-z-rozvitku-miskogo-arkhitekturnogo-prostoru/#.YGJraa8zZhE, accessed July 15, 2021.

15 »Design School for Kids and Youngsters«, in: dash! https://dash.vision/#about, accessed July 15, 2021.

16 »House of Actor after Les Serdyuk«, in: Dom aktera, https://domaktera.kharkiv.ua/theaters, accessed July 15, 2021.

the national theater festival »Kurbolesiya« (2010–2017) and the international festival of works in progress »Theatronic« (2011–2017) as well as the puppetry and mixed media festival »ANIMA« (2017) it basically becomes an open space for new theater initiatives.

Coming back to our gastro-enthusiasts' start-up, it is worth taking a look not only at the numerous alliances they created with other associations and urban communities, but assessing what those efforts contributed to the significance of the urban space. Basically, what we are seeing is the community grounding its activities in the rebirth of interest in the city. Here is an example of how the organizers of the food festival »Luk Fest« describe their choice of venue:

> »The venue of the new festival is the courtyard of the former estate of the professor of the Kharkov Imperial University, researcher and ornithologist Nikolai Somov. The building was constructed according to the design of A.N. Beketov. Today it is home to the ›House of the Doctor‹—and the Kharkov Medical Society. [...] A large green courtyard stands in the center of the estate, and you will surely be surprised by the rear facade of the building. On September 12, you will discover a slightly different side of our city.«[17]

The downtown arena seems to be attracting advocacy from new urban communities, and as the first »Luk« Festival at Kharkiv's Literature Museum demonstrates,[18] location matters. The long list of various organizations partnering with food festivals displays how colorful and variable these cooperative combinations can be. At different times and at different locations, partner organizations of the gastro-enthusiasts at the »Luk Fest« were: Ziferblat Free Space (later the Lacan intellectual bar),[19] the combined area of the gallery and cafe »Ampersand food & art«, anti-cafe »Oblomov«

17 »Today we are Going to Tell You About the Holding Place of the Second Food Festival LUK, Which Takes Place on September 12 «, in: Facebook group ›Lukfest‹, August 28, 2015 https://www.facebook.com/lukfestival/photos/a.991177624234508/1022118334473770/, accessed July 15, 2021.

18 Ostapenko, Leonid (2015): »How Was It: Food Festival LUK Took Place at the Literary Museum Garden«, in: VGORODE, June 25, 2015, https://kh.vgorode.ua/news/dosuh_y_eda/262458-20-kylohrammov-rysa-y-25-kylohrammov-miasnoho-farsha-v-kharkove-proshel-festyval-edy-luk, accessed July 15, 2021.

19 »Intelligent Bar Lacan«, in: Facebook group ›Lacan‹, https://www.facebook.com/lacanbar/, accessed July 15, 2021.

and »TEPLO / TEPLO«, cafes of the third wave »A7« and »Bourbon«, educational hub and coworking space »Spalah Edu Hub«, musical project »Kultura Zvuka«,[20] independent city festival »Gesheft Garage Sale« (Odessa), school of young architects »DASH«, the cultural initiative »Fifth Kharkov«, festival »Vertep Fest«, the fair of Ukrainian clothing designers »Design-Market More«, the project »Street Day«, and the festival »Kharkiv Music day«.[21]

The unifying feature of these diverse groups is their recognition of the city as a platform for social engagement. This is a neighborhood with a heterogeneous group of residents, since in addition to local residents, there are those who have recently settled in Kharkiv, and visiting students. The majority are not natives to the city center but they are nevertheless part of the urban society. The common ground for this extended community is the creation of a new collective culture (through cooperation/complicity) not based on historical reflections. These new communities actively participate in advocating for the downtown area and its phenomena, its fulfillment and authenticity (in contrast to interpretation of the territory as a resource for appropriation). It seems that such bottom-up efforts are contributing to the domestication of urban spaces. They revitalize the fabric of the city by incorporating all new sites into shared spaces.

Transformation of Space

A monolith on the outside, the space of consumerism is torn apart by the destructive actions of urban semiotic partisanship. The latter manifest not only as aesthetic qualities, but also as political statements in the public space (Campos 2016). Simultaneously, united by the discovery of the collective, part of the urban community demonstrates a different attitude toward the city. They are attentive toward the location and have a sense of responsibility for the communal (public) space. Regarding the processes that define the reform of urban space, it is this part of the population in collaboration with the art community that becomes the source of »communal tactics« associated with sites of collective endeavor and the creativity of residents, where space is

---

20 »Music Club ›Kultura zvuka‹«, in: https://kulturazvuka.ua/ua/, accessed July 15, 2021.

21 »Music Day will Take Place in Kharkiv«, in: Official Site of Kharkov City Council, Mayor, Executive Committee, June 20, 2014 10:17, https://www.city.kharkov.ua/ru/news/u-kharkovi-vidznachat-den-muziki--24472.html, accessed July 15, 2021.

understood as a common resource for future development (Gielen 2015). This is facilitated by the scale of the central quarters built up along the perimeter of 2–5-story buildings and having a complex structure of multi-story buildings of the second line that divide the interior space into chains of small courtyards.

Governmental strategies of establishing *order* in the form of organized spaces (De Certeau/Mayol 1998[1980]) are limited solely to the facades of main streets and do not encompass courtyards and alleys. Although it seems logical to restore an integral urban fabric, especially since, thanks to collective actions, the city has already been opened up by local residents, and not only in the format of the main streets.

These strategies are largely focused on shaping the media's image of a »successful« Kharkiv and are in line with the liberal rhetoric of capitalism. The argument for this statement is the amount and forms of work carried out in the central part of the city. First, the officials take care of the main streets, or those parts of the city that are always in sight. Second, it's all about the visibility of the results of this work by the municipal authorities. For example, if large mature trees grow on the street, they will be replaced with new decorative ones; the facade of a building (even of an architectural monument) will be painted in a distinct color; the reconstructed sections of the streets will be decorated with diode garlands and facades will be backlit (the simplest way to make taking care of your hometown visible). Third, courtyards will eventually turn into urban voids, since they are not the subject of urban programs.

This is a rhetoric in which:

> »media representation and consumer tastes lubricate the wheels of global urbanism, anchoring the power of capital and state in the vastness of our personal desires, convincing us that the consumption of an authentic city is about aesthetics and has nothing to do with power« (Zukin 2009: 551).

The city's shell does not (physically) change the space and is a collection of beautifying techniques that promote a utopian image. On the other hand, the inner space of the neighborhoods constantly transforms due to the incessant usurpation and appropriation of spaces under the cloak of urban micro-operations by the administration and their »dead« (van Assche et al. 2014) planning practices. It is essential to recall that Ukraine belongs to countries with a transition economy in which many of the rules governing construction do not limit the ambitions of developers. So, according to the current regulations, for the city center, in almost any place, a building up to 100 meters high with 100 percent development of the site can be erected if it does not contradict the national building codes. Such a rule can hardly be called a limitation.

The downtown arena saturated with graffiti has an annual upgrade in August (during the day of the city) when, with the great efforts of the city maintenance crew it is painted over again fresh. Yet this short-lived measure to restore »order« serves as the canvas for new inscriptions and works of graffiti. This is a daily exercise for establishing presence where:

> »public space is understood as an arena of ongoing contestation and nego-tiation wherein different groups' rights and claims to the city are defined. [...] Each of these concerns – exclusion, encroachment, and claim-making – offers a distinct way of attending to contemporary public spaces and the transformations that shape them.« (Koch/Latham 2012: 517).

As illustrated by these activities, the city thrives as a result of a variety of »creative actions« scattered about the common landscape of experience (De Certeau/Mayol 1998[1980]). The way in which we interpret and exper-ience urban character is conveyed by this opinion of Vladislav Krasnoschek (Kharkiv street artist): »I think that an artist who goes out on the street, has to be ready that his [work] will be painted over a minute after he completes it. You can call it an artistic act or performance. One way or another your art will be destroyed. Street art is a fragile endeavor, the walls belong to everyone.«[22] In the ever-changing dynamics of appropriation, transformation, and revi-sion, the aforementioned »creative actions« are characterized by a certain temporality that limits their interference in the urban space.

And this is exactly what happens – not a single new work placed in the city is left without people reacting and can instantly be refuted by other artists or covered up by local residents.26 The compelling aspect of this situation, is that in the city, multiple modes of communication occur on a daily basis and they are simultaneously peppered by destructive episodes in the form of »semiotic partisanship« that violate or interrupt official order (Campos 2016).

---

22 Kalita, Nastya (2019): »Vladyslav Krasnoshek: About ›Completed dissertation‹ and Medical Practice«, in: Yourart, July 17, 2019, https://supportyourart.com/conversations/krasnochek/, accessed July 15, 2021.

In some cases, this palimpsestic layering of various interventions culminates in a collective clash (for example, local residents and street artists) .[23]

The heterogeneous body of the city also includes public spaces in decline – abandoned places (beyond the reach of utility crews and city administration), which, however, play an important role as open zones for meeting and the communal activities of citizens. Paradoxically, here the inactivity of the authorities leads to the initial neglect and decline of these spaces. These are areas near historical and architectural monuments (usually small buildings), which, according to legislation, do not have the potential for expansion and, as a result, do not attract investment capital. All these sites are »dormant«, waiting for a chain of micro-processes to begin, in order to be appropriated.

These spots in Downtown Kharkiv can be called »abandoned lands« or »the neglected parts« of the city. Each place like this belongs either to the city or to a private owner. Formally, these places are not urban voids. Moreover, covered with numerous signs of »semiotic partisanship« they resemble ruins, but still remain a living space. The encroaching appropriation of this downtown real estate and restriction of free access to it seems to be refuted only by these interconnected cells of »constant presence«. These spaces, free from excessive regulation, are important for collective action and create a rewarding environment for mutual support. They are the places where local communities (or groups) maintain and manifest their identity. But, as Castells says: »these identities, in most cases, are defensive reactions against the impositions of global disorder and uncontrollable, fast-paced change. They do build havens, but not heavens« (Castells 2011: 68). That is why these spaces can be called »urban lagoons« in a binary opposition to the public spaces created by the authorities.

Discussion

The communal actions of the residents contribute to the assimilation (domestication) of the urban landscape, but have little to do with its physical transformation. Rather, we speak of assimilation by means of »temporary use« and communal activity (Koch/Latham 2013: 9). In the context of prospectively

---

23 Nikitenko, Ekaterina (2020): »I Will Overpaint You: Why Do Some Graffiti Live No Longer Than One Night«, in: Nakipelo.ua, November 13, 2020, https://nakipelo.ua/ya-tebya-per-ekroju-pochemu-nekotorye-graffiti-zhivut-ne-dolshe-odnoj-nochi/, accessed July 15, 2021.

difficult interactions between formal and informal institutions, in regard to the question of spatial planning (van Assche et al. 2014; Waibel 2016) (especially for countries with transitional economies) issues of developing public (civil) spaces in Ukrainian cities (and Kharkiv in particular) look quite contradictory.

On the one hand, government planning and »order« (De Certeau/Mayol 1998[1980]) requires the creation of public spaces. This can be attributed to the desire of cities to become attractive, making them an artifact of appreciation by tourists (Campos 2016: 53). We cannot overlook the fact that public spaces (as a symbol of democratic power) are gradually taking precedence (in the urban landscape) over heroic national monuments aimed at strengthening the collective spirit and other material manifestations of authority (ibid.: 59). The paradox however, is that spaces initially created for public use (inclusive by definition), in countries with transitional economies, are being captured for exclusive use by fractions of civil society (Douglass 2007: 49). Originally intended for eating, walking, and possibly taking selfies (as the »showcases« of modern development) these spaces become cluttered with rules of exclusion, prohibition, and control. At times one may think that the Ukrainian administration is intensely studying academic urban criticism (Jackson 1998; Allen 2006; Zukin 2009) and purposefully reinforcing securitization, pacification, ordering, disciplining, homogenizing, commercializing, and controlling in all facets of public spaces. Respectively, with the loss of inclusive spaces, the efforts of urban planners are rather reduced to the creation of »decorations« for public spaces, and as such, these spaces are deprived of the crucial function of interaction between local residents (Schönfeld/Bertolini 2017).

At the same time, one part of the urban community (united by collective actions and interests) demonstrates attentive care to specific places and shares a sense of responsibility for the communal (public) space. In this case, the researcher is dealing with existent (not developing) spaces understood as places of collective activity and co-creation (Gielen 2015). Thus, the main emblematic faculty of such spaces is the inclusiveness of the latter. It is inclusiveness that transforms these (free) spaces into places of collective action and a rewarding environment of mutual support. These places are situational; they are created through implicit and explicit negotiation, as well as through broadening the array of opportunities and privileges to become places for the exchange of ideas and cooperation (Douglass 2007).

Concluding Remarks

Group identity in the local community – and urban culture as a result is not homogenous. On the one hand it involves tendencies of urban space consumption, rather than the tradition of co-activity. At the same time, the fact that certain local residents cooperate and re-adapt the city to modern life, proves the phenomena of a new urban culture. The city is rediscovered through collective endeavors, including: festive processions, urban »occupation«, artistic happenings and social engagement. Locally, spontaneous groups emerge, reviving the culture of collective and communal actions. Simultaneously, the public/civic space is perceived as a platform for groups with varying identities to meet. If we accept movement as one of the ways of temporarily assigning space to influencing the perception of the latter, it is possible to define public space as a process. In this case, the question should be asked: »What exactly is the result of the planner's work? – a place or a space?« If space is a process then: »What means does the planner have (not have) to organize it?«

In the context of augmenting the capacity of urban planning, one approach may be to use »domestication« of the adopted plans (as a follow-up process of incorporating political and social projects into the daily practices of citizens) (Koch/Latham 2013). In this case, the traditional approach to planning is preserved and all questions about the relevance of the adopted planning decision are transferred to the implementation (domestication) specialist. Another approach can be based on identifying (when preparing the initial data) and preserving unused areas (»urban lagoons«) for natural social reproduction by the local community when planning urban development, the functions of interaction, and co-creation.

References

Allen, John (2006): »Ambient Power: Berlin's Potsdamer Platz and the Seductive Logic of Public Spaces«, in: *Urban Studies 43/2*, 441–455. doi: 10.1080/00420980500416982

Assche, Kristof van/Beunen, Raoul/ Duineveld, Martijn (2014): »Formal/ Informal Dialectics and the Self-transformation of Spatial Planning Systems: An Exploration«, in: *Administration & Society 46/6*, 654–683, doi: 10.1177/0095399712469194

Bozhenko, A.O. (2018): *Formation of the Urban Way of Life in the Second Half of the XIXth–Beginning of the XXth Century (on the Materials of the City of Kharkiv).*

Bresnihan, Patrick/Byrne, Michael (2015): »Escape into the City: Everyday Practices of Commoning and the Production of Urban Space in Dublin«, in: *Antipode 47/1*, July 2014, 36–54, doi: 10.1111/anti.12105

Campos, Ricardo (2016): »Visibilidades e Invisibilidades Urbanas«, in: *Revista de Ciências Sociais: RCS 47/1*, 49–76.

Castells, Manuel (2011): *The Power of Identity Vol. 14*, Hoboken, NJ: John Wiley & Sons.

De Certeau, Michel/Mayol, Pierre (1980): *L'invention du quotidien.* – English translation: *The Practice of Everyday Life: Living and Cooking.* transl. by Steven Rendall, Minneapolis: University of Minnesota Press, 1998.

Douglass, Mike (2007): »Civil Society for Itself and in the Public Sphere: Comparative Research on Globalization, Cities and Civic Space in Pacific Asia«, in: *Globalization, the City and Civil Society in Pacific Asia*, New York: Routledge, 45–67.

Gielen, Pascal (2015): »Performing the Common City: On the Crossroads of Art, Politics and Public Life«, in: Pascal Gielen/ Sander Bax/Bram Ieven (eds.), *Interrupting the City: Artistic Constitutions of the Public Sphere*, Amsterdam: Valiz, 273–297.

Goffman, Erving (2008): Behavior in Public Places, New York: Simon and Schuster.

Harvey, David (2012): *Rebel Cities: From the Right to the City to the Urban Revolution*, New York: Verso Books.

Jackson, Peter (1998): »Domesticating the Street«, in: Nicholas Fyfe/Jon Bannister (eds.), *Images of the Street: Planning, Identity and Control in Public Space*, London: Routledge, 176–191.

Koch, Regan/Latham, Alan (2012): »Rethinking Urban Public Space: Accounts From a Junction in West London«, in: *Transactions of the Institute of British Geographers 37/4*, 515–529, doi: 10.1111/j.1475-5661.2011.00489.x

Koch, Regan/Latham, Alan (2013): »On the Hard Work of Domesticating a Public Space«, in: *Urban Studies 50/1*, 6–21, doi: 10.1177/0042098012447001

Latham, Alan (2003): »Urbanity, Lifestyle and Making Sense of the New Urban Cultural Economy: Notes from Auckland, New Zealand«, in: *Urban Studies 40/9*, 1699–1724, doi: 10.1080/0042098032000106564

Lefebvre, Henri (1968): *Le Droit à la Ville.* – English translation: *The Right to the City, Writings on Cities*, transl. by Eleonore Kofman/Elizabeth Lebas, Oxford: Basil Blackwell, 1996.

Lefebvre, Henri (1974): *La Production de l'espace.* – English translation: *The Production of Space*, transl. by Donald Nicholson-Smith, Vol. 142, Oxford: Basil Blackwell, 1991.

Martin, Deborah (2003): »›Place-framing‹ as Place-making: Constituting a Neighborhood for Organizing and Activism«, in: *Annals of the Association of American Geographers 93/3*, 730–750, doi: 10.1111/1467-8306.9303011

Schönfeld, Kim Carlotta von/Bertolini, Luca (2017): »Urban Streets: Epitomes of Planning Challenges and Opportunities at the Interface of Public Space and Mobility«, in: *Cities 68*, 48–55.

Tarasova, Julia (2012a): »Thousands of Holland fans marched through the center of Kharkov to the Metalist Stadium«, in: *STATUS QUO*, June 09, 2012, 17:19, https://www.sq.com.ua/rus/news/videonovosti/09.06.2012/tysyachi_gollandskih_bolelschikov_idut_shestviem_po_centru_harkova_k_stadionu_metallist/, accessed July 15, 2021.

Tarasova, Julia (2012b): »Camping for Holland fans has been officially opened on Zhuravlevka«, in: *STATUS QUO*, June 08, 2012, 23:15, https://www.sq.com.ua/rus/news/fotoreportazh/08.06.2012/na_zhuravlevke_oficialno_otkryli_kemping_dlya_gollandskih_bolelschikov/, accessed July 15, 2021.

Tarasova, Julia (2012c): »Holland fans with posters ›Thank you, Kharkov‹ are marching again to the Metalist Stadium«, in: *STATUS QUO*, June 17, 2012, 19:35, https://www.sq.com.ua/rus/news/videonovosti/17.06.2012/gollandskie_bolelschiki_s_plakatami_spasibo_harkov_vnov_idut_shestviem_k_stadionu_metallist/accessed July 15, 2021.

Vaiou, Dina/Kalandides, Ares (2016): »Practices of Collective Action and Solidarity: Reconfigurations of the Public Space in Crisis-ridden Athens, Greece«, in: *Journal of Housing and the Built Environment 31/3*, 457–470, doi: 10.1007/sl0901-015-9468-z

Waibel, Michael/McFarlin, Colin (2016). *Urban Informalities: Reflections on the Formal and Informal*, New York: Routledge.

Zukin, Sharon (2009): »Changing Landscapes of Power: Opulence and the Urge for Authenticity«, in: *International Journal of Urban and Regional Research 33/2*, 543–553, doi: 10.1111/j.1468-2427.2009.00867.x

Dimensions of Architectural Knowledge, 2021-02 ⊚
https://doi.org/10.14361/dak-2021-0215

Rewriting the Journey of the Mantua-Peschiera Railway: A Moving Experience

Federico Marcolini

Abstract: The research presented in this article is embedded in the context of the on-going doctoral thesis titled *The Mantua-Peschiera Railway: A Case Study for the Historical Analysis and Design Methodology of a Regeneration Project*. The research focuses on the decommissioned railway that once connected the city of Mantua to Peschiera del Garda in the north of Italy and questions its possible future. Nowadays, the railway is not perceived as it was, because, without any specific or recognizable appearence, its few remains, such as the passenger stations, are in ruins. The historical data helped to reshape the original project of the line and its deep inter-dependence with its environment showing peculiar and original characters as a branch line. The author's research aims to create a possible scenario in which the former railway guarantees a continuous connection between the object and its territory within its new function as a *Cultural Route*.

Keywords: Literature Journey; Railways; Landscape; Historical Data.

This article refers to the theoretical framework used to retrace the experience of the railway journey – approaching the complexity of its context and its history – and allows us to move through the heterogeneity of the landscape using a different point of view. Starting from the information contained in the historical documents of the railway and enriched by maps and photographs, the territory of the Mincio Valley is described in order to emphasize the technical description of the territory. Moreover, the importance of a subjective approach is explained here with reference to the possibility of the Valley as a space in between and connecting cities, and in reference to the Grand Tour experience and the idea of a journey.

Corresponding author: Federico Marcolini (Polytechnic University of Milan);
federico.marcolini@polimi.it; https://orcid.org/0000-0002-4748-5186

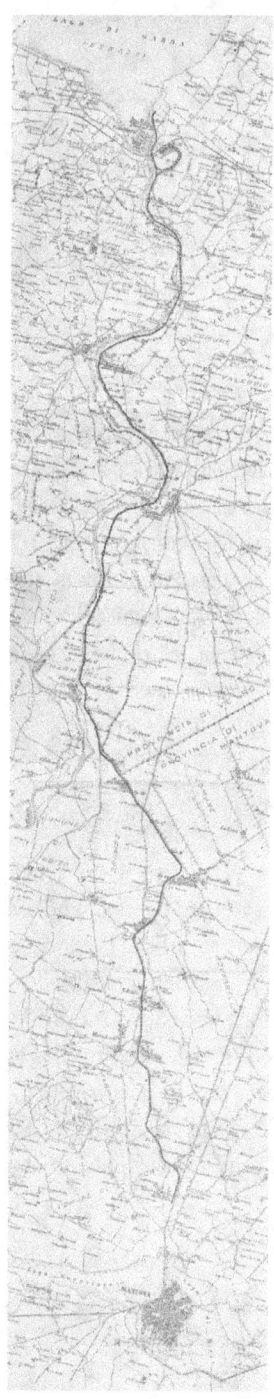

1.
Ferrovia Mantova-Peschiera, 1:25000 orig. Scale,
General Plan, Ing. Arvedo Arvedi, 1905, Archivio
di Stato di Mantova, Fondo Camera di Commercio,
Parte Seconda, Busta 286,
Courtesy: Archivio di Stato di Mantova.

Introduction

In 1905, the Italian Ministry of Transport required the submission of a preliminary draft of plans for the construction of a secondary railway line between the city of Mantua and Peschiera del Garda in the north of Italy. The preliminary draft was designed by the local engineer Arvedo Arvedi in the same year and it is the only document that has survived in which the railway is described. The folder contains several pamphlets including: a general plan (fig. 1.a–b), a technical report, a section on the various heights of the line and a financial report, proving its convenience and economic sustainability.

Retracing the route drawn in the plan, assisted by the description contained in the technical report, it is now possible to rewrite an *immaginario*[1] of the Mantua-Peschiera journey. A journey characterized not by the mere technical description of the railway, but in which the territory and its various landscapes are introduced: quoting ancient and partly forgotten toponyms and monumental features of the built environment (fig. 2) that have disappeared or transformed profoundly, and creating a hypothetical itinerary that, such as the *immaginario* of the railway itself with its layout and its artifacts, is made up of traces, whether they are still recognizable or have completely disappeared.

The journey offers a sequence of complex images which represent a contemporaneity, abstracted and suspended in an indeterminate space. The journey becomes the key to understanding the profound relationship between the railway infrastructure and its territory. A complex environment characterized by distinctive features, of which the Mincio river is the most dominant one. The particularity of this waterway, whose waters are never impetuous or violent, allowed the inhabitants of the valley to get closer to its banks, along which they have built mills, farms, noble residences, villages, and hamlets. Following the morphology of the Valley, it is possible to identify two different areas: The hills in the north part and the plain in the south. These peculiar characters defined different environments in which the anthropization process generated a heterogeneity of landscapes. Since ancient times, these places have been characterized by the strong presence

---

1 The Italian term *immaginario* (*imaginarius* in Latin) is considered here as a function and content of the imagination. A controlled imaginative, as suggested by Kant, in which limits upon the surreal are placed, a productive imagination is that which coincides with the functions of the pure intuition of space and time.

2.
The armory's ruins of Bosco Fontana. This building was formally composed by a convent of the Camaldolesi's order, a church and a small palace. Built in 1632, the building was partially demolished in 1793 and transformed into an armory, bombed during World War II.
Photographer: Federico Marcolini.

of mankind. During the Roman era, centuriation came to surround the limits of the Valley without ever getting to occupy it because of its soil characteristics. It is in fact its nature that imposed a continuous domestication of the land, with the construction of terraces on the slopes facing south and continuous tilling of the land from the stones brought to the valley when the primitive Benaco Glacier melted.

The imagined journey is considered as »a condition of a hermeneutic activity towards the built environment« (Lampugnani Savi 1987: 14), said Vittorio Magnago Lampugnani upon the occasion of the XVIIth edition of the Milan Triennale of 1987 entitled *Un Viaggio in Italia, Nove Progetti per Nove Città*. It is a subjective reading in which architectures, villages, and landscapes are in sequence, creating heterogeneity that, in the case of the Mantua–Peschiera experience, leads back to a contemporary unique layer of coexistence identified in the Mincio Valley and its river.

The »Paese Reale« of the XVIIth Triennale

The key contributions of this territorial's reading starts from the experiments conducted by Vittorio Magnago Lampugnani and Vittorio Savi for the construction of the above mentioned XVIIth Milan Triennale. At that time, the authors aimed to describe the *Paese Reale*[2] (de Seta 2014), the real country, through an interpretation of the built environment, created by selective and arbitrary choices, and without claiming to be exhaustive. The co-curator, Pierluigi Nicolin, justifies this choice, saying that the city, like the anthropized territory, does not present itself as an organic unit and is exposed to different interpretations. The goal of Lampugnani's work was to look for models in the places he passed through and to »start to solve those environmental and redevelopment issues« (Nicolin 1987: 11, author's translation) and to be useful for the city, as Nicolin himself writes in the introduction to the exhibition catalog.

The reference materials attest to the journey of the imagined character Vittorio Valori Perduti and consist of paintings, drawings, models, and

---

2 The *Paese Reale* (the Real Country) to which Cesare De Seta refers, is the Italian Country »discovered« by the European consciousness in the modern age, thanks to the complex and tangled experience of the Grand Tour. A significant contribution to the culture of cosmopolitanism, in which the role assumed by Italy was fundamental as an aggregation center of civilization in modern Europe.

publications »which guarantee the necessary arbitrariness of the point of view« (Nicolin 1987: 12, author's translation). The imagined traveler is at the same time a man of science who asks questions and looks for solutions, and a romantic one who leaves himself open to deeper and more emotional interpretations of the areas that lie between cities.

»Io Osservo«, I Observe

Looking at the *Casabella* editorials by Vittorio Gregotti, collected in »96 ragioni critiche del progetto« (Gregotti 2014), the architect talks about architecture's character as an artistic practice and its specialties with the empiric world of situations and conditions. He underlines the relevance of architecture's critical relationship with the real, and the context into which architecture fits as a fundamental reference: »I write about Homer telling that Ulysses heard the mermaids sing« (Calvino 1980: 322, author's translation), wrote Italo Calvino in a famous essay on the ways and levels in which the notions of reality arrange themselves for the writer's sake, beginning with that »I write« and to what Gregotti says »is not an observation point but the ground for reality's transformation into literary substance« (Gregotti 2014: 2, author's translation).

Within the transcription and narration of reality some transformation and interpretation takes place. Like a poem, the observer clarifies the subjective point of view of the literary documentation in which architecture seeks to embody the depth of »its layers of implications and connections with the different levels of both the real and its disciplinary schematizations, by means of the project's »I write« (ibid.). A subjective position, it is strenuously defended in order to guarantee the value of architectural projects and, therefore, of architecture itself.

A journey into culture, as Carlo Quintavalle reminds us in the introductory essay for the catalog of another exhibition: *Viaggio in Italia*. Curated by Luigi Ghirri and displayed in Bari in 1984, the exhibition »favors some objects over others in various eras« (Ghirri 1984: 8, author's translation). The imagined journey is a subjective experience that reconstructs the memories of places and through them reveals their original nature. An experience described by Gianni Celati in the contribution *Verso la foce* tells the story of traveling along the Po river in literary form as a reporter for his photographer friend (Ghirri 1984: 20–35). A trip similar to the one commissioned to Luigi Ghirri by Vittorio Savi for the *paesaggio immagine e realtà* exhibition, whose catalog was published by Electa in 1981 and in which the architect, Savi, leaves it to the photographer, »who had set a goal, free from aesthetic prejudices towards today's artificial environment« (Savi 1981: 275, author's translation); searching for a real country made up of things and in which people »have escaped from his frames, in which things and substitute goods have replaced them, in order to form an effective synecdoche: anthropological« (ibid.).

More recently, Marco Belpoliti, in his book *Pianura*, retraces the places he lived in the Po Valley and their memories, restoring a subjective reality formed by his culture and memory. An itinerary that recounts some peculiar features, such as the Roman centuriation or monumental buildings such as the Cathedral of Modena, helped by characters such as Christian Tuxen Falbe or friends of the past such as Luigi Ghirri and Gianni Celati (Belpoliti 2021). Here, architecture becomes an emblem of the history of a place, a transposition of a shared culture often cited in the works of those who describe it in literary form or through the poetics of photography.

It is an approach that shows visions of landscapes starting from the subjective mental disposition of those who place themselves on the observer's side:

> »An unprecedented design dimension, where space and time enter, [...] in which the final image is the result of choices made more or less unconsciously by the subject: an experience that implies modes of representation coming from different cultural fields« (Spinelli 2019: 13, author's translation).

An internal point of view, an *inscape*, as the Irish Jesuit Gerard Manley Hopkins defined it, in which the natural landscape becomes the object of reflection upon his tormented vision of reality, like in his poems *Binsey Poplars* and *Spring and Fall*.

The Journey of »Vittorio Valori Perduti«

In 1987, one year before the publication of Gregotti's original work in *Casabella* (Gregotti 1988), the Milan Triennale hosted the exhibitions »Viaggio in Italia« and »Nove progetti per Nove città«[3], under the direction of Pierluigi Nicolin.

A journey that, through the gaze of a heteronomous character, like the ones described by Pessoa, crosses a sequence of places made by their architectures, cities, and landscapes, intended to declare their problems and to suggest new paths (Pessoa 2020). A visit to nine cities in which the protagonist collects the character for each one, »or rather the dominant flavor and behavior of it« (Lampugnani/Savi 1987: 14, author's translation). Through the heteronomy of the imagined protagonist and through the metaphor of travel, the places become the space of the project.

Along this journey, looking at the territories in between cities, the traveling experience is based on a narrative. The materials are chosen through the traveler's particular point of view and recall the different moments and situations related to the journey's experience. The different situations are: the start, the learning, the railway'quête, bewilderment, the stop, the endlessness, the death-city, the nostalgia, and the arrival. These are specific situations that define different sequences of architecture to be interpreted through the reading of an architect: Vittorio Valori Perduti (fig. 4) (Dal Lago 1987: 230).

The exhibition starts from history as a documentary basis for the definition of reference models for the construction of future cities and draws inspiration from identifying the environmental requalification themes necessary for the construction of new development scenarios for cities and territories.

Like the exhibition, the author's research also looks toward history for a model that can be used as a reference, a tool for the redevelopment of territories. An environmental redevelopment that takes issues related to the setting of architectural interventions on the remains of the former

---

3 The XVIIth Triennale di Milano with the exhibition »Le Città Immaginate: Un Viaggio in Italia. Nove progetti per nove città«, »Il progetto domestico« and »Il luogo del lavoro«, completed a series focused on Italian urban and architectural history. This was a trilogy related to the International Exhibition »Le città del mondo e il futuro delle metropoli« displayed at the Palazzo dell'Arte in Milan at the end of 1987.

3.

*Catalog Cover of the XVIIth Milan
Triennale, 1987. Courtesy: Triennale
di Milano, Biblioteca e Archivi.*

MI CHIAMO

*Vittorio Valori Perduti. Quando pronunzio questo nome, mi credono di rado. Pensano sia un nome d'arte.
Tuttavia conta poco che sia autentico; è rilevante che non esprima la contraddizione di cui sono preda. Per-
ché da un lato provo un'infinita nostalgia per i valori dell'Italia fisica e dell'Italia sociale che, assai prima della nascita di mio padre, cominciarono a franare; e, con la seconda rivoluzione industriale, rovinarono; e, sot-
to i miei occhi, per vari motivi da non rivangare qui, si dissolsero. Dall'altro il movimento della cultura archi-
tettonica, il movimento della ricerca professionale, il mio carattere, e tutto, tutto mi spinge a un lavoro positi-
vo, di ricomposizione, reintegrazione, insomma riavvalorizzazione. Cercherò di avanzare un esempio.
Stamane sono passato dall'Eur. Eur: Esposizione universale di Roma... ho trascorso un'infanzia che mi ha
dato pochi ricordi, come quando assisto alla proiezione di un film muto, o parlato in lingua straniera, senza
sottotitoli in italiano. Fra i pochi c'è quello di una improvvisa breve visita alle costruzioni monumentali del-
l'Eur, sospese nel 1941, non ancora terminate, già in rovina. Era appunto il primo dopoguerra. Gli zii mi avevano prelevato a Termini e mi avevano portato a casa loro. Abitavano in un intensivo fuori Porta Metronia.
Di lì si faceva presto ad "andare al mare". E subito mi avevano ricaricato sulla 1100 per una gita. Lo zio era
un piccolo imprenditore edile, che aveva costruito per l'Italia fascista, e, prima di imboccare la strada, voleva
mostrarmi un quartiere mai terminato, mai entrato in funzione. Bastava un giro d'automobile: mi sarei me-
ravigliato e avrei imparato qualche cosa. Sic transit... Una landa desolata. Al fondo di strade sterrate sorge-
vano vaste architetture... Si conserveranno pure delle stampe di foto scattate ai palazzi abbandonati sopra il
logoro tappeto erboso: palazzi della Civiltà, dei Congressi, dell'Ina e dell'Inps.
Rimasi a bocca aperta; non so se fui ammaestrato.
Era bello, quel torso di città. E, quali che siano stati i giudizi formulati in seguito, mi pare di poter sostenere
che non sarebbe stato mai più così attraente e importante.
Doveva rimanere nello stato in cui lo rimirai allora. Al massimo, secondo che era stato programmato, biso-
gnava completarlo con edifici residenziali, in stile 1942. Ma ormai...
Eppure. Vorrei mi affidassero l'incarico di provvedere al restauro dell'E42. Proverei a disegnare la forma di
alcuni isolati che, innestati in posizioni opportune, farebbero balenare l'immagine di un'E42 integra o, se vo-
lete, propizierebbero un retto completamento mentale.
Fallissi io, forse non avrà fallito il coetaneo, lo stimato architetto F.P., che, a quanto mi consta, dell'Eur
si è occupato progettualmente. E se lui, come gli accade, avesse scambiato la necessità di disegnare credi-
bili unità abitative con l'occasione per disegnare una scena a base di quinte, facciate dalle finestre tutte
eguali e gran cornicione, potrebbe tentare un terzo collega.
Guidando, fantasticavo; mi sono persino scordato di guardare la Piramide di Caio Cestio e il palazzo posta-
le di Libera, con un colpo d'occhio che mi è caro.
La marea montante del traffico mi ha depositato nei pressi del Colosseo.*

4.

*The description of »Vittorio Valori Perduti« within the
catalog of the XVIIth Triennale.*

Mantua–Peschiera railway and how they relate to their heritage and the landscapes it crosses.

Choosing the anthropized territory as our reference, we realize how the entire built environment cannot offer itself to our eye as an organic unit. The object of our interest is revealed as a text with multiple meanings, open to different readings. Looking for qualifying and functional interpretations, the metaphor for the journey became a means of accessing different interpretive materials from the territory once crossed by the railway. A look toward the horizon of those who, like Moby Dick's eager to travel boy, want to embark to see the world, and, approaching the old captain, was challenged to observe the infinity of the ocean. In the novel by Herman Melville, the old man posits the question: »Take a peep out that way and tell me what ye see there«, and the boy replies »not much stuff, nothing but water«, and the old man says: »Well, what dost thou think then of seeing the world? Do ye wish to go round Cape Horn to see any more of it, eh? Can't ye see the world where you stand?« (Melville 1892: 78).

This is an episode in which »there is no more radical and at the same time modest denial of the idea of travel as a physical fact« (Pontiggia 1987: 78, author's translation), a provocation through which it is suggested we approach the world without leaving the door, a mental journey, just like the one imagined by the protagonist of *Viaggio in Italia*, curated by Vittorio Magnago Lampugnani and Vittorio Savi. A mental journey because, as Lao Tzu suggests, we should know the world without going out of the door (Pine 2009: 94).

Here, the journey is considered as a »condition of a hermeneutic activity towards [...] the built territory« (Nicolin 1987: 12, author's translation) which offers a sequence of complex images, which seem to represent an equally complex abstract and suspended contemporaneity within an indeterminate space (Camerlenghi 2003). It is an imagined journey that reshapes what anyone could have encountered crossing the Mincio Valley with its railway and beyond. It is a journey certified by materials such as the technical reports of the railway projects, images, and *immaginari* that, like the remains of the railway itself, have survived, even if only as signage in the landscape.

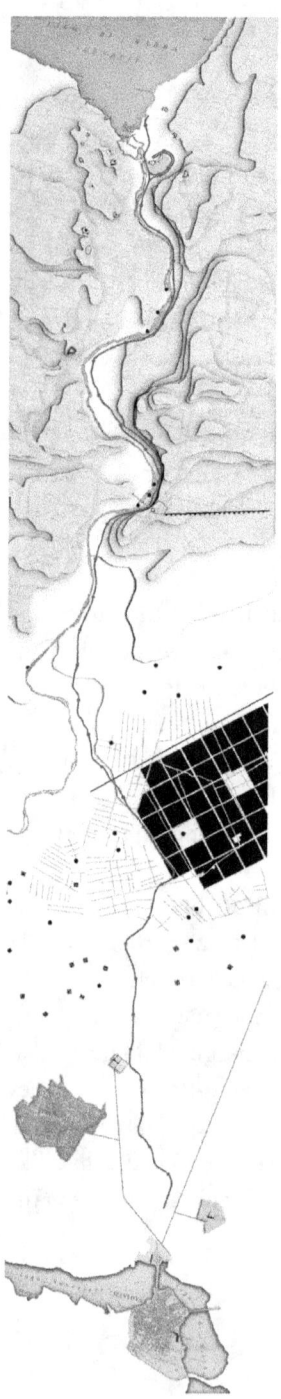

5.
*The Ponte Visconteo in Valeggio
sul Mincio, Calzolari, 1930(?),
Archivio di Stato di Mantova
Fondo Calzolari. Courtesy:
Archivio di Stato di Mantova.*

6.
*The graphic representation of the Mantova-
Peschiera Journey, 2020.
Mapping: Federico Marcolini.*

The Image of the Mincio Valley

Like the imagined character of Vittorio Valori Perduti, who came out of Vittorio Lampugnani's mind, the traveler is, here too, a figure accompanied by different materials, able to guarantee the necessary arbitrariness of his point of view. The imagined journey is a subjective reading of a sequence of architectures, villages, and landscapes, a heterogeneity that leads back to a unique layer of coexistence and contemporaneity that could be identified in the Mincio Valley and its river.

Like Vittorio Valori Perduti, we can imagine his homonymous, a user of the short railway that connected the city of Mantua to the warm and welcoming shores of Lake Garda. This is a journey imagined and reconstructed through the railway projects, whose technical reports return short descriptions of the crossed landscapes, the photographs belonging to the Calzolari and Giovetti Fund of the Archivio di Stato di Mantua and the scientific publications relating to the Mincio and its territory (fig. 5).

It is therefore the interpretive dimension that characterizes the drafting of this imagined journey between Mantua and Peschiera. Within the author's research, the journey follows the description provided by the technical report of the general project carried out by the engineer Arvedo Arvedi in 1905, assisted by extracts from the general plan of the same project. Thanks to that, some elements of the territory are highlighted and used to introduce an in-depth study useful to the definition of the *immaginario* linked to travel and places.

In turn, the insights are built on the basis of original documents such as descriptions, photographs, historical maps or drawings. Therefore, the journey is rewritten through a method which, having the railway as its incipit, opens up the territory without ever disconnecting from it. In addition the railway, being parallel to the course of the river, manages to become part of the landscape, thanks to the interaction among their elements.

Conclusion

From the different modes in which Vittorio Valori Perduti traveled, we refer here to the *andare*, »to go«, in which the protagonist is accompanied in this vision by a *connaisseur*, a modern Virgilio, who is left with the burden of »providing the text, a story of experience, result of a protracted meditation and therefore a broad report, characterized by analytical thrusts«

(Lampugnani/Savi 1987: 15, author's translation). At each crossing, a report is drawn up, a document that shows itself as a chronicle of the itinerary and which, instead of being a text, becomes its graphic representation in the form of a map (fig. 6), which, by its nature defined within a frame, focuses on the places imagined and lost in the memory of those who are accompanying us on this journey.

Another way of traveling is the stop. In the case of the Triennale, it refers to large cities in which the heteronomy of the protagonist allows for a new approach to the object, abandoning the *connaisseur* in favor of a scholar, a luminary capable of contributing to a critical and unique cut and reconstructing, through *microstorie narrate*, small stories, the tiles of a fundamental mosaic to »trace the authentic metonymic profile of the city« (Lampugnani/Savi 1987: 16, author's translation). Yet, if the city is not the protagonist of this work, the stop is, in analogy with the railway and its main artifacts, such as the stations and stops that represent nothing but this. In these cases, the stop always takes place at an inhabited center, in an urbanized and highly man-made place, or a reference to a more or less large area, also man-made but characterized by a greater natural component.

As for the cities of Vittorio Valori Perduti, we look for the authenticity of places where the railway stopped and which today are still there in the form of a ruin, from which it is possible to trace a metonymic profile through the *microstorie* of these *microgeografie* that the great Italian geographer Eugenio Turri reads approaching the Mincio Valley (cf. De Marinis/Franchini/Jacometti 1993).

This is a personal story made by visions and images, descriptions that contain the references and the spirit of their authors. The architectural project becomes the outcome of a subjective culture that relates project and landscape through their representation and interpretation.

References

Belpoliti, Marco (2021): *Pianura (Plain – The Po Valley)*, Torino: Einaudi.

Calvino, Italo (1980): *Una pietra sopra: discorsi di letteratura e società (A Stone Above: Discourses of Literature and Society)*, Torino: Einaudi.

Camerlenghi, Eugenio (2003): *Lineamenti di geografia e storia del paesaggio agrario mantovano (Outlines of Geography and History of the Mantuan Agricultural Landscape)*, Mantua: Tre Lune Edizioni.

Dal Lago, Alessandro (1987), »La città immaginate: Viaggio in Italia a tappe. Parte I« (Imagined Cities. A Nine-Stage Journey around Italy. Part I), in: *Architettura Cronache e Storia 377*, 225–240.

De Marinis, Rafaele C./Franchini, Dario A./Jacometti, G./Lanza, C./Laureti, L./Lonardi, G./Marinelli, S./Monicelli, F./Palvarini Gobio Casali, M.R./Perbellini, G./Turri, E. (1993): *Il Mincio e il suo Territorio (The Mincio and its Territory)*, Verona: Cierre Edizioni.

De Seta, Cesare (2014): *L'Italia nello specchio del Grand Tour (Italy in the Reflection of the Grand Tour)*, Milan: Rizzoli.

Ghirri, Luigi/Leone, Gianni/Velati, Enzo (1984): *Viaggio in Italia (An Italian Journey)*, Alessandria: Il Quadrante.

Gregotti, Vittorio (1988), »Io scrivo che Omero racconta« (I write about Homer telling), in: *Casabella 546*, 2–3.

Gregotti, Vittorio (2014): *96 ragioni critiche del progetto (96 Critical Reasons for the Project)*, Milan: BUR Saggi.

Lampugnani Magnago, Vittorio/Savi, Vittorio (1987): »Cronache di un Viaggio in Italia, del catalogo e della mostra« (Chronicles of a Journey in Italy, the Exhibition Catalog), in: XVII Triennale di Milano (eds.), *Le città immaginate, un viaggio in Italia, nove progetti per nove città*, Milan: Electa, 13–17.

Melville, Herman (1892): *Moby Dick Or, the White Whale*, Boston: L.C.Page & Company Publishers.

Nicolin, Pierluigi (1987): »Introduzione« (Introduction), in: XVII Triennale di Milano (eds.), *Le città immaginate, un viaggio in Italia, nove progetti per nove città*, Milan: Electa, 11–12.

Pessoa, Fernando (2020): *Teoria dell'eteronimia (Theory of Heteronymy)*, Macerata: Quodlibet.

Pine, Red (2009): *Lao-tzu's Taoteching With Selected Commentaries from the Past 2,000 Years*, Port Townsend, WA: Copper Canyon Press.

Pontiggia, Elena (1987), »Le Città Immaginate, un viaggio in Italia« (Imagined Cities, A Journey in Italy), in: *Domus 683*, 78–84.

Savi, Vittorio (1981): »Il paesaggio della pianura Padana« (The Landscape of the Po Valley), in: *paesaggio immagine e realtà*, Milan: Electa, 275–282.

Spinelli, Luigi (2019): *La visione soggettiva: progetti e paesaggi (The Subjective Vision: Projects and Landscapes)*, Milan: Franco Angeli.

Triennale di Milano (1987): *Le città Immaginate. Un viaggio in Italia, Nove progetti per nove città (Imagined Cities. A Journey through Italy, Nine Projects for Nine Cities)*, Milan: Electa.

Contributors

»Since I've had this studio, I realized that I could invite anybody into this building and talk. So we've had everything from neuroscientists, to geographers, to visual artists, to engineers, to architects. And, you know, once you've taken on the sort of big subject of the body of course everybody has a relationship to that, because that's what they're dealing with.

So, although you have to be careful not to sort of make this hugely, unwieldy set of subjects meet each other – you can find the fine lines, the fine draws, and that moment you can talk about those two little things in that space together. And you can find common language, or argument, or agreement, or just the joy of people speaking together, working together.«

Siobhan Davies 2017.

Davies, Siobhan (2017): *Rambert Voices: An Interview with Siobhan Davies*, February 9, 2017, 40:35–41:34.

https://vimeo.com/236578550, accessed September 15, 2021.

Biographies

Inkeri Aula (PhD)

is an anthropologist who specializes in multi-site and multi-sensorial ethnography. In recent years, she has researched the sensory transformations in transgenerational environmental relationships in European citiesin the *Horizon2020* funded transdisciplinary project *SENSOTRA* (2017–2021). She defended her doctoral dissertation at the University of Eastern Finland on Afro-Brazilian wording in translocal fight-dance-art capoeira in 2020. Her versatile research topics include environmental relationships, relational ontologies, utopias, cultural imaginaries, forest myths, weedy landscapes, sensorial atmospheres, Afro-Brazilian culture, and multi-sensory methodologies. Aula is heavily involved in art and research cooperation, including sound installations based on ethnographic research results and materials that are presented on the site *www.gardenofbecomings.com*.

Lisa Beisswanger (Dr.)

is an art historian and postdoctoral research assistant in the Department of Architectural Theory and Science at the Technical University of Darmstadt, Germany. She works at the intersection of architecture and the visual arts. Her current project focuses on building systems and systems thinking in post-war educational architecture. After graduating from the University of Freiburg, she worked as a curatorial trainee and research assistant in the field of contemporary art, at Villa Merkel, Esslingen and Schirn Kunsthalle, Frankfurt. She was a research assistant at the Institute for Art Education at Giessen University and a member of the interdisciplinary graduate center GCSC (International Graduate Centre for the Study of Culture). In 2020 she completed her doctorate *Performance on Display* on the history of performance in museums with distinction. The respective book publication is scheduled for autumn 2021.

Fabio Colonnese (PhD)

is an architect, fellow researcher, and adjunct professor at Sapienza University of Rome, Italy, where teaches Descriptive Geometry, Architecture Survey, and Architecture Drawing. He took part to major survey campaigns, such as Castel Sant'Angelo, the Royal Palace of Caserta and several Rupestrian monasteries in Cappadocia, Turkey. His PhD dissertation on the labyrinth and its manifold relationships with art, architecture, and the city was published in *Il Labirinto e l'Architetto* (*The Labyrinth and the Architect*, 2006). While attending his Rome post-doctoral fellowship in Digital Survey and Representation of the City, he focused on the relationship between the multi-sensorial experience of space and the image of architecture, whose early results can be read in his book *Movimento Percorsi Rappresentazione* (*Movement, Routes, Representation*, 2012). His latest articles focus on perspective illusory devices in Baroque architecture, digital reconstruction after literary architecture, and architecture modeling.

Sergiy Ilchenko

was born in Ukraine in 1963. He graduated from the Kharkiv Civil Engineering Institute, majoring in architecture in 1986. As a student, he undertook an internship at design institutes in Latvia and Estonia. For ten years, he worked at *Sumy Branch* (leading in the region) of Miskbudproekt Design Institute, there he authored projects of different scales – from urban ones to detached buildings and complexes. In 1996, he returned to Kharkiv and taught architecture at Kharkiv National University of Construction and Architecture until 2019, while simultaneously being engaged in architectural practice. In 2016 he started a postgraduate course in architecture at the Kharkiv National University of Construction and Architecture that he passed successfully in 2020. Since then, he has been teaching architecture at the Kharkiv State Academy of Design and Fine Arts.

Federico Marcolini

was born in Italy in 1985. He completed his master's studies at IUAV in Venice (M.Arch.) and is an architect and PhD Student in Architecture and Urban Design at Politecnico di Milano, Department of Architecture, Built Environment and Construction Engineer. Since 2016, he has been a teaching assistant for Design Studio courses at Politecnico di Milano – Polo Territoriale di Mantova, working with international architects such as Eduardo Souto de Moura and Carrilho da Graça. His research topics include architectureal design in historical context and he specialises in regeneration project of abandoned infrastructures such as railways. He has also contributed to the publication: *Ignazio Gardella other architecture* as a result of a research project in collaboration with the Parma CSAC archive, the University of Parma and Politecnico di Milano, focusing on the work of the Italian master Ignazio Gardella. In 2020, he taught the course »Ideal City Theory« at the Hochschule in Kaiserslautern.

Anja Ohliger (Prof.)

studied architecture and urban design at the Technical University of Darmstadt. In addition to her work as a freelance architect and partner at osa_office for subversive architecture, she has been teaching for 20 years. Her main focus is experimental didactic methods in design fundamentals at the interdisciplinary interface between architecture, art, and urbanism. Since 2017 she has been a professor of design and architectural theory in interdisciplinary discourse at the School of Design, Coburg University of Applied Sciences and Arts.

Sarah Robinson (Prof.)

is an architect, writer, and educator whose practice is based in Pavia, Italy. Her writing and research is concerned with the many ways that the built environment shapes the body, mind, and culture. Her books, *Nesting: Body, Dwelling Mind* (William Stout, 2011), *Mind in Architecture: Neuroscience, Embodiment, and the Future of Design* with Juhani Pallasmaa (MIT, 2015) and *Architecture is Verb* (Routledge, 2021) are among the first works to engage with the dialogue between architecture and the cognitive sciences. Holding degrees in both philosophy and architecture, she was the founding president of the Frank Lloyd Wright School of Architecture board of governors. She is also an adjunct professor in Architecture, Design, and Media Technology at Aalborg University, Denmark, and teaches and is a member of the scientific board of NAAD at IUAV, Venice.

Virginie Roy (Prof.)

studied dance at Conservatoire National Supérieur de Musique et de Danse de Lyon (CNSMD) and dance pedagogy at Centre National de la Danse (CND) in Lyon, and completed her master's degree in clinical psychology and her diploma in art therapy at the University of Paris 8. Furthermore, Virginie Roy earned a postgraduate diploma in clinical and health psychology from the University of Vienna. She combines these experiences in her practice as a clinical health psychologist and sport psychologist, as a dancer/performer, as a professor of contemporary dance in the faculty of performing arts at the Music and Art University, and a lecturer on movement and psychology at Sigmund Freud University, both in Vienna. Her research, publications, and collaborations are motivated by the idea of movement in physical and psychic spaces, in the fields of contemporary dance, architecture, and the artistic diversity practice.

Wiktor Skrzypczak

is a licensed architect and dance artist. They are currently working on a doctoral thesis about the correlations between bodily self-consciousness and space perception in architecture at HafenCity University, Hamburg. After graduating in architecture from the Technical University Łódź, they have been planning social housing in Hamburg. They are trained in dance improvisation and somatic pedagogy. Their practice has been shaped through training with Contact Improvisation pioneers: Nancy Stark Smith, Nita Little, Sara Shelton Mann, and Martin Keogh, as well as Body-Mind Centering practitioners: Sigrid Bohlens, Ka Rustler, Walburga Gatz, Anne Expert, Jens Johannsen, Friederike Tröscher, Nina Wehnert, and dance artists Thomas Kampe and Andrew Wass. They have been facilitating movement since 2014, by, among others: *Queer Tango* classes in Hamburg, the *Queer Contact Improvisation* symposium and dance festival in Hamburg, the *Space, Body and Architecture* workshop in Tel-Aviv, the *Architecture: Imaginary Inhabitation, Bodily Imagination* workshop in Hamburg, and the *Spatial Imagination in Contact Improvisation* workshop in Burdąg. Since 2016 they have been a member of *Triade Tanzforum e.V.*

Katja Vaghi (Dr.)

studied dance at Ballet Arts in NYC and then literature and linguistics at Zurich University. She holds a PhD in dance philosophy from the University of Roehampton and lectures at *Die ETAGE*, School for Performance and Visual Arts, in Berlin, and at the Rambert School for Ballet and Contemporary Dance in London and the University of Roehampton. She also lectures on somatic approaches to space at the Coburg University of Applied Sciences and Arts.

Katharina Voigt

studied architecture in Hamburg, Munich, and Stockholm. She worked for Stölken Schmidt Architekten BDA in Hamburg and Heim Kuntscher Architekten und Stadtplaner BDA in Munich. She researches and teaches at the Chair of Architectural Design and Conception, at the Technical University of Munich. Her research focuses on transdisciplinary investigations of architecture, highlighting the lived experience as significant for the anticipation of architectural design, and investigating the integration of sensuality and bodily knowledge in architectural research. Her doctorate on dance practices as a medium and tool of architectural experience, research, and design is associated with the doctoral program Epistemologies of Aesthetic Practices at the Collegium Helveticum. She is a founder and member of the advisory board for *Dimensions. Journal of Architectural Knowledge.*

Tijana Vojnović Ćalić (Dr.)

studied architecture in Belgrade, Serbia, where she completed her PhD. She has worked in architectural offices in Serbia and Germany. Since 2016 she has been a lecturer at the School of Design, Coburg University of Applied Sciences and Arts. Her research focusses on the interdisciplinary approach to design and sustainability in architecture.

Palimpsest: Landscape Traces
Tideways, Northern Sea 2021.
Photographer: Katharina Voigt.

Architektur und Design

Daniel Hornuff
Die Neue Rechte und ihr Design
Vom ästhetischen Angriff auf die offene Gesellschaft

2019, 142 S., kart., Dispersionsbindung, 17 SW-Abbildungen
19,99 € (DE), 978-3-8376-4978-9
E-Book:
PDF: 17,99 € (DE), ISBN 978-3-8394-4978-3

Katharina Brichetti, Franz Mechsner
Heilsame Architektur
Raumqualitäten erleben, verstehen und entwerfen

2019, 288 S., kart., Dispersionsbindung, 57 Farbabbildungen
29,99 € (DE), 978-3-8376-4503-3
E-Book:
PDF: 26,99 € (DE), ISBN 978-3-8394-4503-7

Annette Geiger
Andersmöglichsein. Zur Ästhetik des Designs

2018, 314 S., kart., 175 SW-Abbildungen
29,99 € (DE), 978-3-8376-4489-0
E-Book:
PDF: 26,99 € (DE), ISBN 978-3-8394-4489-4

**Leseproben, weitere Informationen und Bestellmöglichkeiten
finden Sie unter www.transcript-verlag.de**

Architektur und Design

Christoph Rodatz, Pierre Smolarski (Hg.)
Wie können wir den Schaden maximieren?
Gestaltung trotz Komplexität.
Beiträge zu einem Public Interest Design

April 2021, 234 S., kart.
29,00 € (DE), 978-3-8376-5784-5
E-Book: kostenlos erhältlich als Open-Access-Publikation
PDF: ISBN 978-3-8394-5784-9
€

Tim Kammasch (Hg.)
Betrachtungen der Architektur
Versuche in Ekphrasis

2020, 326 S., kart., Dispersionsbindung, 63 SW-Abbildungen
30,00 € (DE), 978-3-8376-4994-9
E-Book:
PDF: 29,99 € (DE), ISBN 978-3-8394-4994-3

Thomas Hecken, Moritz Baßler, Elena Beregow,
Robin Curtis, Heinz Drügh, Mascha Jacobs,
Annekathrin Kohout, Nicolas Pethes, Miriam Zeh (Hg.)
POP
Kultur und Kritik (Jg. 10, 1/2021)

April 2021, 178 S., kart.
16,80 € (DE), 978-3-8376-5393-9
E-Book:
PDF: 16,80 € (DE), ISBN 978-3-8394-5393-3

GPSR Authorized Representative: Easy Access System Europe, Mustamäe tee 50, 10621 Tallinn, Estonia, gpsr.requests@easproject.com

www.ingramcontent.com/pod-product-compliance
Lightning Source LLC
Chambersburg PA
CBHW081655120626

46550CB00010B/2913